Facilitating Trade through Competitive, Low-Carbon Transport

DIRECTIONS IN DEVELOPMENT
Countries and Regions

Facilitating Trade through Competitive, Low-Carbon Transport

The Case for Vietnam's Inland and Coastal Waterways

Luis C. Blancas and M. Baher El-Hifnawi

THE WORLD BANK
Washington, D.C.

© 2014 International Bank for Reconstruction and Development / The World Bank
1818 H Street NW, Washington DC 20433
Telephone: 202-473-1000; Internet: www.worldbank.org

Some rights reserved

1 2 3 4 16 15 14 13

This work is a product of the staff of The World Bank with external contributions. Note that The World Bank does not necessarily own each component of the content included in the work. The World Bank therefore does not warrant that the use of the content contained in the work will not infringe on the rights of third parties. The risk of claims resulting from such infringement rests solely with you.

The findings, interpretations, and conclusions expressed in this work do not necessarily reflect the views of The World Bank, its Board of Executive Directors, or the governments they represent. The World Bank does not guarantee the accuracy of the data included in this work. The boundaries, colors, denominations, and other information shown on any map in this work do not imply any judgment on the part of The World Bank concerning the legal status of any territory or the endorsement or acceptance of such boundaries.

Nothing herein shall constitute or be considered to be a limitation upon or waiver of the privileges and immunities of The World Bank, all of which are specifically reserved.

Rights and Permissions

This work is available under the Creative Commons Attribution 3.0 Unported license (CC BY 3.0) http://creativecommons.org/licenses/by/3.0. Under the Creative Commons Attribution license, you are free to copy, distribute, transmit, and adapt this work, including for commercial purposes, under the following conditions:

Attribution—Please cite the work as follows: Blancas, Luis C., and M. Baher El-Hifnawi. 2014. *Facilitating Trade through Competitive, Low-Carbon Transport: The Case for Vietnam's Inland and Coastal Waterways*. Directions in Development. Washington, DC: World Bank. doi:10.1596/978-1-4648-0105-1. License: Creative Commons Attribution CC BY 3.0

Translations—If you create a translation of this work, please add the following disclaimer along with the attribution: *This translation was not created by The World Bank and should not be considered an official World Bank translation. The World Bank shall not be liable for any content or error in this translation.*

All queries on rights and licenses should be addressed to the Office of the Publisher, The World Bank, 1818 H Street NW, Washington, DC 20433, USA; fax: 202-522-2625; e-mail: pubrights@worldbank.org.

ISBN (paper): 978-1-4648-0105-1
ISBN (electronic): 978-1-4648-0106-8
DOI: 10.1596/978-1-4648-0105-1

Cover photo: © Tran Thi Hoa / World Bank
Cover design: Debra Naylor

Library of Congress Cataloging-in-Publication Data

Blancas, Luis C., author. Facilitating trade through competitive, low carbon transport : the case for Vietnam's inland and coastal waterways / Luis C. Blancas and M. Baher El-Hifnawi.
    pages cm — (Directions in development / World Bank)
  Includes bibliographical references.
  ISBN 978-1-4648-0105-1 (alk. paper) -- ISBN 978-1-4648-0106-8
  1. Inland water transportation—Vietnam—Economic aspects. 2. Coastal water transportation—Vietnam—Economic aspects. I. El-Hifnawi, M. Baher, author. II. Title. III. Series: Directions in development (Washington, D.C.)
  HE884.5.B53 2013
  333.91'509597—dc23   2013039699

Contents

Foreword		*xiii*
Acknowledgments		*xv*
About the Authors		*xvii*
Abbreviations		*xix*
	Overview	1
	Note	6
Chapter 1	**Introduction**	7
	Context	7
	Objectives of the Report	8
	Scope and Methodology	9
	Key Data Sources	11
	Structure of the Report	11
	Note	12
Chapter 2	**Demand for Waterborne and Multimodal Transport**	13
	Size and Historical Growth Patterns of IWT and Coastal Shipping	13
	Growth Projections for IWT and Coastal Shipping	15
	Commodity Tonnage and Tonnage Distribution by Mode	16
	Inland and Coastal Shipping Lengths of Haul	16
	Main Freight Flows	18
	Coastal Shipping	28
	Supply Chains and Logistics Costs in Vietnam	36
	Conclusions on Demand	41
	Notes	42
	References	42
Chapter 3	**Supply-Side Considerations: Waterways, Ports, and Fleet**	43
	Institutional Framework for the Waterway and Port Sectors	43
	Waterway Infrastructure	48
	Ports	56
	Fleet	57

	Conclusions on Waterways, Ports, and Fleet	70
	Notes	71
	References	72
Chapter 4	**Modal Differences in Fuel Efficiency and Greenhouse Gas Emissions**	**73**
	Relative Carbon Intensity among Transport Modes	73
	Indicative Estimates of GHG Emission Reductions	77
	Conclusions	79
	Notes	79
	References	79
Chapter 5	**Main Challenges and Recommendations**	**81**
	Planning	81
	Institutional/Regulatory Environment	83
	Physical Bottlenecks	86
	Financing	91
	Reference	92
Chapter 6	**Strategy and Action Plan**	**93**
Chapter 7	**Estimated Impact of Public Sector Interventions in IWT and Coastal Shipping**	**97**
	Translating the IWT/Coastal Shipping Strategy into Tangible Interventions	97
	Methodology: Translating Interventions into Impacts	98
	Modal Shift and Emissions Impact of the Proposed Interventions	100
	CBA Results	101
	Conclusions	106
	Reference	107
Appendix A	**List of Stakeholders Interviewed**	**109**
	Private Sector Stakeholders Interviewed (2010–12)	109
	Public Sector Stakeholders Interviewed (2010–12)	110
Appendix B	**Major Waterway Routes in the Northern and Southern Regions**	**113**
	Reference	118
Appendix C	**General Considerations on DWT Capacity Increases in the National IWT Fleet**	**119**
	Length Increase	119
	Beam Increase	119

	Draft Increase	120
	Hydraulic Impact	120
Appendix D	**Cargo Data and Modal Split Model**	**121**
	The VITRANSS-2 Dataset Structure	121
	Cargo Data and Other Inputs Used from the VITRANSS-2 Database	123
	Design of the Logit Model Using VITRANSS and Other Data	146
	The Modal Split Model as Developed in This Report	149
	The Impact of Lower Transport Costs on Modal Split	155
	Notes	167
	References	167
Appendix E	**Detailed Description of Proposed Interventions**	**169**
	Detailed Discussions of Each Intervention	169
	Notes	179
	Reference	179
Appendix F	**Detailed Impacts of Proposed Interventions**	**181**
	Project Impacts in 2020 and 2030 Resulting from the Modal Split Model	181
	CBA Methodology and Results	190
	Notes	195
	References	195

Boxes

2.1	A New Container Route in the Mekong Delta	27
2.2	Container Transferium near the Port of Rotterdam	35
2.3	Speed and Reliability as Barriers for IWT in Europe	37
2.4	Cooperation in Logistics Networks and Infrastructure Incentives in Western Europe	39
3.1	Institutional Organization of a Typical Dutch River Port	46
3.2	Classification of European Waterways	53
3.3	Sea-River Vessels in Europe	66
3.4	Fleet Renewal Policies in the Netherlands	67
3.5	Dutch IWT Vessel Fleet Evolution, 2000–08	69
4.1	CO_2 Emissions from Inland Shipping in the Netherlands, 1995–2005	76
D.1	VITRANSS-2 Scenarios	122
E.1	Estimating Investment Costs	171
E.2	Extended Gateway Concept	172
E.3	Coastal Container Shipping in Vietnam	175
E.4	The Marco Polo Program	179

Figures

1.1	Analytical Approach	9
1.2	Structure of the Report by Chapter	12
2.1	Tonnage Throughput at Vietnam's Seaports by Flow Type, 1995–2008	29
2.2	Container Throughput at Vietnam's Seaports by Flow Type, 1995–2008	31
2.3	Largest Container Ports in Vietnam by Throughput, 2007	32
3.1	Congestion on the Cho Gao Canal	45
3.2	Vietnam: Number of Vessels by DWT Class as a Share of Total Fleet, 2000–10	61
3.3	Vietnam: Carrying Capacity by DWT Class as Share of Total River-Going Cargo Fleet, 2000–10	63
3.4	Vietnam: Number of Ocean-Going Vessels by Type, 2010	64
3.5	Vietnam: Ocean-Going Vessels by DWT Class, 2010	65
3.6	Average Increase in Tonnage (DWT) in the Western European (Belgium, Germany, and the Netherlands) IWT Fleet Relative to Vietnam's Position	68
4.1	CO_2 Intensity of Selected Freight Transport Modes, Log Scale	75
4.2	CO_2 Emissions, Long Distance (>150 km) Freight Transport, 2010	75
4.3	CO_2 Emissions for Long Distance Bulk Freight Transport, 2000	76
B4.1.1	Inland Shipping CO_2 Emissions in the Netherlands, 1995–2005	76
6.1	Schematic of the Proposed IWT and Coastal Shipping Strategy	94
7.1	Analytical Tools and Assessment Outputs	99
D.1	Options to Estimate the Parameters of a Logit Model	149

Maps

1.1	Main Areas of Study in Vietnam	10
2.1	Main Corridors in the Northern Delta	19
2.2	Main Corridors in the Mekong Delta	21
2.3	Cross-Border River Transport between Vietnam and Cambodia	34
3.1	Inland Waterways in Vietnam's North Region	49
3.2	Inland Waterways in Vietnam's South Region	50
5.1	Main Inland Waterways and Ports in the North Region	86
5.2	Main Inland Waterways and Ports in the South Region	87

Tables

O.1	Proposed Interventions to Enhance IWT and Coastal Shipping Performance	2
O.2	Cost-Benefit Analysis (CBA) Results for the Proposed Interventions	3
O.3	Sources of Economic Benefits by Intervention	4
2.1	Vietnam: Interprovincial Freight Volumes by Mode, 2008 and Forecast to 2030	14

2.2	Modal Share of Surface Freight Volumes in the Netherlands, 2011	15
2.3	Freight Transport Volumes (Tons per Day) and Modal Shares by Commodity, 2008	16
2.4	Freight Transport Volumes (Tons per Day) and Modal Shares by Length of Haul, 2008	17
2.5	Red River Delta: Current/Projected Road and Waterway Interprovincial Flows	19
2.6	Current and Projected Main Interprovincial Cargo Flows in the Mekong Delta	20
2.7	Road and Coastal Containerized Cargo Flows for the North-South Axis	22
2.8	Origin-Destination Cargo Flows for Corridor 1 in the Red River Delta, 2008	23
2.9	Origin-Destination Cargo Flows for Corridor 2 in the Red River Delta, 2008	24
2.10	Origin-Destination Cargo Flows for Corridor 3 in the Red River Delta, 2008	24
2.11	Origin-Destination Cargo Flows for Corridor 1 in the Mekong River Delta, 2008	25
2.12	Origin-Destination Cargo Flows for Corridor 2 in the Mekong River Delta, 2008	26
2.13	Cargo Volume Handled at Vietnam's Seaports, 1995–2008	29
2.14	Container Volume Handled by Vietnam's Seaports, 1995–2008	30
2.15	NRCTSS 2005 Base Case IWT Volumes and Transport Costs in the North Region	34
B2.4.1	Public Subsidy Program for Transshipment Facilities in the Netherlands, 1996–2004	41
3.1	Scale of Inland Waterways in Vietnam	48
3.2	Vietnam: Technical Classification of Waterways	51
3.3	River Fleet by Waterway Class for 50 and 90 Percent Load Factors	52
B3.2.1	Classification of European Inland Waterways	53
3.4	Allocated Public Investments in Transport by Subsector, 1999–2007	54
3.5	Major Channel Development Projects as of 2010	55
3.6	Vietnam: Technical Classification of Freight River Ports	57
3.7	Major Port Development Projects	58
3.8	Profile of Major Terminals in Selected Operational Class 1 Seaports	59
3.9	Vietnamese Inland Waterway Ships above 20 Meters in Length	60
3.10	Vietnam: Size Class (DWT) of River-Going Cargo Vessels, 2000–10	60
3.11	Vietnam: DWT Carrying Capacity of River-Going Cargo Vessels by Size Class, 2000–10	62

3.12	Characteristics of Barge Convoys in the Mekong Delta, 2002	64
3.13	Vietnam: Ocean-Going Container Vessel Fleet Characteristics, 2010	65
3.14	Typical Container Vessel Characteristics by Size Class, Based on World Fleet	65
B3.4.1	Fleet Renewal and Modernization in the Netherlands	67
3.15	Constraints for Vessel DWT Capacity Increases	68
B3.5.1	Vessel Count in the Dutch Inland Waterway Fleet by DWT Category, 2000 vs. 2008	69
B3.5.2	Tonnage Deployed in the Dutch Inland Waterway Fleet by DWT Category, 2000 vs. 2008	69
4.1	Indicative Evolution of Vietnam's Average IWT Vessel Fleet Emissions	77
4.2	Indicative Gain from Fleet Modernization and Upgrading	78
4.3	Indicative Gain from Modal Shift from Road to Waterway Freight Transport	78
6.1	Recommended Actions for IWT and Coastal Shipping Development in Vietnam	95
7.1	Proposed Interventions to Enhance Performance	98
7.2	Long-Term Emission Reduction and Modal Share Impacts of Proposed Interventions	100
7.3	CBA Results for the Proposed Interventions	102
7.4	Sources of Economic Benefits by Intervention	102
7.5	Sensitivity Analysis	106
B.1	Major Routes in the North Region	114
B.2	Major Routes in the South Region	116
D.1	VITRANSS Zones: Vietnamese Provinces	123
D.2	VITRANSS-2 Commodity Groupings	123
D.3	Road Distances from Northern and Southern Provinces to the Northern Provinces	124
D.4	Road Distances from Northern and Southern Provinces to the Southern Provinces	126
D.5	IWT Distances between Northern Provinces	128
D.6	IWT Distances between Southern Provinces	129
D.7	Northern Provinces: Road Cargo Flows in 2008	130
D.8	Northern Provinces: Road Cargo Flows in 2020	131
D.9	Northern Provinces: Road Cargo Flows in 2030	132
D.10	Northern Provinces: IWT Cargo Flows in 2008	133
D.11	Northern Provinces: IWT Cargo Flows in 2020	134
D.12	Northern Provinces: IWT Cargo Flows in 2030	135
D.13	Southern Provinces: Road Cargo Flows in 2008	136
D.14	Southern Provinces: Road Cargo Flows in 2020	137
D.15	Southern Provinces: Road Cargo Flows in 2030	138
D.16	Southern Provinces: IWT Cargo Flows in 2008	139
D.17	Southern Provinces: IWT Cargo Flows in 2020	140

D.18	Southern Provinces: IWT Cargo Flows in 2030	141
D.19	Outgoing Commodities for the North Region	142
D.20	Incoming Commodities for the North Region	143
D.21	Outgoing Commodities for the South Region	144
D.22	Incoming Commodities for the South Region	145
D.23	Main Performance Indicators of IWT Vessels in Vietnam	150
D.24	Example of Road and IWT Shipping Costs per O-D Pair for Corridor 1	151
D.25	Example of Road and IWT Transit Times per O-D Pair for Corridor 1	152
D.26	Summary of Shipping Costs and Operational Data of Containerships	153
D.27	IWT Shipping Costs per O-D Pair at Corridor 1 for Class 1 Vessels	155
D.28	IWT Volumes for the Red River Delta with and without a One-Class Increase in Ship Size	156
D.29	IWT Volumes Mekong River Delta with and without a One-Class Increase in Ship Size	156
D.30	Estimated Impact of a Hypothetical 10 Percent Decrease in Terminal Handling Charges on the Modal Split of the North-South Trade	158
D.31	Main Cost Components	159
D.32	Round-Trip Time Components and Related Costs	160
D.33	Cost Components of Coastal Transport (HCMC to/from Haiphong)	161
D.34	Trucking Costs for 15-Ton Trucks on North-South Axis	163
D.35	Trucking Costs per Ton on the North-South Axis and within the Red River Delta	163
D.36	Trucking Cost as a Function of Truck Size for Transport in River Deltas	164
D.37	Ship Particulars and Capital Related Costs of Self-Propelled Barges	164
D.38	Non-Capital-Related Costs and Operational Data	165
D.39	Operational Data, Costs, and Emissions by Ship Size and Trip Length	166
D.40	General Data	167
E.1	Summary Overview of the Proposed Interventions	170
F.1	Estimated Impact of Project 1 by 2020 and 2030: Red River Delta Corridor 1	184
F.2	Estimated Impact of Project 2 by 2020 and 2030: Red River Delta Corridor 2	185
F.3	Estimated Impact of Project 3 by 2020 and 2030: Red River Delta Corridor 3	185
F.4	Estimated Impact of Project 4 by 2020 and 2030: Red River Delta Extended Gateway	186

F.5	Estimated Impact of Project 5 by 2020 and 2030: Mekong Delta Corridor 1	187
F.6	Estimated Impact of Project 6 by 2020 and 2030: Coastal Shipping Container Terminal Development	188
F.7	Estimated Impact of Project 7 by 2020 and 2030: Charging for Waterway Maintenance	189
F.8	Estimated Impact of Project 8 by 2020 and 2030: Engine Modernization Program	189
F.9	CBA Results for the Proposed Interventions	193
F.10	Sources of Economic Benefits by Intervention	194
F.11	Sensitivity Analysis	194

Foreword

Vietnam's economic achievements of the past 25 years are impressive. Market-based reforms that were initiated in 1986 and continue to be perfected to this day pave the way for rapid and sustained economic growth. At the same time, pro-poor social policies address access to basic services and economic resources such as land combined with strong growth to dramatically reduce the incidence of poverty, from 58 percent in the early 1990s to approximately 10 percent today. By 2012, Vietnam had transitioned from being a low-income nation to attaining lower middle-income status.

This is a remarkable success story of development. Yet much remains to be done to continue building on the achievements of the past two and a half decades. In particular, Vietnam faces the challenge of further promoting economic growth, while also reducing the carbon intensity of its economy.

With a vast coast line, two large river deltas, and an economic structure led in part by weather-dependent sectors such as rice and coffee cultivation and aquaculture, Vietnam is among the countries most exposed to the impacts of climate change. Finding ways to support low-carbon growth strategies should be seen as a critical component of any long-term plan toward building Vietnam's future development trajectory.

The need to drive long-term, sustained growth continues to be imperative as well. In the wake of the economic crisis of 2008–09 and the protracted period of stagnant growth in Western Europe—a key Vietnam export market—domestic growth has slowed while the global competition to attract foreign direct investment has intensified. Many of those who have been lifted out of poverty remain close to the poverty line and under risk of falling back into poverty if past growth is not sustained. Increasing competitiveness and lowering the cost of doing business are two ways in which Vietnam can generate new sources of future growth.

This report argues that promoting inland waterway transportation and coastal shipping offers Vietnam a path of lower-carbon growth. Waterborne transport captures a significant share of the freight tonnage moved daily in Vietnam. Yet many waterways remain constrained in depth and width, their banks unprotected and their maintenance underfunded. The vessels used on these waterways remain small by international standards, reducing fuel efficiency per ton transported and limiting the environmental advantages of such equipment. Multimodal connections linked to the waterways could also be improved, which can reduce transportation and logistics costs.

Another contribution of the report is that it explicitly takes into account local pollutant and greenhouse gas emissions when economically assessing infrastructure and policy-based interventions in the inland waterway sector. This type of analysis will likely increasingly become the norm in the appraisal of transportation projects around the world, and not least in developing countries, in much the same way as it is already happening in the energy sector.

I hope the report can help inform the wider stakeholder community about the remarkable contributions of the inland waterway transport sector to Vietnam's economic development. Most important, I hope it can stimulate policy discussions that may lead to sound investments in the type of economically and environmentally robust solutions for transport and logistics that can be found in Vietnam's rivers, deltas, and coast lines.

John A. Roome
Director
Sustainable Development
East Asia and the Pacific
World Bank

Acknowledgments

This report has been prepared by the East Asia and Pacific Region of the World Bank in collaboration with Ecorys Research and Consulting. The research team was led by M. Baher El-Hifnawi (Lead Transport Economist, ECSTR) and Luis C. Blancas (Transport Specialist, EASIN) of the World Bank, under the overall guidance of John Roome (Sector Director, EASSD), Victoria Kwakwa (Country Director, EACVF), Jennifer Sara (Sector Manager, EASVS), Abhas Jha (Sector Manager, EASIN), and Paul Vallely (Senior Transport Specialist and Transport Cluster Leader, EASVS). Ecorys staff that contributed to this report included Johan Gille, Simme Veldman, Katrien Dusseldorp, and Marten van den Bossche.

Drafts of the report were reviewed by the following Peer Reviewers and staff of the World Bank: Simon David Ellis (Lead Transport Specialist, ECSTR), John Morton (Senior Urban Environment Specialist, LCSDU), Myla Taylor Williams (Country Program Coordinator, EACVQ), Monica Alina Antoci (Senior Private Sector Development Specialist, CICTI), Paul Amos (Transport Advisor), Duc Minh Pham (Senior Economist, EASPV), Wenlai Zhang (Senior Transport Specialist, EASCS), Reynaldo Bench (Senior Ports Specialist, EASIN), Christopher De Serio (Operations Analyst, EASIN), and Reindert Westra (Senior Urban Transport Specialist, EASIN). Thao Phuong Tuong (Team Assistant, EACVF), Teresita Ortega (Program Assistant, EASWE), and Cristina Hernandez (Program Assistant, EASWE) provided excellent logistical support.

The work benefited from valuable technical help provided by the staff of the Department of Planning and Investment of Vietnam's Ministry of Transport, particularly with regard to access to transportation data.

Finally, the support of the Energy Sector Management Assistance Program (ESMAP), the World Bank–managed Trade Facilitation Facility (TFF), and the Australian Agency for International Development (AusAID) is gratefully acknowledged. ESMAP is a global knowledge and technical assistance program administered by the World Bank that assists low- and middle-income countries to increase know-how and institutional capacity to achieve environmentally sustainable energy solutions for poverty reduction and economic growth. ESMAP is funded by Australia, Austria, Denmark, Finland, France, Germany, Iceland, Lithuania, the Netherlands, Norway, Sweden, the United Kingdom, and the World Bank Group.

About the Authors

Luis C. Blancas is a Transport Specialist with the Sustainable Development Department in the East Asia and the Pacific region of the World Bank. Since 2010, he has led and participated in the preparation and supervision of several World Bank-financed transport infrastructure projects in Vietnam, including interventions to expand capacity and increase efficiency in the country's Red River Delta and Mekong River Delta inland waterway networks and projects to develop Vietnam's expressway sector. He has also conducted public sector technical assistance and analytical work in transport and logistics in China, Malaysia, and Vietnam. Prior to joining the World Bank, he was an Associate with MergeGlobal, a financial and strategic advisor to firms in the global transport and logistics industry; a Research Analyst at the Fiscal Affairs Department of the International Monetary Fund; and a management consultant with Deloitte Consulting's Mexico and Central America practice. Mr. Blancas holds a Master's degree in Management Science and Engineering from Stanford University and a B.A. in Economics from Mexico's Monterrey Institute of Technology.

M. Baher El-Hifnawi is a Lead Transport Economist in the Europe and Central Asia region at the World Bank and is Program Team Leader for the Western Balkan countries. He is also a member of the Bank's Global Expert Team (GET) in Trade Logistics. Prior to this position, he worked in the East Asia and the Pacific region, where he led and participated in the preparation and supervision of numerous transport infrastructure development projects as well as sector reports and technical assistance activities in Mongolia, the Philippines, and Vietnam, including a multimodal transport and logistics regulatory review in the latter. Prior to joining the World Bank, Mr. El-Hifnawi was a Director of Cambridge Resources International, USA, where he worked on advising and capacity building for developing country governments and development institutions. He has both lectured on and conducted financial, economic, risk, and social analyses of investments in transport and infrastructure in a number of countries in East and South Asia, Africa, and Europe. He was Co-Director of the Program on Investment Appraisal and Management run by the Harvard Institute for

International Development (HIID). His private sector experience includes working as a Senior Advisor at KPMG Egypt and at the Egyptian Stock Exchange. Mr. El-Hifnawi has a B.S. in Civil Engineering from Cairo University, a Master's degree in Public Administration, and a Ph.D. in Transport Economics from Harvard University.

Abbreviations

3PL	third-party logistics/third-party logistics services provider
ABS	articulated barge system
B/C	benefit/cost ratio
CAGR	compounded annual growth rate
CBA	cost-benefit analysis
CO_2	carbon dioxide
CT	container transferium
CTT	Combi Terminal Twente
DoT	Department of Transport (under MoT)
DWT	deadweight tonnage
ECMT	European Conference of Ministers of Transport
EF	emission factor
eIRR	economic internal rates of return
EU	European Union
GDP	gross domestic product
GHG	greenhouse gas
GoV	Government of Vietnam
HCMC	Ho Chi Minh City
HFO	heavy fuel oil
HP	horsepower
IFI	International Financial Institutions
IMO	International Maritime Organization
ITF	International Transport Forum
IWT	inland waterway transport
JICA	Japan International Cooperation Agency
JSC	joint stock company
LOA	length overall
MDTIDP	Mekong Delta Transport Infrastructure Development Project
MoF	Ministry of Finance

MoT	Ministry of Transport
MPI	Ministry of Planning and Investment
MTRR	Multimodal Transport Regulatory Review
NCPFP	National Committee for Population and Family Planning
NDTDP	Northern Delta Transport Development Project
NIWTC	Northern Inland Waterway Transport Corporation
NO_x	nitrogen oxide
NPV	net present value
NRCTSS	Northern Region Comprehensive Transport Strategy Study
O-D	origin-destination
ODA	official development assistance
PMU	project management unit
PPP	purchasing power parity
RoRo	roll on/roll off
RP	revealed preference
SB	state budget
SBV	Subsidy Private Inland Waterway Connection
SO_x	sulfur oxide
SOE	state-owned enterprise
SOIT	Subsidy Scheme for Public Use Inland Terminals
SOWATCO	Southern Inland Waterway Transport Corporation
SP	stated preference
TBBV	Temporary Policy Regulation on Subsidies for (Private) Inland Waterway Links
TEU	20-foot equivalent unit
ton-km	ton-kilometer
VICT	Vietnam International Container Terminal
Vinalines	Vietnam National Shipping Lines
Vinamarine	Vietnam Maritime Administration
Vinashin	Vietnam Shipbuilding Industry Group
Vinawaco	Vietnam Waterway Construction Corporation
VITRANSS	Comprehensive Study on the Sustainable Development of the Transport System in Vietnam
VIWA	Vietnam Inland Waterway Administration
VND	Vietnamese dong
WMF	Waterway Maintenance Fund

Overview

Inland waterway transport (IWT) and coastal shipping are essential to the everyday functioning of the Vietnamese economy, which is endowed with two large river deltas and more than 3,000 kilometers of coastline. Yet over the past 15 years the economics and environmental sustainability of these vital modes have been undermined by insufficient investments in expanding, improving, and preserving the country's waterborne transport networks and key nodes such as river and ocean ports—despite sustained levels of rapid economic growth. This has resulted in reduced waterborne freight transport efficiency (e.g., higher transport costs and elevated congestion levels); has weakened incentives for transport carriers to invest in larger-scale, less-polluting vessels; and has likely increased national logistics costs. Furthermore, in the selected markets where modal shift from roads to the waterways may be economically and operationally viable, the case for such a shift has been equally undermined.

Given Vietnam's increasing integration into the global economy on the one hand and exposure to climate change risks—such as rising sea levels and unpredictable weather patterns—on the other, a more efficient, sustainable use of IWT and coastal shipping for freight transport may be an effective, economically feasible way to both increase competitiveness and curb emissions of pollutants and greenhouse gases.

This report presents the results of qualitative and quantitative assessments designed to test the above premise. Specifically, the report (a) identifies institutional, regulatory, and infrastructure bottlenecks that reduce inland and coastal waterway transport efficiency; (b) analyzes the bottlenecks' root causes; and (c) evaluates and proposes policy- and infrastructure-based interventions to address them. The conclusions stemming from the report aim to support the Government of Vietnam (GoV) in its stated goal of promoting economic growth, expanding opportunity, and increasing competitiveness while bolstering environmental sustainability.

The report finds that improving the efficiency and attractiveness of IWT and coastal shipping requires a multipronged approach based on targeted interventions to (a) upgrade and provide sustainable, predictable maintenance to key corridors and nodes of the core waterway network; (b) facilitate multimodal transportation and value-added logistics services (e.g., handling and storage); (c) attain a broader awareness among shippers—particularly small and medium enterprises—of modal choice tradeoffs; and (d) introduce mechanisms to promote fleet modernization.

To determine which specific interventions should be pursued, the report proposes nine potential public sector measures, listed (in no particular order) in table O.1. Based on a modal split model that utilizes a unique origin-destination dataset of interprovincial freight flows by mode, the report estimates the long-term economic impacts of each measure, including impacts on transport cost savings, emission reductions, and transport safety improvements. The modal split model allowed for estimates to be made on the likely changes in modal shares (e.g., between the roads sector and the waterways) and emission volumes that would result from the implementation of the proposed measures.

Subsequently, a standard discounted cost-benefit analysis methodology was utilized to estimate the economic rate of return to investing in each intervention,[1]

Table O.1 Proposed Interventions to Enhance IWT and Coastal Shipping Performance

No.	Intervention name	Intervention summary	Implementation time frame	Estimated costs ($)
1	Upgrade waterway Corridor 1 of the Red River Delta	Raises Corridor 1 (Quang Ninh–Haiphong–Pha Lai–Hanoi–Viet Tri) from waterway Class II to Class I	2016–20	150 million – 250 million
2	Upgrade waterway Corridor 2 of the Red River Delta	Raises Corridor 2 (Haiphong–Ninh Binh) from waterway Class III to Class II	2014–16	150 million – 300 million
3	Upgrade waterway Corridor 3 of the Red River Delta	Raises Corridor 3 (Hanoi–Day/Lach Giang) from waterway Class III to Class II	2013–15	100 million – 200 million
4	Enable extended gateway facility in the Red River Delta to serve the Hanoi market	Development of an inland waterway and cargo-handling facility near Hanoi to serve (mostly import/export) container flows between Haiphong and Hanoi	2014	10 million
5	Upgrade Waterway Corridor 1 of the Mekong Delta	Raises Corridor 1 (HCMC–Ben Tre–My Tho–Vinh Long) from waterway Class III to Class II	2013–16	150 million – 250 million
6	Upgrade a coastal shipping container terminal in Northern Vietnam	Modernization of a container terminal in Haiphong dedicated to domestic container shipping services	2014–15	40 million
7	Introduce user charges to fund waterway maintenance	Imposition of user charges on IWT vessel operators to cover the existing waterway maintenance financing gap	2014–ongoing	0.0003 (VND 6) per ton-km
8	Promote engine and fleet modernization in IWT	Provision of public subsidies (with private sector matching) for engine improvement	2014[a]	20 million
9	Showcase IWT as an enabler of efficient logistics	Promotion campaign on the use of inland water transport and demonstration projects to illustrate its attractiveness	2014–23[a]	30 million

Source: Ecorys/World Bank analysis.
Note: IWT = inland waterway transport.
a. Or until funds are fully disbursed.

by comparing estimated investment costs with the expected benefit streams over time. Those interventions with an economic return in excess of Vietnam's economic cost of capital—set at roughly 10 percent—would be deemed economically viable and therefore desirable for the GoV to pursue. The results of this analysis are summarized in tables O.2 and O.3.

The following key conclusions emerge from the above findings:

- Investments in the waterways can deliver attractive economic returns, but these are heavily dependent on the expected intensity of future traffic.

- Among all main inland waterway corridors in Vietnam's two river delta networks, the upgrading of Corridor 1 of the Mekong Delta (Intervention 5)—including the 29-kilometer Cho Gao Canal, the most pressing bottleneck in the Mekong Delta network for flows to and from Ho Chi Minh City (HCMC)—yields the most attractive economic returns to infrastructure improvements and should be seen as a development priority. The upgrading of Corridor 1 of the Red River Delta (Intervention 1) is also economically viable, albeit yielding slightly lower economic returns than its Mekong Delta counterpart.

- Even though upgrading Corridor 2 of the Red River Delta (Intervention 2) may appear economically unattractive at a 6 percent economic internal rate of return, it may still be desirable for Vietnam to pursue this investment once

Table O.2 Cost-Benefit Analysis (CBA) Results for the Proposed Interventions

No.	Intervention name	Implementation time frame	Financial cost ($ million)	Net present value at 10% ($ million)	eIRR (%)	B/C ratio
1	**Upgrade waterway Corridor 1 of the Red River Delta**	2016–20	200	0.6	10	1.0
2	Upgrade waterway Corridor 2 of the Red River Delta	2014–16	225	−83	6	0.5
3	Upgrade waterway Corridor 3 of the Red River Delta	2013–15	150	−102	2	0.2
4	Introduce an extended gateway facility in the Red River Delta to serve the Hanoi market	2014	10	−2.3	8	0.7
5	**Upgrade waterway Corridor 1 of the Mekong Delta**	2013–16	200	209	16	2.3
6	**Upgrade a coastal shipping container terminal in Northern Vietnam**	2014	40	22.7	13	1.7
7	**Introduce user charges to fund waterway maintenance**	From 2014	—	32	—	—
8	**Promote engine and fleet modernization in IWT**	From 2014	20	0.6	10	1.0

Source: Ecorys/World Bank analysis.
Note: B/C = benefit/cost; eIRR = economic internal rate of return; — = not available. Economically viable interventions shown in boldface.

Table O.3 Sources of Economic Benefits by Intervention

No.	Intervention name	Benefit source (%)			IWT modal share gain by 2030 (percentage points)
		Transport costs savings	Emission reductions	Safety improvements	
1	**Upgrade waterway Corridor 1 of the Red River Delta**	75.5	27.1	0.4	0.6
2	Upgrade waterway Corridor 2 of the Red River Delta	76.1	23.5	0.4	1.1
3	Upgrade waterway Corridor 3 of the Red River Delta	75.5	23.8	0.7	0.5
4	Introduce an extended gateway facility in the Red River Delta to serve the Hanoi market	99.6	−1.5	1.9	3.0
5	**Upgrade waterway Corridor 1 of the Mekong Delta**	75.3	24.1	0.6	1.8
6	**Upgrade a coastal shipping container terminal in Northern Vietnam**	71.7	26.8	1.4	2.9
7	Introduce user charges to fund waterway maintenance	33.9	65.4	0.8	0.0
8	**Promote engine and fleet modernization in IWT**	31.8	68.1	0.1	0.0

Source: Ecorys/World Bank analysis.
Note: IWT = inland waterway transport. Economically viable interventions shown in boldface.

other criteria are taken into consideration. For example, from a network resiliency perspective, Corridor 2 provides a key north-south alternative route to coastal shipping during portions of the year when ocean conditions are unsafe for coastal navigation.

- Upgrading Corridor 3 of the Red River Delta (Intervention 3) and providing an extended container-handling gateway to Haiphong port in the vicinity of Hanoi (Intervention 4) are found to produce economic returns below the economic cost of capital—particularly in the case of the former intervention. The primary reasons for this are low overall volumes in the case of Corridor 3, and low containerized volumes at the target corridor in the case of the extended gateway project.

- Left to market forces, the potential for modal shift from roads to waterways in Vietnam is limited (to within 1–3 percentage points over the long term). The main reason for this is that the waterway network offers limited and largely east-west geographical coverage, which critically limits waterway lengths of haul. As a result, the average length of haul for waterway transport in Vietnam (112 kilometers) is shorter than that of road transport (143 kilometers). Trucks are inherently more flexible in servicing short-haul itineraries, particularly for containerized shipments that may require extra handling at ports when containers are moved via barges. For shipments of nonbulk commodities, experience in North America and Western Europe shows that waterway transport can become economical only at much longer lengths of haul than Vietnam's average. As for bulk commodities, which account for over 75 percent of Vietnam's freight mix, many such products (e.g., construction materials, coal, and fertilizer) are substantially captured by the waterways already, leaving limited room for further gains away from trucks.

- This being the case, the majority of benefits associated with waterway infrastructure upgrading (e.g., Interventions 1 through 6) stem from within-mode (i.e., IWT-specific) transport cost efficiency improvements, as larger ship sizes enable lower transport costs—including environmental externalities—for commodities already captured by the waterways. For most of the proposed infrastructure upgrading interventions, 25–30 percent of economic benefits are generated through emission reductions, making environmental sustainability considerations a key driver of the economic viability of these investments. Indeed, long-term CO_2 emission reductions are projected to reach up to 18 percent, depending on the intervention. Projected safety gains are modest, owing to the modest expected modal shift.

- Two key factors prevent emission reductions associated with the proposed infrastructure upgrading interventions from being even higher: (a) the constrained window of viability for modal shift away from trucks and (b) the fact that emission performance per ton-kilometer (ton-km) of IWT in Vietnam is not as strong relative to road transport as it is in more developed markets (e.g., Western Europe) due to the still small average scale of Vietnam barges.

- Even at moderate shift levels, it is not surprising that the intervention that would lead to the largest modal shift is the coastal shipping project (Intervention 6), since this corridor is by far the most open to modal competition between roads and waterways owing to the much longer lengths of haul involved. Building on this effect, and the fact that terminal handling charges account for a significant share of coastal shipping costs between Haiphong and HCMC, the results suggest that it is economically desirable to upgrade the container-handling infrastructure at the port of Haiphong to reduce the cost of north-south coastal shipping.

- It is noteworthy that Intervention 4, the extended gateway linking Hanoi and Haiphong, would be expected to increase rather than reduce emissions (i.e., the contribution of changes in emission volumes to the project's benefits pool is negative). The reason for this is that the waterway route between Hanoi and Haiphong (142 kilometers) is longer than the road route (105 kilometers). The impact of a longer route, as suggested by the above analysis, in the end offsets the modest gains in emissions per ton-km from the induced modal shift. This exemplifies the many complexities that characterize modal policy and the need to consider the underlying demand-supply and economic geography features of each case.

- The main source of benefits for the non-infrastructure-based interventions (Interventions 7 and 8), on the other hand, is the reduction of emissions. In the case of maintenance charges, this is because such charges would actually increase IWT transport costs, although these cost increases are expected to be more than offset by the benefits of better-maintained waterways. Meanwhile, emissions are reduced as network availability improves, allowing carriers to better deploy larger vessels at segments that may be unable to handle such equipment year-round with insufficient maintenance coverage. In the case of the engine modernization program, new engines are expected to provide significantly better emissions performance compared with current equipment. While some modest transport cost savings will be obtained via fuel efficiency gains, the larger impact of newer engines is expected to originate from lower emission levels per ton-km transported.

- Better maintenance pays for itself. Those parties responsible for waterway maintenance often do not fully account for the negative implications of lagging maintenance expenditures, many of which are borne by society. And given that the majority of benefits expected to be obtained from a more complete funding of waterway maintenance manifest themselves, as suggested by the above results, in the form of lower emissions—the value of which is not captured in transport rates or public sector revenues—it is not surprising that maintenance of the waterway network is underfunded. But the above analysis suggests that fully funding maintenance would be expected to generate transport cost savings above and beyond the value to society of reduced emissions, thereby more than offsetting the cost impact of a maintenance charge.

Note

1. Except for Intervention 9 (IWT promotion program), for which a break-even analysis was conducted. The required road-to-waterway modal shift for this intervention to break even is estimated at roughly 0.5 percent. This is found to be reasonably attainable given the magnitude of the expected modal shift from some of the other interventions evaluated by this report.

CHAPTER 1

Introduction

Context

Transport demand and economic growth are closely linked: In Vietnam, sustained high rates of growth in gross domestic product (GDP)—averaging 7.2 percent per year over the past 20 years and facilitated by the country's increasingly deeper integration into the world economy—have resulted in higher demand for freight transport. In the process, the composition of Vietnam's freight transport demand has changed drastically. Economic openness has given rise to supply chains that are more exposed to competition, domestically and globally, and more likely to be linked by more complex (e.g., multimodal) logistics itineraries than ever before. These chains increasingly rely on efficient and reliable multimodal transportation, storage, handling, and value-added services in order to remain competitive. As Vietnam looks to continue on a path of sustained economic growth, it faces the challenge of better aligning demand and supply of logistics services and improving the overall efficiency of its freight transport system.

While greater international integration has turned trade competitiveness into one of Vietnam's major national objectives, the risks posed by climate change underscore the need for the country to simultaneously address the challenge of reducing greenhouse gas (GHG) emissions—including those from freight transport. Among non-air-freight transport modes (air freight, by far the most carbon-intense transport mode, captures a negligible share of Vietnam's freight mix), road transport typically produces more carbon dioxide (CO_2) emissions per ton-kilometer (ton-km) than any other form of rail or waterborne transport. On average, rail and barge transport are 2.5–3.0 times and 3.5–4.0 times more fuel efficient than truck transport, respectively, on a ton-km basis. And Vietnam is increasingly becoming a road-intensive economy. Vietnam's roads account for approximately half of all freight flows by tonnage and for almost 40 percent of national freight ton-km. Perhaps of more significance, road freight volumes have grown faster than those hauled by rival modes over the recent past and are projected to continue to do so for years to come. Given the existence of capacity constraints in the country's road network and the increasingly costly environmental impact of road use for freight movements, it is desirable for Vietnam to develop and maintain viable, competitive alternatives to road freight transport.

A more intense use of waterborne freight transport can be a particularly effective way of both promoting growth and reducing emissions. Since transport—along both the infrastructure provision and service delivery dimensions—is widely considered a fundamental facilitator of economic growth, it is a common concern, shared by developed and developing countries alike, that efforts to reduce emissions from the transport sector may adversely impact economic growth. Primarily due to favorable economic geography features, Vietnam has in inland waterway transport (IWT) and coastal shipping a promising platform to transition toward a lower-carbon freight transport system without jeopardizing long-term prosperity.

Vietnam's dense river network and long coastline can be seen as a growth sustainability platform. The country's main economic centers—around Hanoi in the Northern region and around Ho Chi Minh City (HCMC) in the Southern region—have historically developed in proximity to coastal areas, along rivers, and in river deltas. Greater use of IWT and coastal shipping, particularly when efficiently linked to other transport modes (e.g., drayage trucks for short-distance haulage) and logistics services (e.g., warehousing and container handling), can produce significant cost reductions for shippers and carriers. And it can do so while producing meaningful economic returns to society at large, including freight and nonfreight vehicle operating cost reductions, travel time savings, reductions in accident and fatality rates, and less environmental degradation.

However, since Vietnam's road sector is typically the recipient of the bulk of public spending devoted to transportation, improving the efficiency and accessibility of IWT and coastal shipping requires the deliberate design and implementation of a mix of public policies, programs, and projects expressly geared to that objective. At present, approximately 80 percent of public spending in transportation is devoted to expanding (primarily) and preserving (secondarily) the road network. This report aims to support Vietnam in the challenge of making the economic case for more strategic investments in waterborne freight transportation.

Objectives of the Report

The report has three objectives. The first is *to identify targeted policy and infrastructure interventions in IWT and coastal shipping* that can enhance the competitiveness and environmental sustainability characteristics of Vietnam's freight transport system. These are interventions that will ideally contribute to achieving lower levels of fuel consumption and GHG emissions as well as to reducing congestion and accident costs system-wide. The second objective of the report is *to estimate the economic benefits and costs associated with the interventions identified*, and to use that information to produce a prioritized list of evaluated recommendations for implementation. Finally, the report seeks *to inform interested*

Introduction

stakeholders, including public sector authorities, the shipper and carrier community, donors, academia, and the general public about the current status, composition, and key challenges and opportunities facing Vietnam's domestic waterborne transport sector.

Scope and Methodology

The report presents the findings of a five-step analytical methodology (see figure 1.1). Steps 1 through 3 utilize supply-demand indicators, findings from stakeholder interviews, qualitative analyses, and comparisons to relevant global benchmarks to identify the main impediments to the further development and use of IWT and coastal shipping—as well as interventions to address them. Step 1 describes the key components comprising Vietnam's IWT and coastal shipping logistics, including the regulatory and institutional setting, the provision of public infrastructure assets, the current and projected freight composition, the size and vessel-type breakdown of carriers' installed capacity, the GHG emissions profile, and the service-delivery market structure. Step 2 assesses the adequacy of these features relative to shipper needs and highlights the most relevant bottlenecks influencing each sector's performance. Step 3 makes preliminary recommendations to drive enhancements. Step 4 adopts a quantitative approach to estimating efficiency and economic return indicators associated with the proposed recommendations stemming from Step 3. For example, estimates were made of the impact that various interventions would have on average vessel sizes, transport operating costs, modal shift, and GHG emissions. These impacts were then used to calculate the net change in economic costs and benefits associated with particular recommendations—including both policy- and infrastructure-based interventions—relative to a "business as usual" baseline. Step 5 concludes the analysis by making more definitive, economically evaluated recommendations for the implementation of targeted public sector interventions.

The report's scope comprises the three most important sources of freight activity in Vietnam, namely, road, IWT, and coastal shipping transportation. This is a reflection of the country's economic and industrial landscape, where most freight itineraries are linked to (a) the Red River Delta and portions of the

Figure 1.1 Analytical Approach

Source: Ecorys/World Bank analysis.
Note: IWT = inland waterway transport.

surrounding Northeast and Northwest regions (with metro Hanoi as a focal point), (b) the Mekong River Delta and portions of the Southeast region (with metro HCMC as a focal point), and (c) the two-way trade linking the two deltas (see map 1.1). Although the road network serves all three trades with varying degrees of efficiency and reliability, IWT is a relevant mode for intraregional freight flows, while coastal shipping is most attractive for interregional flows linking the Northern and Southern regions.[1]

Map 1.1 Main Areas of Study in Vietnam

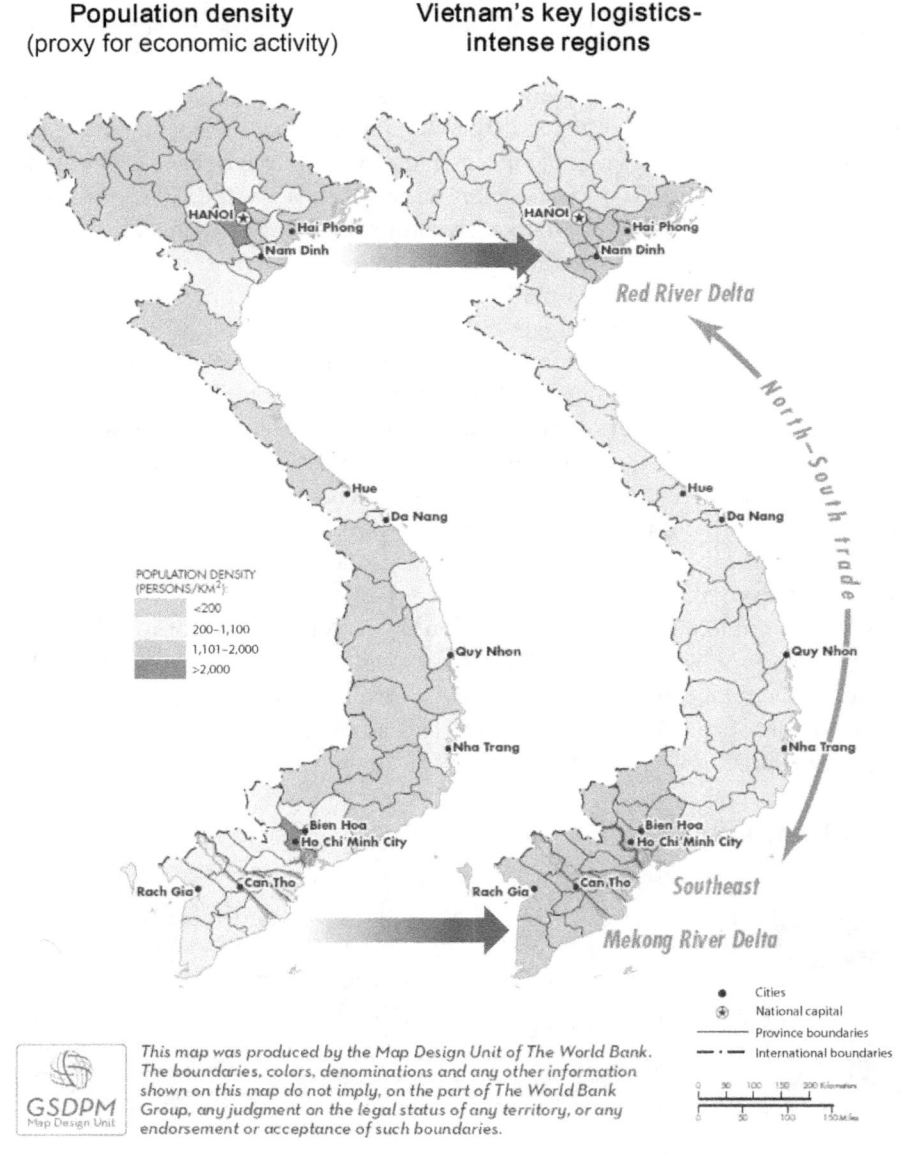

Source: World Bank analysis with data from General Statistics Office of Vietnam.

Key Data Sources

The findings presented in the report were informed by numerous in-country interviews with transport sector stakeholders and builds on data and findings provided by previous studies on the performance of Vietnam's transport and logistics sector. The latter include the Vietnam Inland Waterway Administration (VIWA) IWT Sector Forecast; the second update of the Comprehensive Study on the Sustainable Development of the Transport System in Vietnam (referred to as VITRANSS-2), produced by the Vietnam Ministry of Transport (MoT) in association with the Japan International Cooperation Agency (JICA); the Northern Region Comprehensive Transport Strategy Study (NRCTSS); the World Bank–financed Northern Delta Transport Development Project (NDTDP) and Mekong Delta Transport Infrastructure Development Project (MDTIDP); the World Bank–commissioned Multimodal Transport Regulatory Review (MTRR); and MoT's Transport Development Strategy up to 2020 with a Vision Towards 2030, approved by the prime minister of Vietnam in March 2009. In particular, VITRANSS-2 is widely recognized as the most reliable and up-to-date source of current and projected origin-destination freight traffic matrices available for Vietnam, amid an environment where availability of data of this type is limited. As such, VITRANSS-2 forms the basis of this report's baseline for all traffic and economic impact calculations.

Structure of the Report

The structure of the report, depicted graphically in figure 1.2, is divided into seven chapters. The report opens with a stock taking of current developments and expected trends in IWT and coastal shipping from the perspective of market demand (chapter 2) and market supply (chapter 3). Chapter 4 assesses, on an indicative basis, the environmental implications (in terms of CO_2 emissions) of these transport trends. Chapter 5 defines and assesses the main bottlenecks impacting the development of inland and coastal waterborne transport. A preliminary strategy for developing IWT and coastal shipping is presented in chapter 6. The chapter discusses both the overall strategic approach and a series of proposed remedial actions, including public policy and infrastructure provision interventions. A set of specific IWT and coastal shipping interventions (also referred to as "projects"), informed by the latter analysis, are further developed and evaluated in chapter 7. The evaluation is based on an intervention-specific model methodology that includes modal split modeling combined with a cost-benefit analysis (CBA). These models are used to calculate economic internal rates of return (eIRRs) of recommended interventions.

Six appendices are provided at the end of the report. Appendix A lists the stakeholders interviewed. Appendix B describes the physical characteristics of the major waterway routes in Northern and Southern Vietnam in tabular form. Appendix C summarizes key considerations in IWT fleet scaling up.

Figure 1.2 Structure of the Report by Chapter

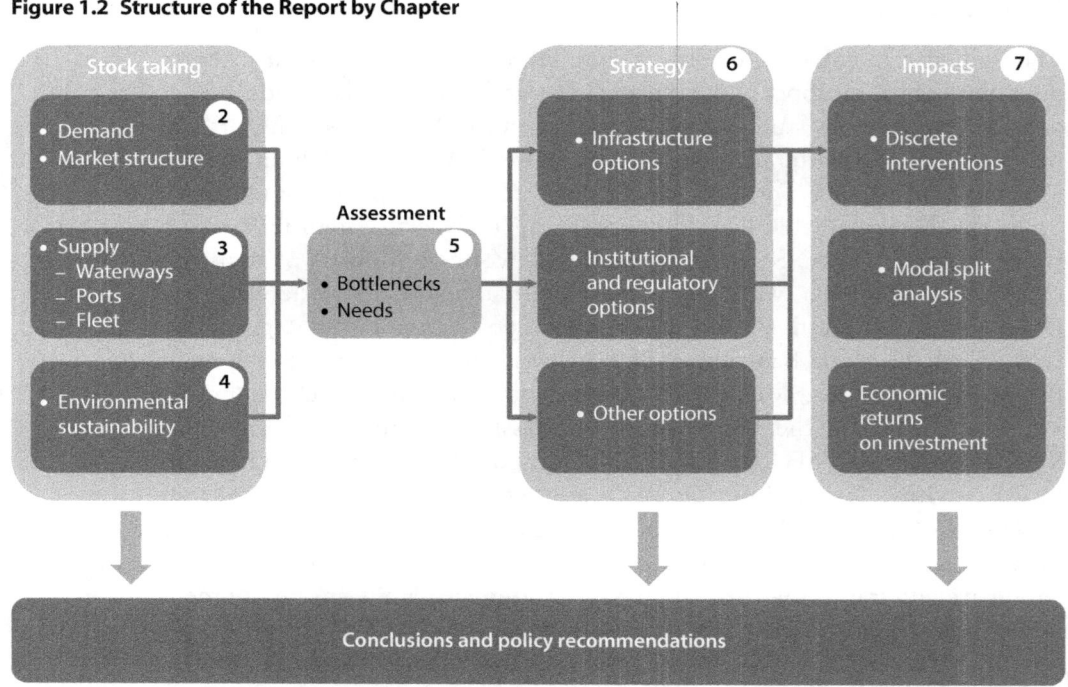

Source: Ecorys/World Bank analysis.
Note: Number in circle indicates chapter of this report where the topic is covered.

The output of the scenario-based CBA (chapter 7) is chiefly determined by the underlying estimation of changes in modal choice for the routing of freight triggered by a particular intervention. Given the relevance of estimating modal shift as reliably and meaningfully as possible, a modal split model has been developed, which was utilized to assess the impact of recommendations on modal choice (and subsequent GHG emissions). This model is described in appendix D.

Detailed descriptions of the interventions proposed are presented in appendix E. Finally, details on estimating the economic impact of these projects using the modal split model and CBA are presented in appendix F.

Note

1. For brevity in the discussion, the remainder of the report will refer to the Red River Delta and portions of the Northwest and Northeast regions closest to Hanoi, collectively, as "the North region," "the Northern region," "Northern Vietnam," or, for simplicity, the Red River Delta (as this is the dominant of the three regions from a logistics standpoint). Similarly, it will refer to the Mekong Delta and portions of the Southeast region (where the latter includes, notably, HCMC), collectively, as "the South region," "the Southern region," "Southern Vietnam," or, for simplicity, the Mekong River Delta region. The report will refer to the trade corridor between the North and South regions as the "North-South axis" or "North-South trade."

CHAPTER 2

Demand for Waterborne and Multimodal Transport

Size and Historical Growth Patterns of IWT and Coastal Shipping

Vietnam's interprovincial freight transport market is largely dominated by two modes: inland waterway and road transport (see table 2.1). Together, these modes account for 94 percent of the tons and 67 percent of the ton-kilometers (ton-km) transported annually between provinces nationwide. While inland waterway transport (IWT) tonnage has been growing at a healthy rate, 1.5 times that of gross domestic product (GDP), over the past several years, the road sector has managed to grow even faster. According to Vietnam's General Statistics Office, in the 10 years to 2008 IWT freight tonnage grew at an average annual rate of 10.5 percent, compared with 14.1 percent for road tonnage over the same period. In other words, IWT has been losing tonnage share to the roads since at least 1998. Such share erosion over the recent past stems from a combination of factors, including increasing production levels of time-sensitive goods (e.g., seasonal products and high-end electronic components), economic (and population) growth in areas outside the geographic coverage of the IWT network, plummeting truck transport rates in an environment of deregulated competition and low barriers to entry, and a significant expansion of the road network.

Yet, and despite having lost share to the road sector over a number of years, IWT still accounts for the highest tonnage share among all modes, at 48.3 percent (slightly higher than the road sector's share of 45.4 percent). Simply put, the IWT sector remains essential to the everyday functioning of the Vietnamese economy. When demand is measured in ton-km, which better reflects the transport intensity of a given mode, IWT's 30.4 percent share is also significant and not far from the road sector's 36.6 percent. The fact that the road sector has a lower demand share than IWT on a tonnage basis but a higher demand share than IWT on a ton-km basis implies that the average length of haul for a load moved over the road (143 kilometers) is higher than that of a load moved by inland waterways (112 kilometers).

Table 2.1 Vietnam: Interprovincial Freight Volumes by Mode, 2008 and Forecast to 2030

Year	Road	Rail	IWT	Coastal shipping (Domestic)	Air	All modes
Volume (millions of tons per year)[a,b]						
2008	181	8	193	17	0.1	400
2030	640	47	395	38	0.3	1,119
Modal shares, % (based on tons)						
2008	45.4	1.9	48.3	4.4	0.0	100
2030	57.2	4.2	35.3	3.4	0.0	100
Average trip length (km)						
2008	143	400	112	1,161	1,404	178
2030	201	509	122	1,107	1,348	217
Volume (billions of ton-km per year)[a]						
2008	26	3	22	20	0.1	71
2030	129	24	48	42	0.4	243
Modal shares, % (based on ton-km)						
2008	36.6	4.3	30.4	28.5	0.1	100
2030	53.0	9.8	19.9	17.2	0.2	100
Annual growth rates 2008–30 (%)						
Tons	5.9	8.5	3.3	3.6	6.5	4.8
Ton-km	7.5	9.7	3.7	3.4	6.3	5.7

Source: Data from JICA 2009.
Note: IWT = inland waterway transport.
a. Per-day data as reported by JICA 2009 multiplied by 300.
b. It is noted that JICA 2009 data for 2008 differ from statistics published elsewhere by the Vietnam Inland Waterway Administration (VIWA). For this report, the authors determined that JICA 2009 data were preferable, to be consistent with forecast data from the same source for 2020 and 2030, which are not available from VIWA.

Although coastal shipping carries a tonnage share that, at 4.4 percent, is markedly lower than that of both IWT and the road sector, the mode's ton-km share (28.5 percent) is practically at par with that of IWT. This is due to the nature of coastal shipping loads, which on average are considerably longer than those of any other mode except air freight. Thus, both IWT and coastal shipping (a) attract meaningful demand levels in the freight market and (b) cater to unique shipment types.

Official statistics from the Vietnam Maritime Administration (Vinamarine) show that, between 1998 and 2008, coastal shipping tonnage grew at an average annual rate of 13.2 percent—faster than IWT tonnage but still slower than road tonnage. This masks, however, the impressive growth performance of the containerized portion of coastal shipments, where 20-foot equivalent units (TEUs) grew at an average annual rate of 35 percent over the same 10-year period, although starting from a small base. This is further evidence that Vietnam's production and transportation profile has changed over the past 10 years to accommodate higher manufactured-commodity volumes, which are typically containerized and more dependent on higher-service-level (typically intermodal) logistics.

Demand for Waterborne and Multimodal Transport

At anywhere between 1.5 and 2.0 times the rate of growth of GDP, depending on mode, it is clear that the growth rates for the road, inland waterway, and coastal shipping freight sectors are placing strain on transport sector infrastructure and service delivery. Critically, the strain does not necessarily relate only to specific shipping routes, but also to key supply chain "handoff" links, such as transshipment terminals, storage areas, and intermodal hinterland connection points.

Growth Projections for IWT and Coastal Shipping

Vietnam's road freight volumes are projected to see faster long-term growth than IWT or coastal shipping volumes (see lower panel of table 2.1). Specifically, it is expected that the road sector will grow at an average annual rate of 5.9 percent in terms of tons and 7.5 percent in terms of ton-kms over the next 20 years, compared with 3.3 percent and 3.7 percent, respectively, for IWT. Coastal shipping is also projected to lose share to the roads over the next 20 years, under both demand measures.

As a means to assess the reasonableness of the long-term forecasts presented in table 2.1, one can compare Vietnam's projected freight flows with current freight activity in the Netherlands—an advanced economy with heavy use of inland waterways (see table 2.2). Data from 2011 for the Netherlands indicate that the market share of IWT is 32 percent in tonnage terms. This is far lower than Vietnam's current share but closer to what is expected for Vietnam by 2030. Conversely, IWT's current ton-km share in the Netherlands (37 percent) is higher than the corresponding figure for Vietnam (about 30 percent and projected to fall over the next 20 years). Both findings suggest that IWT in the Netherlands typically delivers shipments over longer distances compared with those traveling by roads, while in Vietnam the opposite is true. Network differences between the countries account for this discrepancy.

Table 2.2 Modal Share of Surface Freight Volumes in the Netherlands, 2011

Road	Rail	IWT	All
Volume (millions of tons)			
694	39	344	1,077
Modal share, % (based on tons transported)			
64	4	32	100
Volumes (billion ton-km)			
73.3	6.4	46.3	126.0
Modal share, % (based on ton-km transported)			
58	5	37	100
Average trip length (km)			
46	171	95	—

Source: Ecorys/World Bank analysis, with data from Statistics Netherlands 2013 and Eurostat 2013.
Note: — = not available; IWT = inland waterway transport. Average trip length data are for 2006.

Commodity Tonnage and Tonnage Distribution by Mode

Vietnam's inland and coastal waterways are primarily used to transport bulk commodities. Table 2.3 shows the commodity and modal breakdown of Vietnam's freight transportation. Construction materials, coal, and cement register the largest absolute IWT volumes, whereas coal, construction materials, fertilizer, and fishery products are the most IWT-dependent commodities. In coastal shipping, the largest absolute volumes originate from manufactured goods, cement, and coal, whereas petroleum, cement, and coal are the commodities with the highest incidence of coastal shipping use. Notably, the combined tonnage market share of IWT and coastal shipping in the transportation of manufactured goods, which are typically containerized, is currently noticeably low (9 percent), signaling an important market opportunity for these modes.

Inland and Coastal Shipping Lengths of Haul

Most inland waterway freight shipments in Vietnam travel a distance of less than 200 kilometers. Every mode of transport has a certain length of haul range within which it can perform competitively at acceptable operating costs and where it can attract disproportionate share loads relative to other modes. Vietnam's inland waterways perform best for consignments of up to 300 kilometers in trip

Table 2.3 Freight Transport Volumes (Tons per Day) and Modal Shares by Commodity, 2008

Commodity	IWT	Coastal	Road	Rail	Total	% IWT	% Coastal
Rice	36,109	4,261	78,969	204	119,543	30	4
Sugar cane/sugar	4,847	88	3,682	0	8,617	56	1
Wood	11,683	914	11,499	523	24,619	47	4
Steel	1,015	764	41,965	2,156	45,900	2	2
Construction materials	370,787	1,914	129,219	8,213	510,133	73	0
Cement	64,387	13,021	38,965	3,810	120,183	54	11
Fertilizer	28,678	1,168	8,813	2,939	41,598	69	3
Coal	92,549	10,092	12,106	2,377	117,124	79	9
Petroleum	5,018	8,234	33,374	404	47,030	11	18
Industrial crops	2,415	0	5,628	0	8,043	30	0
Manufacturing goods	3,916	13,524	171,895	4,895	194,481	2	7
Fishery products	12,203	0	7,186	0	19,389	63	0
Animal meat and others	9,373	4,118	61,578	0	75,069	12	5
Total (tons/day)	642,980	58,098	604,879	25,521	1,331,729	n.a.	n.a.
Modal share (% tons)	48.3	4.4	45.4	1.9	100	n.a.	n.a.
Average trip length	112	1,161	143	400	178	n.a.	n.a.
Modal share (% ton-km)	30.4	28.5	36.5	4.3	100	n.a.	n.a.

Source: Data from JICA 2009.
Note: Coastal = coastal shipping; IWT = inland waterway transport; n.a. = not applicable.

length and especially for those in the range of 100–200 kilometers (see table 2.4). Within the latter distance range, IWT has a dominant market share, in tonnage terms, of 81 percent. Conversely, coastal shipping performs best in the range of 400–1,800 kilometers and peaks at 1,400–1,600 kilometers, where the mode captures a market share of 71 percent.

The competitive position of transport modes relative to a given shipment is strongly influenced by the distance traveled. It is typically the case that road transport has a competitive advantage over short distances, where flexibility is critical, while other modes are more competitive over longer distances, where cost efficiency can be the key routing decision factor. In Vietnam, the short average length of haul for the relatively less flexible IWT services (112 kilometers) compared with a slightly longer one for road transport services (143 kilometers) could be seen as evidence of the vulnerability of IWT. This is largely explained by the fact that Vietnam's waterway networks are concentrated in the northern and southern provinces, while road transport networks reach places, such as the central provinces, where navigable waterways are limited and where distances relative to the main economic centers in the North and South regions are longer.

Unlike Western Europe, where IWT has a competitive edge at medium to long distances of 200–600 kilometers, in Vietnam IWT must continue to compete with the roads on relatively short distances to gain cargo share. This implies that cost-efficient vessels, accessible loading facilities, and high-quality logistics services need to be available to fulfill the potential of IWT in Vietnam.

Table 2.4 Freight Transport Volumes (Tons per Day) and Modal Shares by Length of Haul, 2008

Trip length (km)	IWT	Coastal	Road	Rail	Total	% IWT	% Coastal
<100	268,974	288	442,294	3,114	714,670	38	0
100–200	363,935	639	77,468	7,188	449,230	81	0
200–300	9,236	2,601	38,388	5,480	55,707	17	5
300–400	834	590	8,361	3,309	13,094	6	5
400–500	1	4,854	2,915	1,154	8,925	0	54
500–600	0	1,614	3,020	546	5,180	0	31
600–700	0	1,628	1,907	217	3,753	0	43
700–800	0	3,531	1,884	345	5,769	0	61
800–900	0	3,751	6,618	596	10,985	0	34
900–1,000	0	225	3,471	283	3,979	0	6
1,000–1,200	0	4,189	3,436	800	8,429	0	50
1,200–1,400	0	6,339	1,476	305	8,121	0	78
1,400–1,600	0	23,756	7,295	2,115	33,379	0	71
1,600–1,800	0	4,093	6,309	69	10,471	0	39
1,800–2,000	0	0	37	0	37	0	0
Total (tons/day)	642,980	58,098	604,879	25,521	1,331,729	48	4

Source: Data from JICA 2009.
Note: Coastal = coastal shipping; IWT = inland waterway transport.

Main Freight Flows

Regional Routes and Modal Competition

Because of the geographic concentration of Vietnam's inland waterway network, which reduces the available lengths of haul for waterway shipments, potential tonnage share gains for the IWT sector can realistically only materialize vis-à-vis the road network. The rail network is primarily used for long-haul, north-south shipments and therefore has negligible geographic overlap with the waterways. And while north-south coastal shipping may in principle be far more exposed to rail competition than inland waterway shipping given the length of coastal hauls, the share of rail transport in the tonnage shipped between the Red and Mekong River deltas is small, mainly a reflection of Vietnam's still low rail service quality and reliability.[1] Consequently, the rest of the report will center on analyzing the relative economic competitiveness of waterway and coastal shipping relative to the road sector.

Primary Intra- and Interregional Corridors
Red River Delta Region

Three freight corridors account for the majority (71 percent) of interprovincial, intraregional road, and inland waterway freight flows in the Red River Delta. These corridors are as follows (see map 2.1 highlighting their location):

- Corridor 1: Quang Ninh–Haiphong–Pha Lai–Hanoi–Viet Tri
- Corridor 2: Haiphong–Thai Binh–Ha Nam–Nam Dinh–Ninh Binh–Quang Ninh
- Corridor 3: Hanoi–Day/Lach Giang

As shown in table 2.5, in 2008, 631,000 daily tons of freight were moved between provinces in the Red River Delta region via the roads or the waterways. Of those, 375,000 moved on the waterways (59 percent of total) and 256,000 moved on the roads (41 percent). It is projected that interprovincial freight flows in the Red River Delta will grow at a rate of 3.6 percent for the 2008–20 period, and at a rate of 2.6 percent between 2020 and 2030.

It is projected that by 2020 some 518,000 waterway tons and 446,000 road tons will move between provinces in the region every day, implying an expected decrease in the modal share of IWT of approximately 5 percentage points, from 59 percent to 54 percent. Such a shift stems from the changing nature of regional flows away from raw materials and more intensively into manufactured products.

Mekong Delta

The comparable interprovincial transport volumes in the Mekong River Delta region for 2008 are 466,000 total tons per day (broken down by 261,000 tons per day via the waterways and 206,000 tons per day via the roads). These are

Demand for Waterborne and Multimodal Transport

Map 2.1 Main Corridors in the Northern Delta

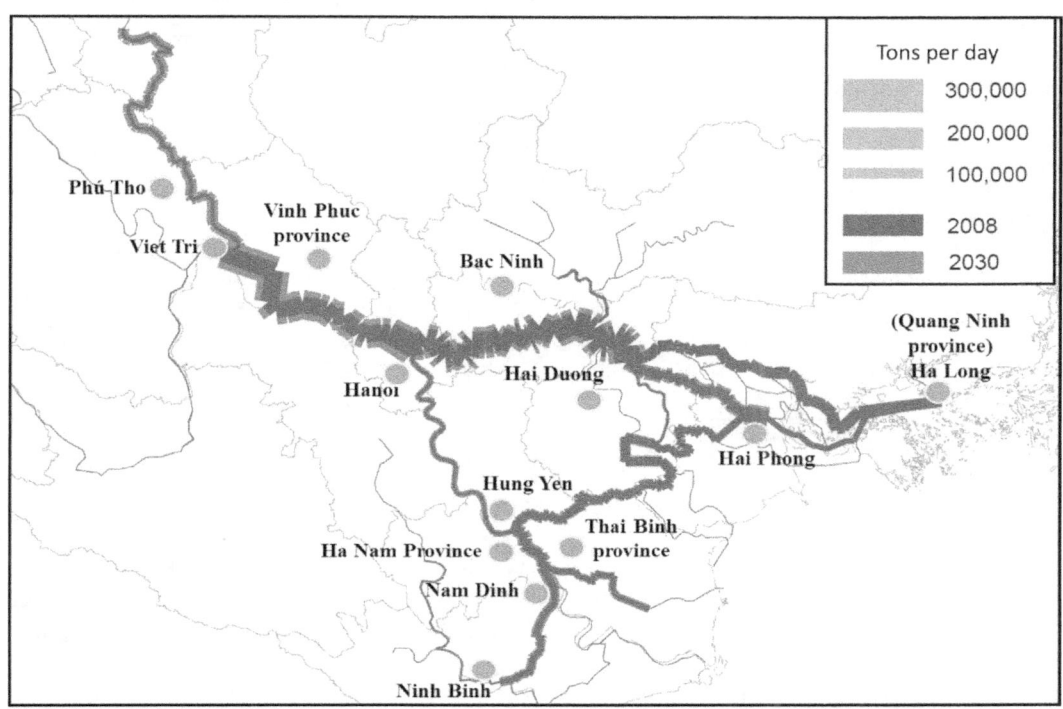

Source: Ecorys, with data from JICA 2009.

Table 2.5 Red River Delta: Current/Projected Road and Waterway Interprovincial Flows

Tons per day	Mode	2008	2020	2030	CAGR 2008–20	CAGR 2020–30
	IWT	374,616	518,361	638,149	2.7	2.1
Total delta	Road	256,203	446,329	604,768	4.7	3.1
	Both	630,819	964,691	1,242,917	3.6	2.6
	IWT	225,671	304,726	370,606	2.5	2.0
Corridor 1	Road	91,186	166,832	229,871	5.2	3.3
	Both	316,857	471,559	600,477	3.4	2.4
	IWT	19,890	37,858	52,832	5.5	3.4
Corridor 2	Road	33,236	50,983	60,149	3.6	1.7
	Both	53,126	88,841	112,981	4.4	2.4
	IWT	62,176	81,096	96,862	2.2	1.8
Corridor 3	Road	16,531	25,706	28,336	3.7	1.0
	Both	78,707	106,801	125,198	2.6	1.6
	IWT	307,737	423,680	520,300	2.7	2.1
All 3 corridors	Road	140,953	243,521	318,356	4.7	2.7
	Both	448,690	667,201	838,656	3.4	2.3

Source: Data from JICA 2009.
Note: CAGR = compounded annual growth rate; IWT = inland waterway transport.

Table 2.6 Current and Projected Main Interprovincial Cargo Flows in the Mekong Delta

Tons per day	Mode	2008	2020	2030	CAGR 2008–20	CAGR 2020–30
Total delta	IWT	260,663	461,606	629,059	4.9	3.1
	Road	205,661	490,279	727,461	7.5	4.0
	Both	466,324	951,885	1,356,520	6.1	3.6
Corridor 1	IWT	115,810	231,839	328,529	6.0	3.5
	Road	21,664	53,519	80,064	7.8	4.1
	Both	137,474	285,357	408,593	6.3	3.7
Corridor 2	IWT	23,452	45,961	64,719	5.8	3.5
	Road	2,615	24,790	43,270	20.6	5.7
	Both	26,067	70,752	107,989	8.7	4.3
Total 2 corridors	IWT	139,262	277,800	393,248	5.9	3.5
	Road	24,279	78,309	123,334	10.3	4.6
	Both	163,541	356,109	516,582	6.7	3.8

Source: Data from JICA 2009.
Note: CAGR = compounded annual growth rate; IWT = inland waterway transport.

lower absolute tonnage volumes than those registered in the Red River Delta for the same year (see table 2.6). Interprovincial Mekong Delta road and waterway volumes are expected to increase at a rate of 6.1 percent per year through 2020, before slowing to 3.6 percent per year between 2020 and 2030. Both projections are significantly higher than those for the Red River Delta, reflecting the expectation of continued dynamism for Southern Vietnam in the manufacturing, aquaculture, and agriculture sectors.

By 2020, it is expected that 462,000 tons per day and 490,000 tons per day, respectively, will move via the waterways and the roads between Mekong Delta provinces. As in the Red River Delta, these projections imply an expected erosion in the modal share of IWT over (roughly) the next 10 years, from 56 percent to 48 percent.

Two main freight corridors are found in the Mekong Delta (see map 2.2 depiction of them):

- Corridor 1: HCMC–Ben Tre–My Tho–Vinh Long
  (HCMC–Tien Giang–Vinh Long–Dong Thap–An Giang–Can Tho–Hau Giang)
- Corridor 2: HCMC–Tien Giang–Ben Tre–Tra Vin–Soc Trang–Bac Lieu/Ca Mau

Coastal Shipping

Owing to the report's emphasis on public sector interventions that may lead to modal shift away from the roads and into waterborne transport, the analysis of freight flows in the domestic North-South trade (defined as freight shipped between the Red River Delta and the Mekong River Delta regions) focuses on the transportation of containerized cargo on trucks and vessels—the type of

Demand for Waterborne and Multimodal Transport

Map 2.2 Main Corridors in the Mekong Delta

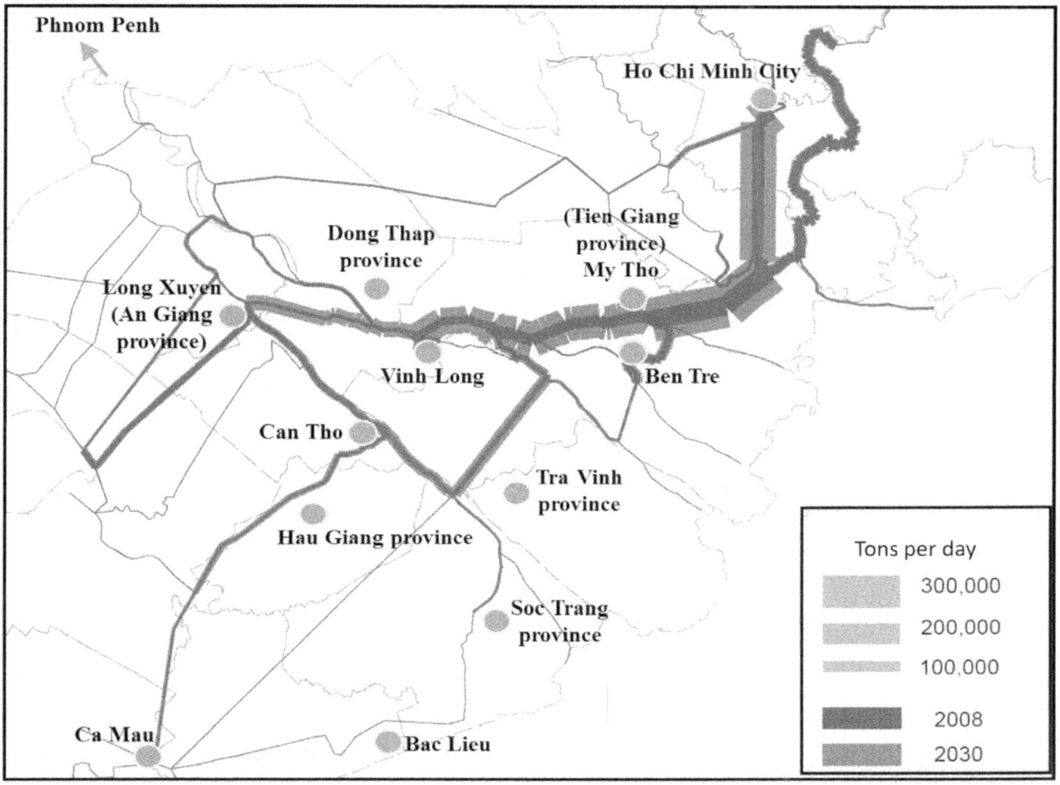

Source: Ecorys, with data from JICA 2009.

freight that is most susceptible to modal shift. Liquid and dry bulk cargo transported by road or vessel between these regions, while prevalent, is not a focus of the report, as it is significantly less prone to modal shift (most bulk commodities in the trade are largely already captured by coastal shipping). North-South cargo flows by rail are also excluded, as rail volumes are comparatively small[2] and the quality of rail service—travel times and travel time variability—comparatively low, signaling limited opportunities for road to rail modal shift based on quality of service improvements.

In 2008, approximately 29,000 tons of containerized cargo were transported daily between the two delta regions, of which about 13,000 tons per day traveled the southbound leg while slightly more than 16,000 tons per day traveled the northbound leg (see table 2.7). In other words, the North-South trade is directionally imbalanced overall, with more volumes traveling from south to north.

However, the story changes when volumes are segregated by mode: the southbound leg is the dominant leg for coastal shipping, while the northbound leg is

Table 2.7 Road and Coastal Containerized Cargo Flows for the North-South Axis

Tons per day	2008	2020	2030	CAGR 2008–20	CAGR 2020–30
Road					
North→South	3,341	22,923	39,241	17.4	5.5
South→North	7,624	20,347	30,950	8.5	4.3
Both directions	10,965	43,270	70,191	12.1	5.0
Coastal					
North→South	9,611	65,945	112,889	17.4	5.5
South→North	8,642	23,064	35,083	8.5	4.3
Both directions	18,254	89,009	147,972	14.1	5.2
Total					
North→South	12,952	88,868	152,130	17.4	5.5
South→North	16,266	43,411	66,033	8.5	4.3
Both directions	29,219	132,279	218,163	13.4	5.1

Source: Data from JICA 2009.
Note: JICA 2009 provides no projections of containerized volumes on the coastal trade beyond 2008. It is assumed that coastal volumes will grow at the same rate as road volumes, where the latter are forecast by JICA 2009 for 2020 and 2030. This seemed appropriate given the similarity between commodity types transported by the two modes on this corridor. CAGR = compounded annual growth rate.

the dominant leg for highway shipping. This pattern may be a reflection of the nature of economic activity in the delta regions, where the Mekong Delta still dominates in industrial production and manufacturing activity, with supply chains that would seem relatively more reliant on road transportation than their counterparts in the Northern Delta. Not surprisingly, JICA (2009) projections indicate that containerized North-South shipping (over-the-road and coastal) will grow over the next 20 years at a multiple of intradelta road and IWT flows, where the latter include (much slower-growing) noncontainerized commodities moved mainly by IWT.

Zooming in on the Red River Delta

Map 2.1 illustrates the three waterway corridors of the Red River Delta region. Corridor 1 (from Quang Ninh to Viet Tri, via Hanoi) is the most active, with a 60 percent share of total regional IWT tonnage. Corridor 2 (from Quang Ninh to Ninh Binh) is the second most important corridor in the region, with 17 percent of all IWT flows, while Corridor 3 (from Ninh Binh to Hanoi) accounts for a further 5 percent. Together, the three corridors capture 82 percent of regional IWT tonnage.

Corridor 1: Hanoi–Haiphong–Quang Ninh

Corridor 1 freight flow data by mode (IWT and road) and origin-destination (O-D) pair (province to province) are presented in table 2.8. Hai Duong, Phu Tho, and Quang Ninh are major sources of outgoing IWT flows, while Hanoi and Haiphong are the two most important destinations. Quang Ninh province is a major coal-producing area that supplies nearly the entire

Table 2.8 Origin-Destination Cargo Flows for Corridor 1 in the Red River Delta, 2008

	Hanoi	Vinh Phuc	Bac Ninh	Hai Duong	Haiphong	Quang Ninh	Phu Tho	Total
IWT tons per day								
Hanoi	n.a.	100	—	300	5,640	880	3,040	9,960
Vinh Phuc	1,430	n.a.	—	—	—	590	30	2,050
Bac Ninh	1,200	—	n.a.	—	—	—	—	1,200
Hai Duong	49,880	—	—	n.a.	—	7,605	5,860	63,345
Haiphong	4,500	—	—	—	n.a.	4,050	5,200	13,750
Quang Ninh	17,400	150	14,720	15,477	560	n.a.	14,280	62,587
Phu Tho	11,400	300	3,010	6,319	44,110	7,640	n.a.	72,779
Total	85,810	550	17,730	22,096	50,310	20,765	28,410	225,671
Road tons per day								
Hanoi	n.a.	2,564	10,835	2,071	2,200	109	214	17,993
Vinh Phuc	7,674	n.a.	35	65	1,591	151	535	10,051
Bac Ninh	5,215	16	n.a.	3	126	60	30	5,450
Hai Duong	1,810	873	964	n.a.	7,606	830	255	12,338
Haiphong	17,462	218	452	10,034	n.a.	1,055	365	29,586
Quang Ninh	376	220	106	2,695	5,910	n.a.	—	9,307
Phu Tho	72	4,818	812	3	755	—	n.a.	6,461
Total	32,609	8,709	13,204	14,871	18,189	2,205	1,399	91,186

Source: Data from JICA 2009.
Note: — = no flows reported; n.a. = not applicable. Origins are shown in leftmost column and destinations as rows across.

demand of the Red River Delta. Moreover, Hai Duong and Phu Tho provinces are important construction material– and cement-producing provinces supplying the high-growing construction markets of Hanoi and Haiphong (and surrounding provinces).

Corridor 2: Quang Ninh–Ninh Binh

Rather than connecting the sea to major population centers like Hanoi, Corridor 2 is aligned parallel to the coastline. As such, the route strengthens network resiliency by functioning as an alternative to coastal shipping between Quang Ninh and Ninh Binh during periods when weather conditions prevent or complicate the latter. Volumes on both the roads and waterways of Corridor 2 are a fraction of those on Corridor 1 (see table 2.9).

Corridor 3: Hanoi–Ninh Binh

Table 2.10 presents O-D freight flows for the north-south Corridor 3. IWT is primarily used for northbound shipments. Reflecting the strong directional imbalance of this trade, no southbound shipments starting at Hanoi or Hung Yen were reported in 2008. The modal share of IWT is very high on a number of O-D pairs at downstream provinces, indicating the importance of bulk commodities for this region. While Hung Yen has a manufactured goods base, Nam Dinh and Ninh Binh mainly provide cement and construction materials and import coal.

Table 2.9 Origin-Destination Cargo Flows for Corridor 2 in the Red River Delta, 2008

	Haiphong	Thai Binh	Ha Nam	Nam Dinh	Ninh Binh	Quang Ninh	Total
ITW tons per day							
Haiphong	n.a.	4.426	280	—	200	4.050	8.956
Thai Binh	—	n.a.	—	500	600	—	1,100
Ha Nam	—	2,000	n.a.	800	—	—	2,800
Nam Dinh	1,500	900	—	n.a.	400	800	3,600
Ninh Binh	5,800	5,000	—	2,250	n.a.	—	13,050
Quang Ninh	560	11,060	300	11,920	8,830	n.a.	32,670
Total	7,860	23,386	580	15,470	10,030	4,850	62,176
Road tons per day							
Haiphong	n.a.	4,789	11	1,475	531	1,055	7,861
Thai Binh	1,308	n.a.	—	75	—	127	1,510
Ha Nam	210	6	n.a.	78	—	9	303
Nam Dinh	444	—	20	n.a.	—	57	521
Ninh Binh	105	248	—	—	n.a.	—	353
Quang Ninh	5,910	—	—	73	—	n.a.	5,983
Total	7,977	5,043	31	1,701	531	1,248	16,531

Source: Data from JICA 2009.
Note: — = no flows reported; n.a. = not applicable. Origins are shown in leftmost column and destinations as rows across.

Table 2.10 Origin-Destination Cargo Flows for Corridor 3 in the Red River Delta, 2008

	Hanoi	Hung Yen	Thai Binh	Ha Nam	Nam Dinh	Ninh Binh	Total
ITW tons per day							
Hanoi	n.a.	—	—	—	—	—	—
Hung Yen	—	n.a.	—	—	—	—	—
Thai Binh	—	—	n.a.	—	500	600	1,100
Ha Nam	1,600	—	2,000	n.a.	800	—	4,400
Nam Dinh	3,340	900	900	—	n.a.	400	5,540
Ninh Binh	800	800	5,000	—	2,250	n.a.	8,850
Total	5,740	1,700	7,900	—	3,550	1,000	19,890
Road tons per day							
Hanoi	n.a.	5,257	54	232	215	88	5,846
Hung Yen	22,426	n.a.	272	26	33	—	22,757
Thai Binh	51	248	n.a.	—	75	—	374
Ha Nam	706	2,818	6	n.a.	78	—	3,608
Nam Dinh	34	—	—	20	n.a.	—	54
Ninh Binh	346	3	248	—	—	n.a	597
Total	23,563	8,326	580	278	401	88	33,236

Source: Data from JICA 2009.
Note: — = no flows reported; n.a. = not applicable. Origins are shown in leftmost column and destinations as rows across.

Zooming in on the Mekong River Delta

Map 2.2 illustrates the freight relevance of the routes to and from Ho Chi Minh City (HCMC) and My Tho/Ben Tre, and further to Vinh Long. Corridors 1 and 2 run parallel through Ben Tre. Volumes decrease with increasing distance from HCMC in both corridors.

Corridors 1 and 2 capture 52 percent of total IWT volumes in the Mekong Delta. Corridor 1, however, is dominant, accounting for 44 percent of Mekong Delta IWT traffic volumes, compared with 8 percent for Corridor 2.

Corridor 1: HCMC–Northwest

HCMC is the main origin and main destination in the Mekong Delta (see table 2.11). Commodities transported in and out of HCMC are relatively diversified, including both raw materials and manufactured goods, as HCMC is both a production center and a consumption province. An Giang and Kien Giang are also important destination provinces. Road transport captures lower volumes than IWT across almost all O-D pairs, except for the routes between Hau Giang and Can Tho. This may be explained by the short distance involved, limiting the advantage of using IWT once all costs (e.g., port handling fees) are taken into account.

Table 2.11 Origin-Destination Cargo Flows for Corridor 1 in the Mekong River Delta, 2008

	HCMC	Tien Giang	Vinh Long	Dong Thap	AG+KG[a]	Can Tho	Hau Giang	Total
ITW tons per day								
HCMC	n.a.	4,100	3,005	100	8,935	27,820	—	43,960
Tien Giang	1,650	n.a.	—	—	108	325	250	2,333
Vinh Long	15,135	54	n.a.	—	56	—	5	15,250
Dong Thap	3,300	—	—	n.a.	3,378	1,210	—	7,888
AG+KG[a]	6,673	702	176	1,349	n.a.	7,915	2,801	19,616
Can Tho	500	55	—	—	22,720	n.a.	2,123	25,398
Hau Giang	250	225	—	—	890	—	n.a.	1,365
Total	27,508	5,136	3,181	1,449	36,087	37,270	5,179	115,810
Road tons per day								
HCMC	n.a.	916	102	179	757	350	48	2,352
Tien Giang	717	n.a.	—	—	—	23	14	754
Vinh Long	177	—	n.a.	—	—	574	80	831
Dong Thap	354	—	—	n.a.	9	16	45	424
AG+KG[a]	1,126	2	—	—	n.a.	3,144	56	4,328
Can Tho	168	242	1,087	—	3,253	n.a.	5,424	10,174
Hau Giang	69	—	15	10	—	2,707	n.a.	2,801
Total	2,611	1.160	1,204	189	4,019	6,814	5,667	21,664

Source: Data from JICA 2009.
Note: — = no flows reported; n.a. = not applicable; HCMC = Ho Chi Minh City. Origins are shown in leftmost column and destinations as rows across.
a. An Giang and Kien Giang provinces.

Table 2.12 Origin-Destination Cargo Flows for Corridor 2 in the Mekong River Delta, 2008

	HCMC	Tien Giang	Ben Tre	Tra Vin	Soc Trang	BL+CM[a]	Total
IWT tons per day							
HCMC	n.a.	4,100	1,380	—	465	—	5,945
Tien Giang	1,650	n.a.	569	—	—	15	2,234
Ben Tre	12,463	1,500	n.a.	—	—	—	13,963
Tra Vin	—	27	73	n.a.	—	—	100
Soc Trang	—	210	1,000	—	n.a.	—	1,210
BL+CM[a]	—	—	—	—	—	n.a.	—
Total	14,113	5,837	3,022	—	465	15	23,452
Road tons per day							
HCMC	n.a.	916	122	80	28	86	1,232
Tien Giang	717	n.a.	—	—	128	—	845
Ben Tre	206	—	n.a.	—	—	32	238
Tra Vin	59	—	—	n.a.	—	—	59
Soc Trang	31	—	—	—	n.a.	—	31
BL+CM[a]	100	110	—	—	—	n.a.	210
Total	1,113	1,026	122	80	156	118	2,615

Source: Data from JICA 2009.
Note: — = no flows reported; n.a. = not applicable; HCMC = Ho Chi Minh City. Origins are shown in leftmost column and destinations as rows across.
a. Bac Lieu and Ca Mau provinces.

Corridor 2: HCMC–Southwest

The northernmost section of this corridor (from HCMC to Tien Giang) overlaps with Corridor 1. Through Ben Tre, volumes are large, but they decline substantially farther away from HCMC (see table 2.12). Ben Tre is an important source for rice and construction materials. Road transport plays a rather marginal role on this corridor, with volumes of around 10 percent of those of IWT.

Container Transport in the Mekong Delta

According to Louis Berger Group and Royal Haskoning (2006), in 2005 the southern river port of Can Tho, one of the busiest in the Mekong Delta, handled some 19,000 TEUs in containerized volume. With regard to the containerized supply chain to/from Can Tho and the various Mekong Delta provinces, the estimated share of containers transported by road and waterways that year was 38 percent and 62 percent, respectively. Between HCMC and Can Tho, in contrast, the roads' share of container traffic is much higher (at about 90 percent), reflecting the demand for more time-sensitive logistics associated with HCMC-linked shipments, which tend to comprise goods with higher value-added content. But as road congestion intensifies, particularly in and around HCMC proper, more competitive barge services linking HCMC with the Mekong Delta are increasingly being introduced (see box 2.1). About a third of the containers handled at Saigon Port are transported by 16–64 TEUs barges to local inland container depots.

Box 2.1 A New Container Route in the Mekong Delta

Tan Cang Logistics, a wholly owned subsidiary of the Sai Gon Tan Cang Corporation, has recently opened a new container river route to the Mekong River Delta by barge, connecting Ho Chi Minh City (HCMC) with the river ports of Can Tho and My Tho (An Giang Province). The barges used are capable of carrying 24–36 TEU, and there is one daily departure from each end.

Goods at that new route are mostly agricultural products for export, which were previously transported in bulk by trucks before being containerized in HCMC at high cost. With the start of the new service, goods can now be containerized at My Tho port and shipped by river to Tan Cang at HCMC and then transferred to larger sea-going ships for export. Such modality reduces transportation costs and lowers the volume burden for roads in the region. It also increases the volume of goods moving between Mekong River Delta provinces, HCMC, and the rest of the world. The time to move goods from Can Tho and An Giang to Europe and the United States is said to have been reduced from 30 to 45 days before the route opening down to 20–27 days.

IWT Market Structure
Shipping Companies

In the North region, large IWT shipments of bulk cargo—such as clinker, sand, gravel, and coal—are transported by state-owned IWT carriers using multiple barge configurations and pusher tugs. In the South region, and especially in the Mekong Delta, IWT services are primarily operated by privately held carriers, utilizing a mix of dumb and self-propelled barges and typically transporting small shipments of rice and other agricultural products. Competition is fierce among private operators, although some long-standing arrangements between state-owned customers and state-owned service providers are still effective. There are two state-owned waterway transport companies operating in the IWT industry: the Northern and the Southern Waterway Transport Corporations. State-owned enterprises (SOEs) under other ministries and own-account operators also provide specialized services to cement plants, paper mills, construction material enterprises, and similar producers.

The Northern Inland Waterway Transport Corporation (NIWTC), an SOE, is the primary provider of river transport services in the Red River Delta region; it also operates river ports. The company accounts for about 75 percent of the IWT tonnage supply in the region. It offers transport services in the northern provinces of Haiphong, Quang Ninh, Bac Giang, Nam Dinh, Thai Binh, and Viet Tri.

The Southern Inland Waterway Transport Corporation (SOWATCO) is the counterpart SOE of its northern sister company and is active in the Mekong Delta. SOWATCO's market share is much lower than that of its northern counterpart because there are more private operators active in the South region than in the North region. In 2005, about 75–80 percent of the South region's total fleet tonnage was operated by private companies/owners, the remainder operated by SOWATCO. Notably in the Saigon River near HCMC, there are major barge movements where shipping interests contract barge owners to move their cargo. Notable privately held waterway transport companies in the South region include the following:

- Rag Dam Tien Giang Cooperative
- Ha Tien Joint Stock Company
- Can Tho Inland Waterway Transport Company
- Falcon Shipping Company
- Vietnam Ocean Shipping Company
- Thong Nhat Shipping Company
- Thanh Long Shipping Company
- Tan Cang Logistics (see box 2.1)

Although SOWATCO does not dominate the South region in terms of relative market share as NIWTC does in the North region, it is the largest company when it comes to container shipping—with about 50 percent of the market. This is because it is the local partner of the joint venture that owns the Vietnam International Container Terminal (VICT) and also participates in the Long Binh. Furthermore, the company operates several container-specialized vessels.

Coastal Shipping

Shipping Volumes

Vietnam's coastal shipping sector is generally concerned with the transportation of bulk cargo along the corridor linking the industrial centers of the North and South regions. About 53 percent of all tonnage transported by coastal shipping comprises cement, coal, and petroleum products, which are typically shipped in bulk (see table 2.3). Still, a non-negligible 23 percent of the cargo moved by this mode is made up of manufactured goods primarily transported in container vessels. The distance by sea between Haiphong and HCMC is about 1,700 kilometers. It is thus not surprising that the average length of haul for coastal shipping load is 1,161 kilometers, or about three times that of the typical rail shipment and more than eight times that of the typical road consignment. It is over such comparatively longer trips that coastal shipping becomes increasingly attractive to shippers (particularly for bulk cargo flows) vis-à-vis the road (primarily) and rail (secondarily) sectors, which are coastal shipping's natural modal competitors.

The total (international plus domestic) cargo throughput handled by Vietnam's seaports increased at an average annual rate of 14 percent between 1995 and 2008, going from 38 to 197 million tons per year (figure 2.1).

From 2001 to 2008, the subset of coastal (i.e., domestic) seaport volumes climbed from 20 to 43 million tons—an average annual rate of 11.4 percent over the period. Throughout the eight-year stretch, coastal shipping's share of total seaport tonnage fluctuated between 21 percent and 24 percent (table 2.13).

Figure 2.1 Tonnage Throughput at Vietnam's Seaports by Flow Type, 1995–2008
Millions of tons

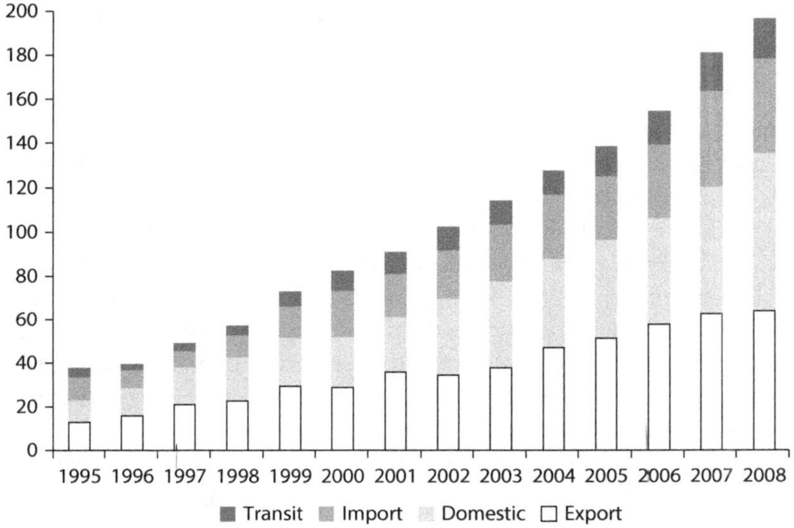

Source: Data from Vietnam Maritime Administration (Vinamarine).

Table 2.13 Cargo Volume Handled at Vietnam's Seaports, 1995–2008
Millions of tons

Year	Export	Import	Domestic	Transit	Total	Share coastal (%)
1995	12.9	10.6	10.5	3.7	37.7	28
1996	15.9	13.1	8.1	2.1	39.2	21
1997	21.2	17.2	7.3	3.2	48.8	15
1998	22.8	20.0	10.0	4.0	56.9	18
1999	29.6	22.3	14.3	6.5	72.8	20
2000	29.0	23.1	21.2	9.1	82.4	26
2001	35.9	25.4	20.1	9.6	91.1	22
2002	34.5	35.0	22.7	10.1	102.3	22
2003	37.9	39.9	25.9	10.6	114.2	23
2004	47.1	41.3	29.0	10.3	127.7	23
2005	51.2	45.8	28.9	12.6	138.4	21
2006	57.6	49.1	33.1	14.7	154.5	21
2007	62.5	58.6	42.9	17.1	181.1	24
2008	63.7	72.4	42.8	17.7	196.6	22

Source: Data from Vinamarine.

Container Flows

Containerized Cargo (Domestic Cargo)

Vietnamese seaports registered a tremendous increase in container volumes between 1995 and 2008 (table 2.14 and figure 2.2). During that period, the annual containerized volume handled by the country's seaports increased from 315,000 to 5,023,000 TEUs—an average annual rate of 24 percent. This volume performance places Vietnam at an equal level with Thailand, where containerization was launched earlier. First introduced in 1997, coastal container shipping (i.e., domestic) services had reached a volume of 876,000 TEUs by year-end 2008. Over the 2001–08 period, coastal containerized volume increased at an average annual rate of 13.2 percent.

Containerized Cargo (Feeder Cargo)

As recently as mid-2009, Vietnam's seaports received no direct calls by container ships deployed on the Asia–Europe and Asia–North America (Transpacific) trade routes. As a result, all Vietnamese containerized trade with Europe, North America, and certain parts of Asia had to be transshipped at "hub" ports, such as those of Singapore and Hong Kong SAR, China. Only the trades with nearby Asian countries were shipped directly without transshipment. This picture has changed, as the first direct calls by container vessels operating intercontinental routes have been established in the vicinity of HCMC. It is expected that similar routes will serve the North region in the medium term.

At present, a number of international container shipping companies carry cargo from Vietnamese ports to the United States (Grand Alliance, Orient

Table 2.14 Container Volume Handled by Vietnam's Seaports, 1995–2008
Thousands of TEUs

Year	Export	Import	Domestic	Total	Share coastal (%)
1995	153	163	0	315	0
1996	226	239	0	465	0
1997	381	372	7	761	1
1998	376	382	42	800	5
1999	440	449	61	950	6
2000	497	513	137	1,148	12
2001	478	501	367	1,346	27
2002	748	730	240	1,718	14
2003	883	875	285	2,043	14
2004	1,059	1,046	333	2,438	14
2005	1,266	1,217	436	2,920	15
2006	1,475	1,428	507	3,411	15
2007	1,837	1,878	774	4,489	17
2008	2,046	2,105	876	5,023	17

Source: Data from Vinamarine.
Note: Transit container volume is not included due to lack of statistical data. TEU = 20-foot equivalent unit.

Figure 2.2 Container Throughput at Vietnam's Seaports by Flow Type, 1995–2008
Millions of TEUs

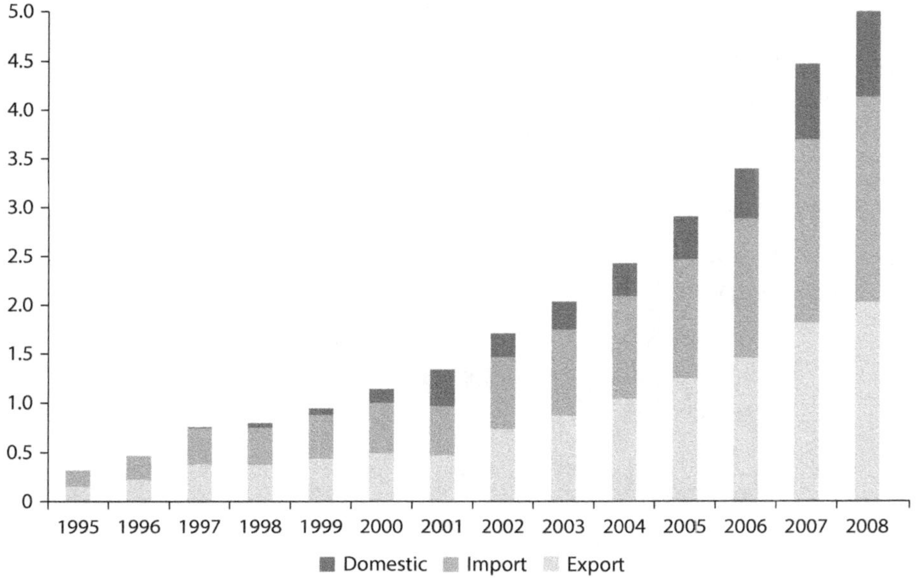

■ Domestic ■ Import ■ Export

Source: Data from Vinamarine.
Note: Transit container volume is not included due to lack of statistical data. TEU = 20-foot equivalent unit.

Overseas Container Line, Hapag-Lloyd, and NYK Line). The international port SP-PSA (at Ba Ria-Vung Tau) announced four shipments a week for a direct ocean route to the U.S. West Coast. The largest ship used on this route has a capacity of 9,000 TEUs, and the shipping time is 16–22 days. Starting in June 2009, Tan Cang-Cai Mep port near HCMC announced direct container routes to Europe and North America. By the first five months of 2009, this port had handled a volume of 100,000 TEUs from ships arriving directly from Europe and North America.

Vietnam's major container ports are located in the northern Haiphong port range and in the southern HCMC port range (see figure 2.3). The largest container throughput by far is concentrated in the HCMC area, which accounts for just over 60 percent of Vietnam's total.

Sea-River Transport

Most major seaports in Vietnam are physically located on rivers. This gives rise to ambiguity as to where IWT ends and coastal shipping begins. This overlap has ramifications and causes ambiguity on the current use of, and the allocation of maintenance responsibilities for, ports and channels.

There are no statistics available that carve out sea-river transport from either IWT or coastal shipping volumes. It is known, however, that seagoing vessels sail upstream both in the Red River and the Mekong River, and that multiple ports in both rivers receive these vessels. For the ports located more upstream, water

Figure 2.3 Largest Container Ports in Vietnam by Throughput, 2007
Thousands of TEUs

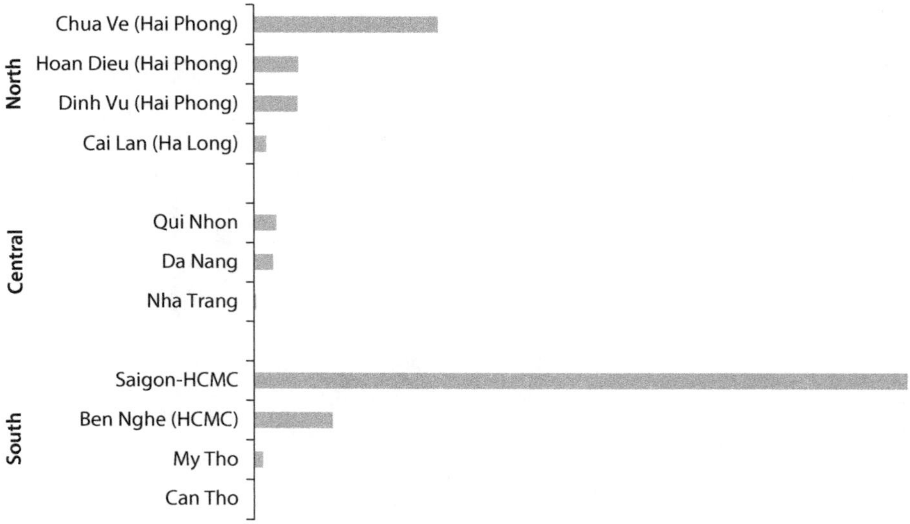

North	Chua Ve (Hai Phong)	▬▬▬▬▬▬▬▬
North	Hoan Dieu (Hai Phong)	▬▬▬
North	Dinh Vu (Hai Phong)	▬▬▬
North	Cai Lan (Ha Long)	▪
Central	Qui Nhon	▪
Central	Da Nang	▪
Central	Nha Trang	
South	Saigon-HCMC	▬▬▬▬▬▬▬▬▬▬▬▬▬▬▬▬▬
South	Ben Nghe (HCMC)	▬▬▬
South	My Tho	▪
South	Can Tho	

Source: Data from OCDI, CMB (Construction Consultation Joint Stock Company of Maritime Building), derived from JICA 2009.
Note: HCMC = Ho Chi Minh City; TEU = 20-foot equivalent unit.

level fluctuations constrain this activity to seasonal periods. For example, the river port of Can Tho services seagoing vessels, which are used to export goods such as sea food products, rice, wood products, cement, coal, ceramics, and fertilizer. Although some stakeholders interviewed mentioned that sea-river vessels can sail the Mekong River up to Phnom Penh in Cambodia, the study team was unable to find evidence confirming that this actually happens.

A separate issue with regard to sea-river transport is the use of river barges at sea. The short distance between river mouths, particularly in the South region, is sometimes sailed using IWT vessels. The same is done in Europe (e.g., in the Black Sea). This type of shipping requires calm waters and is not considered feasible for sailing the longer distance between Southern and Northern Vietnam. Specific data on the number of ships and cargo volumes involved are not available.

Market Structure for Coastal Shipping
Vinalines
Vietnam National Shipping Lines (Vinalines) is an SOE that operates seagoing vessels. It also operates most of the higher-volume commercial ports. In 2006, Vinalines dominated the coastal shipping market (Meyrick and Associates *et al.* 2006). According to JICA (2009) this was still the case in 2009, when its market share was about 60 percent.[3] Although a detailed breakdown of volumes transported by the company could not be obtained, market observers believe that

Vinalines continued to possess a dominant market position in 2010, despite that its market share may have dropped somewhat. The company still mainly focuses on domestic and regional trades and is not involved in intercontinental shipping routes.

Vinalines is virtually the only operator offering scheduled services in north-south coastal shipping. Some other operators (including Nhat Hai Dang JSC–Lighthouse) offer north-south coastal shipping services as well, but they do not deliver regular services. More competition is likely to lower transport tariffs for these services, increase their number and variety, and reduce travel and waiting times.

Competitive Position of IWT and Coastal Shipping
Competitive Position of IWT

In the evaluation of the attractiveness and potential of the actual IWT system in the two river delta systems, one should make a distinction between the following types of hauls:

a. *Short-medium hauls:* local transport taking place within provinces that can be described as internal transport or feeder transport to nodal points, from where cargo is consolidated for further transportation to other provinces and
b. *Medium-long hauls:* interprovincial transport.

Small vessels with a carrying capacity of less than 10 tons or in the range of 10–50 tons are used for the first type of transport. Vessels with a carrying capacity of 50–100 tons are used both in feeder and long-haul transport, while the over-100-ton fleet is exclusively used for longer distances.

The cross-border trade with Cambodia exemplifies the geographic and corridor approach to market (map 2.3). A waterway route already exists and thrives that is currently served by three companies utilizing 50–150 TEU vessels. The one-way journey takes 2–3 days at a freight rate of $250 per TEU. This is competitive over the coastal route, which goes around the Mekong Delta to Sihanoukville port. Maintaining and upgrading this waterway could be considered a central part of a southern regional IWT strategy that would also greatly benefit Cambodia.

There is also a growing need for consolidation of freight[4] and scheduled IWT services, similar to those provided in Europe. Chapter 5 explores possible locations for consolidation facilities.

Based on the assumptions in the IWT model used in ALMEC Corp. (2006) (see table 2.15), the average IWT cost per ton-km including handling cost is estimated to be $0.0257 in the North region (2006 data). This gives IWT a significant advantage over road transport when financial costs are the deciding factor. This report's own calculations confirm this advantage (see appendix E).

Deep-water container terminals, such as those in the Vung Tau range in the South region (both operational and planned), are expected to attract large

Map 2.3 Cross-Border River Transport between Vietnam and Cambodia

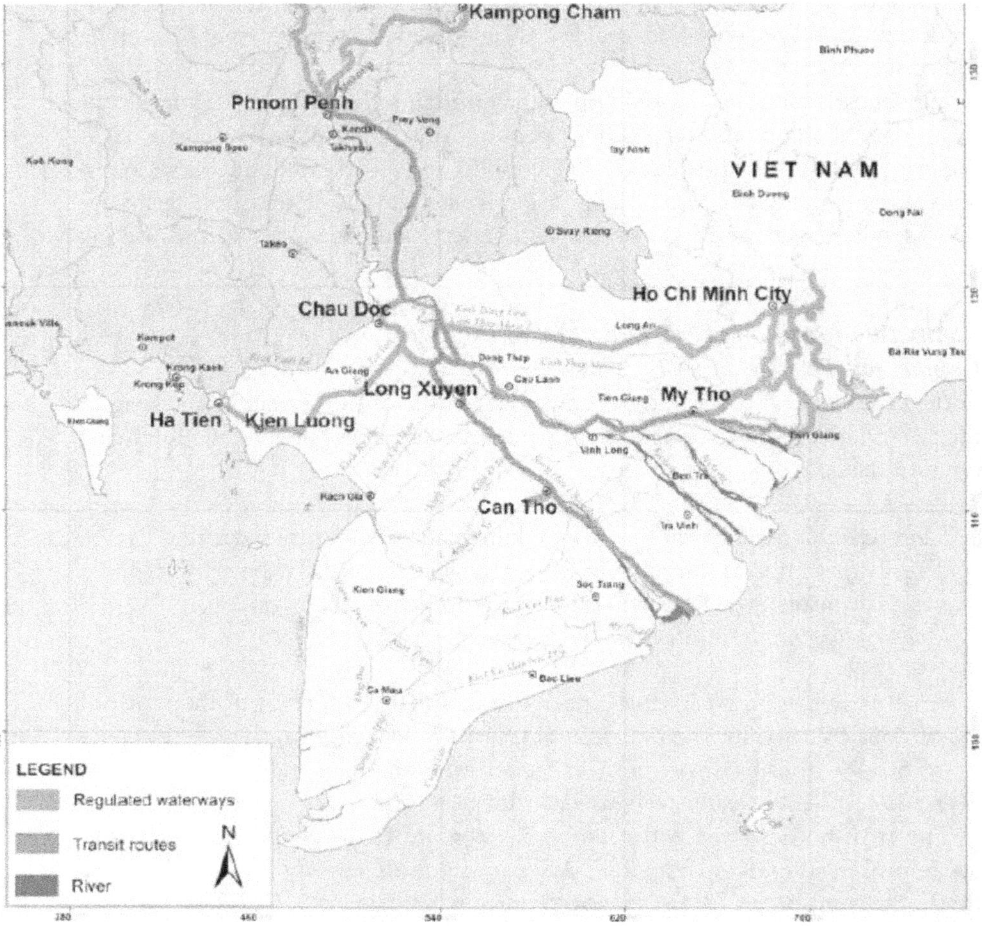

Source: Mekong River Commission.

Table 2.15 NRCTSS 2005 Base Case IWT Volumes and Transport Costs in the North Region

Cargo		Transport costs (Millions of US$)			Cost per ton (US$/ton)			Waterways (US$/ton-km)
Tons (Millions)	Ton-km (millions)	Total	Ports	Waterways	Total	Ports	Waterways	
40.2	5,610	188.1	44.1	144	4.72	1.1	3.62	0.0257

Source: ALMEC Corp. 2006.
Note: IWT = Inland waterway transport; NRCTSS = Northern Region Comprehensive Transport Strategy Study.

volumes of freight over the medium term. A single container service may attract on average 5,000 TEUs per week, or about 250,000 TEUs per year. If all such volumes were transported to/from the hinterland (HCMC and beyond) by road, substantial pressure would be placed on the available road network, causing delays and undermining the container terminals' competitive position and value proposition. Such pressures may be allayed if modern barge services between Vung Tau and HCMC and My Tho were introduced. These could provide similar functionality as that attained by a container transferium (CT) in Rotterdam (see box 2.2). Based on the demand and the experience in other countries, one can expect Vietnam to develop such initiatives organically.

Competitive Position of Coastal Shipping

Vinalines operates nine weekly services between HCMC and Hanoi, transporting a total volume of about 400,000 TEUs per year northbound and 200,000 TEUs per year southbound. Given the north-south directional imbalance, southbound freight rates tend to be 20–25 percent lower than northbound rates. The ships employed range in size from 500 to 1,000 TEUs. According to Vinalines, road transport is dominant for distances below 200 kilometers and coastal transport for distances in excess of 300 kilometers. The comparative advantage for road transport may extend to longer distances in the future as a high-grade road network continues to expand and modernize.

Box 2.2 Container Transferium near the Port of Rotterdam

The port of Rotterdam has accessibility problems by road (A15) due to the clustering of containers transported by large vessels to and from the port (compared to small consignment sizes by small IWT vessels). The Port of Rotterdam Authority has embarked on a project to build a container transferium (CT) in Alblasserdam (close to Rotterdam) as a means to reduce terminal congestion in the seaport itself. The Ministry of Transport will invest in the road connection to this CT. The largest terminal operator in the Netherlands, BCTN, will operate the terminal. The terminal design calls for an area of 4 hectares and a 255-meter quay and is expected to be operational in early 2014.

Within three years of operation, the CT should contribute to a shift of 200,000 TEU from road to water. This equals some 10 percent of the number of container trucks on the main hinterland motorway. Trucks deliver and collect at the CT in Alblasserdam, and the distance of about 50 kilometers with the Rotterdam Maasvlakte (Mainport terminals) is bridged by large inland vessels (more than 200 TEUs in capacity). The final origin and destination of the boxes will usually not be far from the CT. The port authority and ministry have adopted this concept in support of the government's policy to promote transport by rail and water and shift containers from roads to other transport modes.

Source: Data from the Port of Rotterdam.

Preliminary investigation of freight rates for the shipment of a 20-foot container between HCMC and Haiphong by road, rail, and coastal waterway reveals the cost advantage of coastal shipping:

- Road: Vietnamese dong (VND) 25 million ($1,250)
- Rail: VND 16–18 million ($800–900)
- Coastal waterway: VND 6 million ($300)

where rail and coastal rates exclude the costs of pre- and on-carriage.

To increase the role of coastal shipping, it is important that inland multimodal depots are strategically conceived and located as inland collection and distribution centers. IWT is envisaged to play an important role in this, especially in the South region. Vinalines does not see a large role for this in the North region, given the draft restrictions in the dry season. This, however, may be based on their focus on seagoing vessel operations. NIWTC, on the other hand, is planning to add a new inland container port at Phu Dong along the Duong River near Hanoi, with an annual capacity of 75,000 TEUs to accommodate IWT convoys carrying 24–36 TEUs. This shows that there is a lack of consensus on the potential of coastal shipping in the North region and argues for a better analysis of infrastructure constraints in the area.

Supply Chains and Logistics Costs in Vietnam

A supply chain can be defined as the flow of resources and data to fulfill end-customer demand, starting from raw materials sourcing through the various stages of value adding, handling, storage, and transport. Within the management of supply chains, logistics activities are concerned with the transport, storage, and handling of goods at all levels of the chain. Seaports and inland ports play an important role in facilitating supply chain flows through efficient logistics. Their presence is an attractive factor for manufacturing facility location decisions and can spur local job creation. Seaports and inland ports can have three functions:

1. The port as a hub of transport chains (freight transfer point)
2. The port as an anchoring location for industry, services, and as a vital part of industry clusters
3. The port as a node in domestic and international production networks

While all ports form a node in the supply chain or production network, they will not always play the roles of freight transfer points or industry centers. Some ports could serve two functions and others all three. Haiphong port, for example, which provides direct access to the hinterland by road, rail, and inland waterway, serves as a freight transfer point and has encouraged industries to locate along the main transport corridor.

Seaports and inland ports are critical nodes in the supply chain, but they should not be planned and managed in isolation. To strengthen the position of Vietnam's seaports, it is important to improve their links to hinterland areas—where the majority of value-adding activities, such as assembly or manufacturing, are located—via a variety of modes of transport and cargo-handling options: IWT, rail, road, and short sea/feeder connections, as well as multitenant warehousing facilities, including those with special handling capabilities, such as cold chains.

Logistics Costs in Vietnam

Vietnam's rapidly increasing international trade in containerized cargo creates new requirements for the transport sector, especially with respect to foreign customers who emphasize speedy and timely delivery of high-value goods. There is scant evidence of this type of shippers utilizing IWT for such purposes in Vietnam. The commodities that utilize IWT are mainly low-value, bulk cargo, such as cement, coal, and construction materials. Were IWT to try to attract higher-value cargo, it would be necessary to address the reliability, accessibility, and visibility problems it shares with railway transportation (speedy delivery is generally not required for IWT; see box 2.3 for a discussion of speed and reliability in IWT in Europe).

Box 2.3 Speed and Reliability as Barriers for IWT in Europe

A 2010 survey commissioned by the German Federal Ministry of Environment revealed that a majority of shippers have a preference for road transport, as it is considered faster, cheaper, and more reliable than competing modes. Only about 14 percent of shippers surveyed had had positive experiences with rail transport or IWT. This was concluded from an inquiry among 123 shippers conducted by the Technical University of Dortmund. Most companies were interested in consolidating freight flows, reducing empty trips, and other operational improvements within road transport, but largely do not look at modes other than roads.

Nevertheless, inland waterway vessels in Western Europe transport substantial containerized volumes from the seaports of Rotterdam and Antwerp to the German hinterland, as well as to domestic river terminals. Often, these containers carry high-value and time-critical goods. The main reasons for choosing IWT instead of road, however, do not relate to the good traceability or the reliability of services, but rather to geographic factors, for example, the following:

1. Location of the seaports of Rotterdam and Antwerp along main waterways connected to their hinterland (Germany through the Rhine, as well as major canals to regions within the Netherlands and Belgium)
2. Network of terminals within these countries providing access to nearby industrial customers
3. Congestion at seaports and on main highway connections into port hinterlands

IWT in Western Europe continues to face reliability and traceability challenges. Although developments in communication systems like River Information Services aim to reduce these problems, to date they have not provided the overall solution initially hoped for.

Source: Includes information reported by Nieuwsblad Transport 2010.

JICA (2009) provides the following assessment of the current state of Vietnamese logistics:

> There is as yet no multimodal transportation corridor in Vietnam. The need to define improved freight transfers, such as between the road network and ports or airports, between the road network and railway loading bays, or between barge delivery area and trucks is becoming increasingly important.
>
> The reason is mainly institutional. The transportation system is organized by transportation mode, and no single mode is focused on creating "multimodal chains" and "seamless transfers at nodes" that are needed to lower transportation costs.
>
> Inadequate infrastructure has always been cited as the reason for Vietnam's high logistics costs, estimated by some at 25 percent of GDP. This is higher than China, Thailand, or Japan. Accordingly, Vietnam has embarked on aggressive programs to improve ports, road, rail, waterway, and airports infrastructure. More than these, modern logistics demand a parallel development of the "information and communications highway." Here, one may think of electronic documents and web-portals to share travel information. And yet, logistics cannot wait for the completion of all of these elements before it can be globally competitive.
>
> A multimodal framework is invaluable in identifying bottlenecks and weaknesses across the supply chain. Targeted intervention is the key to improving Vietnam's logistics performance. According to the World Bank 2008 survey on logistics performance, domestic transportation cost is not a main issue. Rather, the poor timeliness of shipments is at fault, which, in turn, leads to higher than needed warehousing and inventory costs. Creating electronic portals that can link the various logistics players (such as freight forwarders, Customs, Truckers, Shippers, Rail freight companies, Manufacturers, etc.) will be one important intervention. The easing of cross border trade procedures is another, since Vietnam ranked poorly on this dimension compared to other ASEAN countries.
>
> Nurturing the growth of third-party logistics providers (3PLs) is also imperative to improve Vietnam's trade competitiveness. Such enterprises are accustomed to the just-in-time inventory practices of global trade. To bypass domestic hold-ups, multinationals often bring in their own 3PLs to ensure that their products get to market on time, and that raw materials arrive just in time. Which policy measures will support 3PLs in Vietnam? These will include the liberalization of entry rules for foreign logistics companies and a revision of the licensing rules hindering multi-service logistics businesses.
>
> There are about 1,200 enterprises operating in Vietnam's 3PL industry, including a limited number of world-class logistics multinationals. Although Vietnam's World Trade Organization road map on logistics commitments will not come into effect until 2014, foreign companies have started operating under various forms,

especially for the provision of 3PL services utilizing modern technology and standardized processes linked to developed-country markets.

Vietnam's logistics services industry is growing rapidly from a small base at about 20 percent per year. The export, import, and retail markets have had (and are expected to continue to register) high growth rates, and many logistics services providers are likely to benefit from this trend.

Although access to foreign investment in logistics services remains constrained, existing limitations are scheduled to be phased out under national law. Decree no. 140/2007/CP-ND (dated September 2007) regulates market access for foreign 3PL service providers in Vietnam. It stipulates that no 100 percent foreign-invested capital enterprises are allowed to enter the market prior to 2014 (or 2012 in marine transportation).

Further growth in outsourced logistics operations will depend on the ability of this sector to offer higher and more consistent service levels. Strategic decisions between vertical integration in logistics and outsourcing to 3PLs constantly take place in the global industrial, manufacturing, retail, and services sectors. Since 3PL penetration in Vietnam remains limited and service quality is relatively underdeveloped, shippers may pursue inward-looking operating strategies aimed at maintaining control along the supply chain. In the Netherlands, for example, several incentive programs have been used to promote the use of outsourced intermodal transport (see box 2.4). For Vietnam, the use of incentive programs may be considered as well.

Box 2.4 Cooperation in Logistics Networks and Infrastructure Incentives in Western Europe

Logistics Services Integration

Leading European barge container carriers are increasingly trying to achieve functional vertical integration of the container transport chain by extending their service offering to include complete door-to-door logistics solutions. As a result, the barge market is now dominated by large logistics groups, such as Wincanton, Rhenus Logistics, and Imperial Logistics Group (Zurbach 2005). The integration of leading barge operating companies in the structures of highly diversified logistics groups further strengthens the functional integration of the logistics chain. The logistics groups also fully exploit the complementarities of barge transport with rail and road transport to offer clients (shippers) a complete intermodal product and reliable, cost-effective services.

Intermodal developments in Europe demonstrate that market players are constantly searching for ways to bundle cargo and integrate activities along the supply chain. The focus is most on operational considerations from the supply side, for example, network optimization from the perspective of intermodal operators. Further optimization and expansion of the intermodal offering will also greatly depend on successful actions toward coordination and

box continues next page

Box 2.4 Cooperation in Logistics Networks and Infrastructure Incentives in Western Europe
(continued)

cooperation on the demand side of the market, that is, the shippers and cargo generators. Thus, intermodal services require an innovative range of relationships and network formations with and between intermodal operators and cargo handlers. These coordination problems in hinterland chains have been addressed in Van Der Horst and De Langen (2008) with a strong focus on organizational forms and an institutionalized approach. They distinguish four main categories of arrangements to improve coordination:

- The introduction of incentives (e.g., a bonus or penalty)
- The creation of an interfirm alliance (e.g., through the introduction of standards for quality and service or a joint capacity pool)
- Changing the scope of the organization (e.g., through vertical integration or the introduction of a chain manager)
- Collective action (e.g., through governance by a port authority or a concerted action by a branch association; see also De Langen and Chouly 2004)

In the Netherlands, the government used the first (incentives, subsidy schemes) and last instruments (collective action, such as building the container transferium) to improve the network of seaports, inland ports, and hinterland connections.

Incentives for the Development and Improvement of Transshipment Facilities

The Dutch government actively pursues a policy of replacing freight transport by road with intermodal transport by rail and IWT. Such modal shift requires an efficient intermodal transport system, and transshipment facilities are an essential part of such a system. Since 1996, the Dutch government has designed three schemes to promote the development and improvement of transshipment facilities for individual shippers and stimulate the use of terminals. Two schemes were for private-use terminals (i.e., facilities that are not accessible to all transport users under nondiscriminatory conditions) and one scheme was for public-use terminals:

- Temporary Policy Regulation on Subsidies for (Private) Inland Waterway Links (TBBV) scheme in 1996
- Subsidy Private Inland Waterway Connection (SBV) scheme in 2000
- Subsidy Scheme for Public Use Inland Terminals (SOIT) scheme in 2000

Under the two private-use-terminal schemes, the subsidy recipient was required to provide a five-year transport guarantee whereby the party undertakes to transship at least a pre-declared quantity of goods by means of the private link being subsidized. In addition, the recipient must report annually on the quantity of goods transshipped.

Under the public-use scheme, the state subsidized 50 percent of the construction and equipment cost (subsidy did not cover land) for new terminals or expansions of existing terminals for the transshipment of goods to and from waterways. The recipient was required to finance at least 50 percent of the total cost of the project and provide a market analysis, including an estimate of transshipment volumes during the first five years of operation, corroborated by declarations of intent from shippers.

box continues next page

Box 2.4 Cooperation in Logistics Networks and Infrastructure Incentives in Western Europe *(continued)*

The results of the schemes and investments are shown in table B2.4.1.

Table B2.4.1 Public Subsidy Program for Transshipment Facilities in the Netherlands, 1996–2004

Scheme	Period	Budget	Approved requests	Modal shift
TBBV	1996–00	€20 million	81 of 99	2.0 million tons per year
SBV	2001–03	€1 million	37 of 50	3.6 million tons per year
SOIT	2000–04	€9 million	9 container terminals	About 400,000 TEUs per year

Source: Ecorys 2009.
Note: SBV = Subsidy Private Inland Waterway Connection; SOIT = Subsidy Scheme for Public Use Inland Terminals; TBBV = Temporary Policy Regulation on Subsidies for (Private) Inland Waterway Links; TEU = 20-foot equivalent unit.

Conclusions on Demand

The market for IWT and coastal shipping transport services in Vietnam is substantial, although it faces increasing competition from the road sector. IWT and coastal shipping are better understood when segregated into three different submarkets: one concerning IWT in the North region, another in the South region, and a coastal trade linking the northern and southern economic core regions of the country. Within the North and South regions, IWT freight flows are highly concentrated on a limited number of waterways.

The market shares of IWT and coastal shipping in Vietnam are high, even when compared with that of the road sector. Both sectors are expected to substantially grow further in the future, but other modes, especially roads, are expected to grow faster. While IWT currently serves mainly bulk cargo shippers and captures only a small share of container volumes, experience from Europe suggests that inland waterways, when efficiently connected to ports and roads, can carry higher-value, time-sensitive goods on a more consistent basis. IWT has a fairly strong competitive position for shipments in the 100–300 kilometer length of haul range, with a dominant position for shipments in the 100–200 kilometer range. Coastal shipping, on the other hand, dominates shipments traveling distances of 1,400–1,600 kilometers, which are mostly linked to the trade between the North and South regions. For most other distances, the road sector is the main transport mode.

Vietnam's multimodal transport network, in terms of physical and regulatory infrastructure, is at an early stage of development. Indicators on logistics performance show that Vietnam's logistics costs are relatively high compared to those of some of its regional peers. Efficient handling in ports is a prerequisite for successful competition with other transport modes. The role of 3PLs is still limited, although numerous players have already entered the market, and their role is growing.

Notes

1. The rail sector accounts for a mere 2 percent of Vietnam's nationwide interprovincial tonnage.
2. The rail sector accounts for only 5 percent of tonnage in the North-South trade, despite the long haul nature of the route.
3. JICA (2009). Vinalines operates 60 percent of the national fleet (measured in terms of deadweight tonnage).
4. This was confirmed by multiple private stakeholders during interviews; see appendix A.

References

ALMEC Corp. 2006. *Northern Region Comprehensive Transport Strategy Study (NRCTSS) Baseline Report*. Tokyo: ALMEC Corp.

De Langen, Peter W., and Ariane Chouly. 2004. "Hinterland Access Regimes in Seaports." *European Journal of Transport and Infrastructure Research* 4: 361–80.

Ecorys. 2009. *Platina Good Practices Report I: Navigation and Inland Waterway Action and Development in Europe (NAIADES)*. Brussels: Inland Navigation Europe.

Eurostat. 2013. *Freight Transport Statistics*. http://epp.eurostat.ec.europa.eu/statistics_explained/index.php/Freight_transport_statistics.

JICA (Japan International Cooperation Agency). 2009. *The Comprehensive Study on the Sustainable Development of Transport System in Vietnam (VITRANSS-2)*. Hanoi: JICA.

Louis Berger Group and Royal Haskoning. 2006. *Mekong Delta Transport Infrastructure Development Project (MTIDP) Feasibility Study*. Washington, DC: World Bank.

Meyrick and Associates, Transport Development and Strategy Institute (TDSI), and Carl Bro. 2006. *Vietnam: Multimodal Transport Regulatory Review*. Washington, DC: World Bank.

Nieuwsblad Transport. 2010. "Shippers Dissatisfied with Rail and Barge." *Nieuwsblad Transport*, August 25.

Statistics Netherlands. 2013. *Statistical Yearbook 2013*. The Hague, Netherlands: Statistics Netherlands.

Van Der Horst, Martijn R., and Peter W. De Langen. 2008. "Coordination in Hinterland Transport Chains: A Major Challenge for the Seaport Community." *Maritime Economics & Logistics* 10: 108–29.

Zurbach, Vincent. 2005. "Transport de Conteneurs sur le Rhin: Quelles logiques de fonctionnement?" Master's thesis. University of Paris.

CHAPTER 3

Supply-Side Considerations: Waterways, Ports, and Fleet

Institutional Framework for the Waterway and Port Sectors

The Ministry of Transport (MoT) is responsible for regulating and overseeing all transport modes as well as the shipbuilding industry.[1] It is also in charge of overall national transport planning and is responsible for ensuring that local and provincial infrastructure development is in accordance with the national transport plan. MoT coordinates with other central government agencies, such as the Ministry of Planning and Investment (MPI) and the Ministry of Finance (MoF). MoT reports to the Office of the Government.

MPI is responsible for prioritizing projects and allocating budgets. The cooperation between MPI and MoT is therefore critical for all physical works planned in Vietnam. Budgets are then provided through MoF.

Several specialized management agencies reside under MoT, the most important of which are the Vietnam Inland Waterway Administration (VIWA), Vietnam Maritime Administration (Vinamarine), Vietnam Waterway Construction Corporation (Vinawaco, which specializes in dredging), and Vietnam Register (for fleet registration and quality assurance). The Vietnam National Shipping Lines (Vinalines) and the Vietnam Shipbuilding Industry Group (Vinashin) reside under the Office of the Government. Most of the larger waterways and river ports are managed and administered by VIWA, while Vinamarine administers the coastal waterways and the large seaports.[2] Smaller waterways and ports are controlled directly by provincial governments. MoT also has the administrative responsibility for several education institutes, including Vietnam Maritime University.

Waterways

VIWA is the owner of national waterways (a 6,600 kilometer network) on behalf of the government and the implementing agency for inland waterway policies. It is responsible for the provision and maintenance of infrastructure along national rivers, lakes, and river ports and for the provision of aids to navigation on the waterways. Maintenance dredging works are usually contracted out to Vinawaco. In some cases, dredging is initiated by local authorities (e.g., Ho Chi Minh City [HCMC]). The remainder of the navigable waterways, including small ports, is managed by the relevant provincial departments of transport under the people's committees of the provinces and centrally run cities.

VIWA is subdivided into four regional management units. Management units execute public administration functions in the inland waterway transport (IWT) sector, and are each responsible for various common-use river ports:

1. IWT regional management unit number I is in charge of IWT in the provinces of Haiphong, Quang Ninh, and sections of Hai Duong in Northern and Northeast Vietnam;
2. IWT regional management unit number II is in charge of IWT in the Red River Delta provinces in the North region and in various rivers in Central Vietnam;
3. IWT regional management unit number III is in charge of IWT in eight provinces in the Mekong Delta and in the southern tip of Central Vietnam; and
4. IWT regional management unit number IV is in charge of IWT in the nine southward provinces of the Mekong Delta and the Gulf of Thailand (Can Tho, An Giang, Kien Giang, Vinh Long, Tra Vinh, Hau Giang, Soc Trang, Bac Lieu, and Ca Mau).

In addition, VIWA has 15 river management stations overseeing localized river navigation, including enforcement. Five of these 15 stations (numbers 2, 3, 5, 6, and 8) have been equitized into joint stock companies (JSCs). These JSCs enter into contracts with VIWA to carry out the same responsibilities as the river management stations. Such JSCs operate under the law on enterprises and are partially state-owned. For example, Inland Waterway Management Joint Stock Company No. 2 maintains waterway channels; controls river traffic; removes obstacles; operates (pulling, pushing) vessels to maintain traffic safety and offers pilotage services; manufactures and installs aids to navigation; conducts dredging, irrigation, and civil construction; operates cargo transport and ancillary services related to vessel repair, sale of spare parts, and refueling; and engages in the trading of construction material, agricultural products, real estate, and import-export transactions. IWT projects are implemented by project management units (PMUs) under VIWA or MoT.

Two regional transport and port operating enterprises report directly to MoT, namely, the Northern Inland Waterway Transport Corporation (NIWTC) and the Southern Inland Waterway Transport Corporation (see the discussion in chapter 2).

The Waterway Police are responsible for traffic safety. Traffic management is needed on busy waterway sections such as Kenh Cho Gao (also referred to as the Cho Gao Canal). Figure 3.1 shows congestion on the Kenh Cho Gao, the main artery connecting HCMC to the Mekong Delta. This waterway currently poses the most critical capacity bottleneck in the national inland waterway network.

Figure 3.1 Congestion on the Cho Gao Canal

Source: David A. Biggs, http://www.facultydirectory.ucr.edu/cgi-bin/pub/public_individual.pl?faculty=2317.

River Ports

VIWA assumes sole port authority responsibility for national river ports. In several ports, operational activities are conducted by state-owned enterprises (SOEs) under MoT. This is, for example, the case for Hanoi Port, as well as for Phu Luong Port, about 7 kilometers downstream of Hanoi along the Red River. Furthermore, shipping companies may also own and operate ports. For example, the NIWTC, an SOE under MoT, owns Phu Dong Port, a new port planned to be developed along the Duong River. Box 3.1 describes the institutional organization of a typical Dutch river port, as a comparison with the Vietnamese system.

Seaports, Coastal Shipping, and Maritime Transport

Vinamarine and Vinalines are the two main agencies involved in seaports, maritime transport, and coastal shipping. Vinamarine develops the strategy for the subsector and is the regulatory agency under MoT. It is responsible for preparing policy plans and legislative proposals. It has 23 local branches that act as harbor masters, regulating vessel traffic at ports, and enforcing maritime safety and environmental standards. Search and rescue tasks are also included in its mandate. Vinamarine also operates a few small ports. Furthermore, Vinamarine is responsible for managing the Vietnam Register and for supporting SOEs such as Vinashin and Vinalines in safety and security issues.

Box 3.1 Institutional Organization of a Typical Dutch River Port

River port Hengelo

The river port of Hengelo in the Netherlands (East) is located along the Twente Canal, which is accessible to vessels of up to 2,000 tons. Hengelo is the largest port in Twente, with annual handling volumes of 3.5 million tons, including 100,000 20-foot equivalent units (TEUs) in containerized trade. Responsibilities for the port and canal are allocated as follows:

- The Municipality of Hengelo is responsible for the maintenance of the water area on both sides of the canal for 15 meters from the quay. The municipality is the owner of most of the dam walls and quays (some sections are privately owned). The municipality of Hengelo has the obligation to keep its part of the Twente Canal (2×15 meters width) at the required depth.
- Regulation port and quay fees: These fees, referred to as "port fees," are a levy for the use of public municipal water services.
- Ownership structure: The port basins and marina are the property of the municipality of Hengelo. Maintenance costs (keeping the waterway at the required depth by dredging) for the ports are about €1.2 million per year. Hengelo has invested in the industrial areas along the canal (e.g., by building quays) and now recoups part of the cost through infrastructure usage fees levied on private companies. Hengelo also has its own 500-meter public quay, which can be used by companies in the Hengelo region that are not located on the water.
- The Regional Department of Rijkswaterstaat (executing agency of the Ministry of Transport [MoT]) is responsible for the maintenance and management of the Twente Canal (except for the water sections near the port quays, which are maintained by the municipality, as mentioned above) and the three locks; plans for deepening the canal and building a new lock would take an investment from the MoT of about €120 million.
- Port authority: This task lies with the municipality of Hengelo.
- Some 15 companies located on the water make use of inland waterway transport and port facilities for shipping their cargo.
- CTH Property (100 percent held by Foundation CTH) is the owner of the grounds and infrastructure of the terminal. CTH Property is the tenant (lessee) of the terminal area via a lease agreement with the municipality of Hengelo and Akzo Nobel. The Foundation financed the construction of the quay, a runway for the crane, and hardening of the area. CTH Property rents the terminal area to the private terminal operator Combi Terminal Twente (CTT) for a fixed/variable price.
- CTT is the terminal operator (the container terminal opened in 2001). The company is a joint venture of three private investors and has invested in the crane, office, reach stackers, warehouses, information and communication technology, and other facilities.
- The terminal is a public container terminal by virtue of the distinction between ownership of the quay, infrastructure and land area, and the actual operation of the terminal. More than 30 companies in the region use the CTT terminal.

box continues next page

Box 3.1 Institutional Organization of a Typical Dutch River Port *(continued)*

- The public investments are approximately €2 million, and private investments are approximately €3 million. The container terminal is financed via Foundation CTH through a combination of public contributions from (a) the Province of Overijssel (with funding from the European Regional Development Fund), and (b) the MoT (with a Subsidy Scheme for Public Use Inland Terminals [SOIT] contribution of €0.5 million).
- A 2010 enlargement of the container terminal (from 150 to 300 meters of quay length and from 3 to 5 acres of yard area) was financed in equal parts by MoT and by the Foundation.

Source: Ecorys.

Vinalines is an SOE that provides ocean-going and coastal shipping (through 14 shipping companies), port and terminal operations (18 port and terminal handling companies), and vessel servicing (43 companies). Prior to 1995, Vinalines was part of Vinamarine. In 1995, the two were separated, with Vinamarine being made responsible for policy and strategy issues and Vinalines for operational issues. Still, Vinalines is both regulated and financially backed by the government. In the country's strategy for the maritime sector, the company is explicitly targeted to become the core in ocean shipping, logistics, support services, and seaports. As an SOE, Vinalines benefits from loans explicitly or implicitly backed by government guarantees. Being an SOE with close ties to the government also carries financial risks. For example, Vinalines was "encouraged" to buy ships from Vinashin that had been canceled by some of the shipbuilder's foreign customers as the global economic crisis unfolded. This could end up creating a serious financial burden for the company.

The Fleet

Vietnam Register is an agency under MoT responsible for the technical inspection of ships and other vehicles (e.g., trucks and rail cars). It reviews and approves vessel design, classifies newly built ships, conducts vessel surveys, and registers both seagoing and inland waterway vessels. The register for maritime ships covers all ships under the Vietnamese flag or Vietnamese ownership, as well as all ships surveyed and inspected by the agency. A comparison of Register data with figures from industry experts and operators suggests that the Register does not include all inland waterway vessels in active use.

Vinashin is Vietnam's largest shipbuilder. It owns and operates numerous shipyards located all along the country's coast, representing approximately 80 percent of Vietnam's shipbuilding capacity. While the shipbuilding sector as a whole is under the oversight of MoT, Vinashin management reports directly to the Office of the Government. Vinashin is a signatory party to several joint ventures (some of which with partly foreign-owned enterprises) in the areas of shipyards (e.g., Hyundai) and equipment production. Furthermore, the organization is active in a number of other sectors, including shipping services and nontransport sectors like real estate and construction. Vinashin faced major financial difficulty during the global financial and economic crisis of 2008–09, resulting in a 2010 default on a syndicated loan by international lenders. At the time of writing, Vinashin is undergoing major debt and operational restructuring.

Waterway Infrastructure

The number of rivers and canals in Vietnam is estimated at about 2,360, with a total length of 220,000 kilometers (see table 3.1). Out of the total network, only about 19 percent (41,900 kilometers) is considered navigable, and 7 percent (15,436 kilometers) has been placed under management and operation. The major routes in Northern and Southern Vietnam are 4,553 kilometers long: 2 percent of the length of the full network. The national government manages 65 waterways in the North region (total length of 2,727 kilometers), 21 in the Central region (802 kilometers), and 101 waterways in the South region (3,083 kilometers). Detailed information on the major waterways can be found in appendix B.

Northern Waterways

The North region's river system can be defined by four major corridors: Hong, Thai Binh, Luoc, and Duong (see map 3.1). The minimum channel widths range from 30 to 36 meters, with minimum depths of 1.5–3.6 meters. River conditions are affected by the northern hydrometeorology, where May to October is the wet (rainy) season and November to May is the dry season. The water level difference between the two seasons is 5–7 meters. During the rainy season, the velocity of the river is high, but once the dry season sets in, the depth becomes shallower, and the velocity drops. The sediment at the estuaries is complex and difficult to manage, with shoals changing every year.

Table 3.1 Scale of Inland Waterways in Vietnam

Vietnam inland waterways: 220,000 km			
Navigational length: 41,900 km (19%)			Non-navigational length: 178,100 km (81%)
Under management: 15,436 km (37%)		Not under management: 26,464 km (63%)	
By central government: 6,612 km (43%)	By local government: 8,824 km (57%)		
Of which major Northern routes: 1,506 km (10%) Of which major Southern routes: 3,047 km (20%) Of which nonmajor routes: 10,883 km (70%)			

Source: Data from JICA 2009.
Note: km = kilometer.

Supply-Side Considerations: Waterways, Ports, and Fleet

Map 3.1 Inland Waterways in Vietnam's North Region

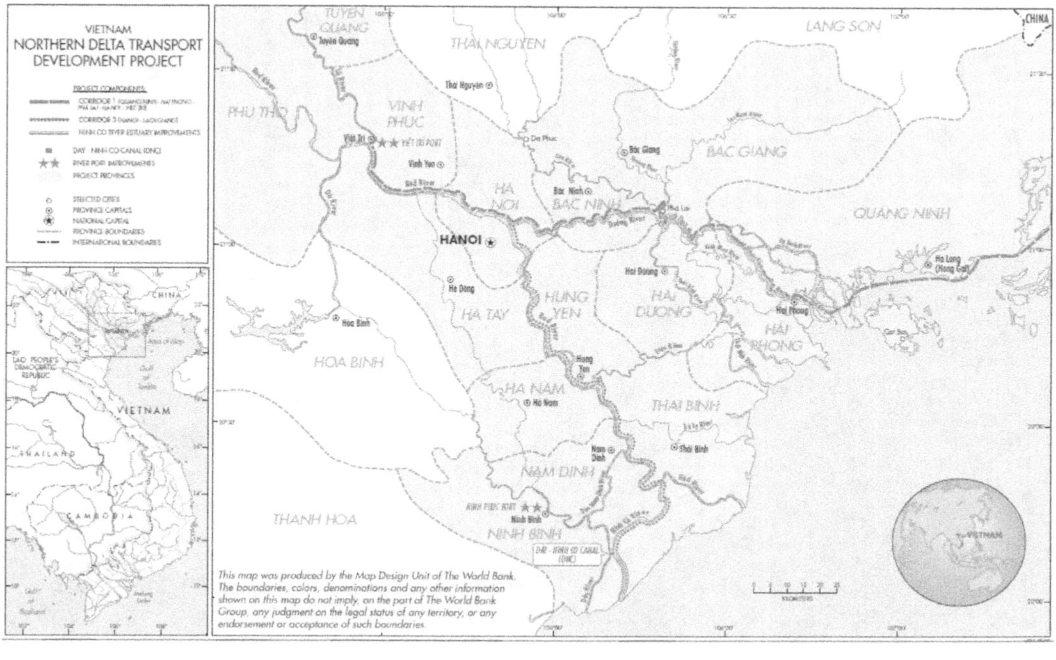

Source: World Bank 2008.

The North region has 55 channels with a length of 2,753 kilometers, of which 12 with a length of 1,506 kilometers are considered major routes. Most of the waterways in the region operate 24 hours a day because of a secured navigational depth. However, the connected waterways are of different grades and feature sharp curves, both of which limit navigational efficiency. In addition, a few waterways have limited vertical clearance under bridges and other river-crossing structures. The most pressing challenges for the northern waterways are, therefore (a) limitations on vertical clearance off river-crossing facilities, (b) a high incidence of sharp curves, and (c) the encroachment on river-banks by housing settlements.

Southern Waterways

IWT in the Mekong Delta relies on two major river channels—the Mekong and Dong Nai rivers (see map 3.2). The channels are more favorable for IWT than those in the North region, with minimum widths of 30–100 meters and minimum depths of 2.5–4.0 meters.[3] River conditions are affected by tidal patterns, but there are not many shoals and the frequency of dredging is low. On the other hand, many channels are constrained by low bridges and narrow clearances. Fourteen inland waterway routes in the South region (with a combined length of 3,047 kilometers) are considered major routes.

Map 3.2 Inland Waterways in Vietnam's South Region

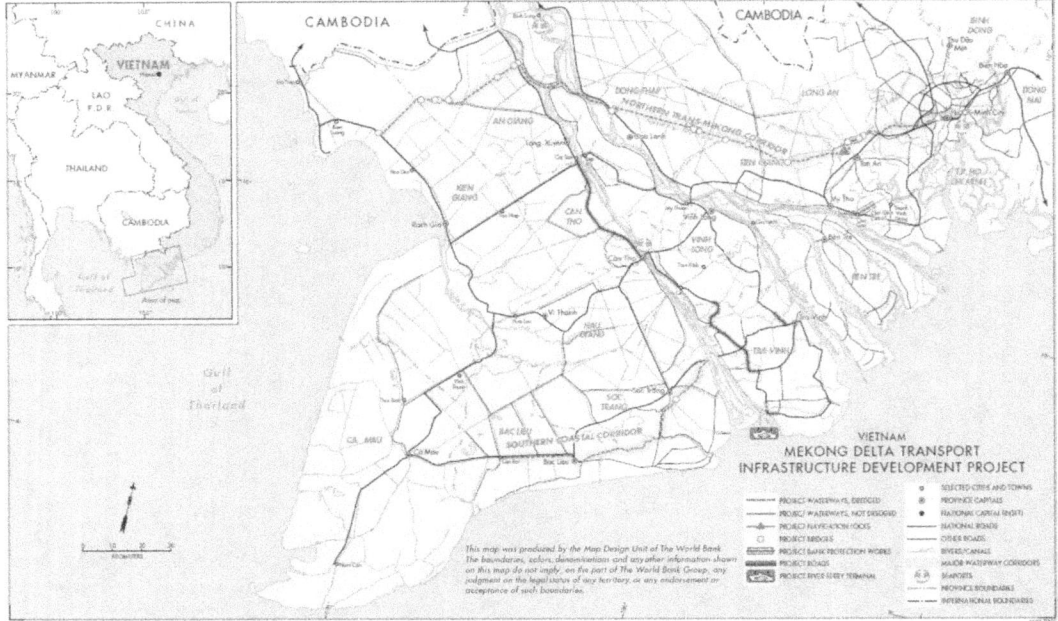

Source: World Bank 2007.

Central Region Waterways

In the Central region, the rivers flow west to east (from the mountains to the sea) independently, without forming a network. Channel lengths span 804 kilometers. In the wet season, the water velocity is high. Conversely, during the dry season the draft is insufficient to support freight traffic. Because of depth limitations and the presence of falls, river navigation is generally not viable except for short 20-kilometer sections near river estuaries.

Technical Classification of the Waterways

To guide the planning, management, and development of inland waterways, the government has adopted a classification system based on channel dimensions and corresponding vessel types. Initially, the classification had six classes for all waterways. These were subsequently revised in consideration of technical differences between the South and North regions, resulting in different class definitions for both regions. Although the various definitions may cause some confusion, this issue has been avoided so far, as inland waterway vessels usually sail only either in the North region or in the South region. A draft version of the classification is shown in table 3.2. It should be noted that in practice, waterways may not always meet the design characteristics associated with their class. Table 3.3 presents the characteristics of river vessels that can be accommodated on each waterway class in the North and South regions for 50 and 90 percent load factors. Box 3.2 shows a similar classification for Europe.

Table 3.2 Vietnam: Technical Classification of Waterways

	Features of the waterways					Minimum size of dry lock				Bridge span		Height of clearance		Depth to lay cable/pipe line	
	River		Channel												
Class	Depth (m)	Width (m)	Depth (m)	Width (m)	Curve radius (m)	Length (m)	Width (m)	Depth level (m)		Channel (m)	River (m)	Bridge (m)	Electric wire (m)	Channel (m)	River (m)
I-North	>3.4	>125	>4.0	>80	>600	145.0	12.5	3.8		>75	>120	11	12+ΔH	2.0	2.0
I-South	>3.4	>125	>4.0	>80	>450	100.0	12.5	3.8		>75	>120	11	12+ΔH	2.0	2.0
II-North	2.5–3.4	40–125	3.1–3.9	70–80	500–600	145.0	12.5	3.4		>75	>120	9.5	12+ΔH	2.0	2.0
II-South	3.0–3.4	50–125	3.7–3.9	35–80	400–450	100.0	12.5	3.5		>75	>120	9.5	12+ΔH	2.0	2.0
III-North	2.0–2.4	35–40	2.5–3.0	30–40	350–500	120.0	10.5	3.3		>28	>38	7	12+ΔH	1.5	1.5
III-South	2.8–3.0	35–50	3.3–3.6	25–35	300–400	95.0	10.5	3.4		>33	>48	7 (6)	12+ΔH	1.5	1.5
IV-North	1.6–1.9	25–35	2.0–2.4	20–30	100–350	85.0	10.5	2.2		>24	>33	6 (5)	7+ΔH	1.5	1.5
IV-South	2.2–2.8	20–35	2.6–3.2	15–25	70–300	75.0	9.5	2.7		>24	>33	6 (5)	7+ΔH	1.5	1.5
V-North	1.4–1.5	12–25	1.8–1.9	10–20	60–100	26.0	6.0	1.8		>15	>24	4 (3.5)	7+ΔH	1.5	1.5
V-South	1.3–2.2	14–20	1.6–2.5	10–15	60–70	18.0	5.5	1.9		>15	>19	4 (3.5)	7+ΔH	1.5	1.5
VI-North	0.9–1.3	<12	0.9–1.7	10	<60	13.0	4.0	1.3		>10	>11	3 (2.5)	7+ΔH	1.5	1.5
VI-South	0.9–1.2	<14	1.0–1.5	<10	<60	12.0	4.0	1.3		>10	>13	3 (2.5)	7+ΔH	1.5	1.5

Source: VIWA 2007.

Note: X-North: Class x as for inland waterway in the North. X-South: Class x as for inland waterway in the South. Safe sideline Δ H is stipulated in Ordinance No.54/1999/ND-CP of the prime minister, July 8, 1999. The depth to lay cable/pipeline: the depth under the design bottom of planned vessel channel.

Table 3.3 River Fleet by Waterway Class for 50 and 90 Percent Load Factors

Class	Weight (tons)	Self-propelled vessel			Pushed barge			
		Length (m) 50%/90%	Width (m) 50%/90%	Draft (m) 50%/90%	Weight (ton)	Length (m) 50%/90%	Width (m) 50%/90%	Draft (m) 50%/90%
I-North	601–1,050	49/52	8.8/9.5	2.5/3.1	4×400/600	121/132	20.0/22.0	1.85/2.70
I-South		44/50	9.0/10.0	2.85/3.1		87/92	20.6/22.0	2.55/2.80
II-North	301–600	44/47	7.50/8.50	2.10/2.60	4×400/600	121/132	20.0/22.0	1.85/2.70
II-South		39/42	7.70/8.80	2.50/2.75		87/92	20.6/22.0	2.55/2.80
III-North	101–300	34/40	6.00/7.30	1.70/2.00	2×200/250/400	104/108	7.0/8.5	1.50/2.70
III-South		25/36	6.50/7.50	2.15/2.55		80/87	8.5/9.4	2.30/2.80
IV-North	51–100	27/30	4.80/6.00	1.35/1.60	2×100	71/79	6.0/9.0	1.10/1.20
IV-South		18/22	5.10/5.80	1.80/2.10		54/68	6.10/8.00	1.20/1.60
V-North	10–50	19/24	4.00/5.20	1.20/1.40	n.a.	n.a.	n.a.	n.a.
V-South		14/16	3.40/4.40	1.05/1.50			n.a.	n.a.
VI-North	<10	12/18	1.90/3.00	0.55/0.85	n.a.	n.a.	n.a.	n.a.
VI-South		11/13	2.30/2.70	0.65/0.85			n.a.	n.a.

Source: VIWA 2007.
Note: n.a. = not applicable.

Box 3.2 Classification of European Waterways

In Europe, inland waterways are classified using the so-called ECEMT categories, defined by the European Conference of Ministers of Transport. Its main feature is that classes are defined on the basis of the maximum size of ships allowed. The categories are as shown in table B3.2.1.

Table B3.2.1 Classification of European Inland Waterways

Class	Type	Standard ships on which classes are based				
		Length (m)	Width (m)	Draft (m)	Tonnage	Height (m)
0	Small craft, recreational	Varies	Varies	Varies	<250	Varies
I	Spits	38.5	5.05	1.8–2.2	250–400	4.0
II	Kempenaar	50–55	6.6	2.5	400–650	4.0–5.0
III	Dordmun-Ems Canal ship	67–80	8.2	2.5	650–1,000	
IV	Rhine-Herne ship	80–85	9.5	2.5	1,000–1,500	5.25 or 7.0
	Push convoy 1 barge	85	9.5	2.5–2.8	1,250–1,450	
Va	Large Rhine ship	95–110	11.4	2.5–2.8	1,500–3,000	5.25/7.0/9.1
	Push convoy 1 barge	95–110	11.4	2.5–4.5	1,600–3,000	
Vb	Push convoy 2 barges	172–185	11.4	2.5–4.5	3,200–6,000	
VIa	Push convoy 2 barges	95–110	22.8	2.5–4.5	3,200–6,000	
VIb	JOWI-type ship	140	15.0	3.9	Not specified	7.0 or 9.1
	Push convoy 4 barges	185–195	22.8	2.5–4.5	6,400–12,000	
VIc	Push convoy 6 barges	270–260	22.8	2.5–4.5	9,600–18,000	
		193–200	30.0–34.2	2.5–4.5	9,600–18,000	9.1
VII	Push convoy 9 barges	285–295	30.0–34.2	2.5–4.5	14,500–27,000	

Source: ECMT 1992.

Planned Investments in Waterways

Between 1999 and 2007, Vietnam allocated Vietnamese dong (VND) 113,000 billion ($5.6 billion) to public transport infrastructure development (see table 3.4). However, only about 45 percent of the planned investments were eventually implemented and the related funds disbursed. On average, Vietnam's 1999–2007 transport investment allocation amounted to VND 14,200 billion (roughly $700 million) annually—or 2.2 percent of the country's gross domestic product (GDP).[4] The low investment realization rate highlights challenges for the transport sector to secure and mobilize funds.

At present, funding for transport-sector investments is allocated on the basis of past trends. The road subsector receives the most funding (80 percent of all transport sector funds between 1999 and 2007). By comparison, the inland waterway and rail subsectors received minimal levels of funding: 2 percent each over the same eight-year period. It is by no means obvious that these percentages represent a balanced transportation strategy, where funding depends on the investment merits and viability of each subsector's project pipeline.

Table 3.4 Allocated Public Investments in Transport by Subsector, 1999–2007
Millions of U.S. dollars

Mode	Total amount	% share
Road	4,500	80
Railway	115	2
Waterway	110	2
Maritime	510	9
Air	415	7
Total	5,645	100

Source: Data from JICA 2009.

The IWT Master Plan for 2020

Guidance for the development of the IWT subsector is provided by the Master Plan for Vietnam Inland Waterway Sector to 2020 (Decision No. 16/2000/QD-TTg, February 2, 2000). This plan has undergone some revisions and adjustments and has been approved by the Minister of Transport (Decision No. 13/2008/QD-BGTVT, August 6, 2008). It comprises programs that VIWA seeks to undertake in the areas of infrastructure, transport services, fleet development, and vessel manufacturing. The basic directions of the master plan are as follows:

1. Exploit the natural advantages of waterways in transporting bulk cargo at lower costs and minimal impact on the environment.
2. Achieve vertical integration within IWT by synchronizing development of routes, ports, handling equipment, vessels, and managerial capacity to meet the demand for cargo and passenger transportation at higher quality and safety.
3. Develop IWT infrastructure to form a seamless system with other transport modes, and in coordination with irrigation and hydropower sectors.
4. Upgrade the fleet with a more efficient configuration that is also safe and better suited to existing conditions in canals and rivers.
5. Broaden the financing base for IWT, with the public sector focusing on the river channels while collaborating with the private sector in port development.

Aside from aiming to expand the IWT network of routes and services, the plan also set objectives for the vessel fleet, navigational channels, and ports:

1. *Vessel fleet:* Capacity of 12 million tons; lower the average age of vessels from 12 to 5–7 years; change the vessel mix to 30–35 percent push convoys and 65–70 percent self-propelled.
2. *Navigational channels:* Increase the length of rivers and channels under government control; ensure the same grade in main channels; modernize marking buoys; and secure channel right-of-way through big cities.

3. *Ports and landing stages:* Modernize selected hub ports, main ports in key regions, and special ports; increase loading and unloading efficiency through mechanization; and build new passenger ports and landing stages.
4. *Capital investment program:* The plan is estimated to require more than VND 73 trillion ($3.7 billion) up to 2020. The sectorial breakdown of the $3.7 billion investment envelope is proposed as follows: investments for channel works will amount to VND 30 trillion ($1.5 billion), divided into VND 24 trillion ($1.2 billion) for construction upgrading and VND 6 trillion ($300 million) for maintenance; a further VND 7 trillion ($350 million) is programmed for ports; VND 36 trillion ($1.8 billion) for vessels; and VND 270 billion ($15 million) for support industries.

Major Channel Projects

There are 10 major ongoing channelization projects to carry out dredging, widening, and radius enlargement (see table 3.5). They will also contribute to smoothing sharp curves, securing banks, and heightening vertical clearances of bridges, among other activities. The original estimated cost for all 10 projects was set at about $330 million, to be partially financed by Official Development Assistance (ODA) (e.g., from the World Bank).

Table 3.5 Major Channel Development Projects as of 2010

	Channel section	Description	Estimated cost (US $ millions)
1[a]	Quang Ninh–Hanoi–Viet Tri	Expanding radius, cutting curves, regulating the field, heightening air clearance of bridges	60
2	Quang Ninh–Ninh Binh (via man-made channel of Haiphong)	Expanding radius, cutting curves, heightening air clearance of bridges	25
3[a]	Lach Giang–Hanoi	Regulating the estuary, dredging the current	75
4[a]	Hanoi–Viet Tri	Widening the radius, regulating the sandbar	20
5	Viet Tri–Yen Bai–Lao Cai	Dredging, building	50
6	Viet Tri–Tuyen Quang	Widening the radius, regulating the sandbar	20
7[a]	Sai Gon–Ha Tien (via Rach Chanh, Thap Muoi 2 canal)	Upgrading, widening, heightening air clearance for bridges	40
8[a]	Sai Gon–Ca Mau (via Tra Vinh canal, Phu Huu–Bai Sau)	Widening, heightening bridge air clearance	40
9	Tien river (section from Vinh Xuong–Vam Nao river)	n.a.	5
10	Phuoc Xuyen canal–4Bis–Canal 28	Upgrading bridge air clearance	5
	Total cost		330

Source: VIWA 2009, World Bank 2007 and 2008.
Note: n.a. = not available. at the bottom of the table.
a. Projects 1, 3, and 4 and Projects 7 and 8 are currently being implemented under Northern Delta Transport Development Project and Mekong Delta Transport Infrastructure Development Project, respectively.

Ports

River Ports

Vietnam's inland waterway network comprises more than 7,000 river ports and landing stages of various categories. According to JICA (2009), there are 126 general-purpose river ports (of which 122 are in operation), 4,809 freight-handling ports (of which 3,484 are licensed), and 2,348 river-crossing docks (of which 1,005 are licensed).[5] As more industries locate along riverbanks, improvised berths of simple design and low cost have also proliferated. While convenient to their owners, such improvised landings tend to hamper navigation and safety. With a few exceptions, throughput in many of the ports is generally low compared to installed capacity.

Small berths operated by local companies can be found in many rural areas, not all of which are licensed or actively regulated by local authorities. Regulating these activities is difficult because the authorities have limited resources and there is a natural incentive to utilize what is perceived to be a free resource. The landing stages can be very basic and in many cases consist only of a ramp and a small mobile crane. Many lack basic cranes, leaving all cargo to be handled manually or by crews and equipment hired for that purpose by the shipper.

River ports and landing stages are managed by different entities (VIWA, provinces, and small private enterprises). Public-sector managed ports (whether under central or local management) are generally of limited scale, have outdated handling facilities and low levels of mechanization, are poorly maintained, and have poor hinterland access. Industrial, dedicated ports appear to be well equipped and periodically maintained. Landing stages and piers are built for specific requirements without any particular pattern or order, although guidelines have been issued by VIWA to mitigate the problem.

There are 11 major terminal/river ports in the North region and about 18 major river cargo ports in the South region. VIWA has drafted the technical parameters to be followed in the preparation of plans and designs for freight ports, passenger ports, freight landing stages, and passenger landing stages. Eight classes of river cargo ports have been defined based on the following factors (table 3.6):

1. Scale of infrastructure (size of the wharf, warehousing space, freight yard, and/or ancillary facilities);
2. Size and type of vessels that the port can accommodate (in terms of deadweight tonnage [DWT] and draft); and
3. Port throughput capacity (tons of cargo per year).

State-run ports tend to cover their operating costs, but any surplus is remitted to the government, as they have no fiscal autonomy. Investment and maintenance costs are treated separately and are dependent on the national budget.

Planned Investments in River Ports

The investment program for nine major ports in the North region, nine ports in the South region, and one port in the Central region is presented in table 3.7.

Table 3.6 Vietnam: Technical Classification of Freight River Ports

Class	Scope of works	Size (type) of accommodated vessel	Throughput capacity (tons)
I-A	RC-bridge or R-bridge Warehouse, freight yard, and supporting facilities	≥1,500 DWT vessel or draft > 3.5 m	>1.5 million
I-B	RC-bridge or R-bridge Warehouse, freight yard, and supporting facilities	≥1,000 DWT vessel or draft > 3.0 m	1.5–1 million
II-A	RC-bridge or R-bridge Warehouse, freight yard, and supporting facilities	≥600 DWT vessel or draft > 2.5 m	>1 million
II-B	RC-bridge or R-bridge Warehouse, freight yard, and supporting facilities	≥400 DWT vessel or draft > 2.0 m	500–1 million
III-A	RC-bridge or R-bridge Warehouse, freight yard, and supporting facilities	≥300 DWT vessel or draft ≥ 1.5 m	>500,000
III-B	RC-bridge or permanent supports Warehouse or freight yard	<300 DWT vessel or draft <1.5 m	200,000–500,000
IV-A	RC-bridge or permanent supports Warehouse or freight yard	≥200 DWT vessel or draft ≥ 1.0 m	>200,000
IV-B	RC-bridge or permanent supports Warehouse or freight yard	<200 DWT vessel or draft <1.0 m	<200,000

Source: VIWA 2007.
Note: DWT = deadweight tonnage; RC-bridge = reinforced concrete bridge; R-bridge = reinforced bridge.

It has a total cost of VND 366 billion (about $19 million), to be funded from local or external sources (e.g., Official Development Assistance). Section 5.2 identifies core routes and recommends priority ports.

Seaports

Based on the Prime Minister's Decision No. 16/2008/QD-TTg (January 28, 2008), seaports are classified into three classes:

1. Class 1 ports are primary ports with high traffic and serving larger vessels operating on foreign and long domestic interregional routes.
2. Class 2 ports function as secondary feeder ports with medium traffic and smaller hinterlands.
3. Class 3 ports are crude oil ports, which in effect are oil tanks adjacent to oil derricks at sea.

Table 3.8 describes Vietnam's main Class 1 maritime ports. It is notable that Cai Mep-Thi Vai is the only port range at present capable of servicing vessels of more than 50,000 DWT.

Fleet

Fleet of River-Going Vessels

The Vietnam Register classifies the inland waterway fleet by vessel length into two categories: vessels 20 meters or less (76,925 units) and vessels longer than 20 meters (130,970 units).[6] Vessels are registered both at the local and

Table 3.7 Major Port Development Projects

Name of port		Description	Cost ($ million)
North			13
1	Hanoi–Khuyen Luong port	Upgrading, expanding	2
2	Phu Dong container port	Newly building	4
3	Ninh Binh–Ninh Phuc port	Upgrading, expanding	1
4	Hoa Binh port	Upgrading, expanding	0.3
5	Viet Tri port	Upgrading, expanding	1
6	Da Phuc port	Newly building	1
7	Hanoi passenger port	Building stage 1	0.5
8	Ben Binh passenger port	Upgrading, expanding	1.5
9	Ha Long passenger port	Upgrading, expanding	1.3
South			5
1	Phu Dinh port	Building	0.8
2	Tan Chau port	Building stage 1	1
3	Ho Phong port	Building stage 1	0.8
4	Giao Long port	Building stage 2	0.3
5	An Phuoc port	Upgrading, expanding	0.3
6	Binh Long port	Upgrading, expanding	0.5
7	Long Duc port	Building stage 1	0.5
8	HCM passenger port	Upgrading, expanding	0.5
9	Can Tho passenger port	Upgrading, expanding	0.5
Central			0.6
	Ho Do port (new)	Building	0.6
	Total		19

Source: VIWA 2009.
Note: Ninh Phuc and Viet Tri ports are being upgraded under the World Bank–financed Northern Delta Transport Development Project (NDTDP), 2009–14.

national levels. Table 3.9 provides key information for the dataset covering vessels over 20 meters long.

The fleet includes a large number of ships of small size. While containerships carry on average the largest tonnage capacity, tankers are also considerably bigger than dry cargo ships. A fleet analysis conducted in preparation of the World Bank-financed MDTIDP (Louis Berger Group and Royal Haskoning 2006) showed that, among the dry cargo fleet in the Mekong River Delta as of November 2004, 24 percent were ships with a carrying capacity of less than 25 tons, 23 percent with a carrying capacity of 25–100 tons, 37 percent with a carrying capacity of 100–500 tons, and 16 percent with a carrying capacity in excess of 500 tons.

Table 3.10 and figure 3.2 show the evolution of the dry cargo vessel fleet by DWT and horse power for the years 2000, 2005, and 2010. As table 3.10 shows, the 95,126 vessels in Vietnam's 2010 river-going vessel fleet were 2.8 times the corresponding number in 2000. The primary reason for an almost tripling in the size of the vessel fleet in the decade to 2010 is the opening up of the Vietnamese

Supply-Side Considerations: Waterways, Ports, and Fleet

Table 3.8 Profile of Major Terminals in Selected Operational Class 1 Seaports

Name of seaport	Name of terminal	Berth Length (m)	Berth Depth (m)	Berth Maximum vessel size (DWT)	Access channel Length (km)	Access channel Minimum depth (m)
Cam Pha		500	9.5–10.5	50,000	40	7.4
Hon Gai	Cai Lan	926	5.0–12.0	45,000	31	7.3
	B12	506	1.6–13.0	40,000	15	8.1
Haiphong	Vat Cach	484	4.0–4.5	3,000	20	3.7
	Hoan Dieu (main port)	1,717	8.4	10,000	37	4.1
	Chua Ve	848	8.5	10,000	37	4.1
	Dinh Vu	238	8.7	20,000	26	5.3
	Doan Xa	210	8.4	10,000	30	4.5
	Transvina	182	8.5	10,000	30	4.5
	Viconship	320	—	10,000	30	4.5
	Cua Cam	348	2.5–7.0	7,000	20	4.5
Nghi Son	Nghi Son General	390	7.5–11.0	10,000	2	7.5
Cua Lo		650	7.5	10,000	4	5.5
Vung Ang		185	10.8	(plan) 45,000	2	9.2
Chan May		420	8.0–12.5	30,000	3	12.0
Da Nang	Tien Sa	595	11.0–12.0	30,000	8	12.7
	Han River	528	7.0	5,000	8	12.7
Dung Quat		110	8.7	20,000	Near sea	8.7
Quy Nhon		830	8.5–11.8	30,000	7	10.5
Nha Trang		552	8.5–11.8	20,000	5	11.5
Vun Tau	Phu My (Ba Ria-Serece)	614	3.0–12.0	60,000	31	12.0
Dong Nai	Dong Nai (Long Binh Tan)	172	3.0–8.3	5,000	100	4.0
Ho Chi Minh City	Sai Gon	2,669	8.5–11.0	36,000	85	8.5
	Ben Nghe	816	9.5–13.0	36,000	84	8.5
	Cat Lai	973	10.5–12.0	15,000	85	8.5
	Tan Cang	706	9.5	36,000	90	8.5
	VICT	486	10.0	20,000	85	8.5
	Nha Be Oil	545	6.8–11.8	32,000	70	8.5
Cai Mep-Thi Vai	TCCT	300	12.0	120,000	n.a	12.0
	TCIT	590	14.0	120,000	33	14.0
	CMIT	600	16.5	160,000	28	14.0
	SITV	730	14.0	120,000	n.a	12.0
	SP-PSA	600	14.5	120,000	n.a	12.0
Can Tho	Can Tho	302	11.0	10,000	120	3.0

Source: JICA 2009 and Ecorys/World Bank analysis.
Note: — = not available; DWT = deadweight tonnage.

IWT market to private operators, which started in 2000. More recently, the 2008–09 economic crisis led to a dramatic drop in trade, and many private vessel operators (particularly small size service providers) have incurred sustained losses or were acquired by larger companies and operators.

Although the growth of the smaller vessel size categories (under 50 DWT) between 2000 and 2010 was a healthy 9.8 percent per year, the number of

Table 3.9 Vietnamese Inland Waterway Ships above 20 Meters in Length

Vessel type	Vessel count	Engine capacity (HP)	Average capacity (HP)	Carrying capacity (tons)	Average capacity (tons)
Dry cargo ships	97,439	5,336,761	55	9,934,020	102
Container ships	440	170,355	387	383,262	871
Tankers	2,383	294,378	124	451,162	189
Tugboats	5,035	1,107,652	220	n.a.	n.a.
Other	25,673	n.a.	n.a.	n.a.	n.a.
Total	130,970	n.a.	n.a.	10,768,444	n.a.

Source: Data fromg Vietnam Register, as of end-April 2010.
Note: HP = horsepower; n.a. = not applicable.

Table 3.10 Vietnam: Size Class (DWT) of River-Going Cargo Vessels, 2000–10

Size (DWT) class river-going vessels	Number of vessels in 2000	Number of vessels in 2005	Number of vessels in 2010
5–15 tons and 5–15 HP	22,531	27,351	53,239
15–50 tons and 15–50 HP	7,875	13,559	23,902
50–200 tons and 50–135 HP	2,749	5,683	9,266
200–300 tons and >135 HP	340	802	1,248
300–500 tons and >135 HP	239	1,059	2,989
500–700 tons and >135 HP	88	578	1,613
700–1,000 tons and >135 HP	33	299	1,641
>1,000 tons and >135 HP	4	60	1,228
Total cargo vessel fleet	33,859	49,391	95,126

Source: Data from Vietnam Register. Mainly for dry cargo ships of more than 20 m or more in length.
Note: DWT = deadweight tonnage; HP = horsepower.

vessels larger than 50 DWT grew at an average annual rate of 18 percent over the same period, and the share of these vessels in the national fleet increased from 10 percent in 2000 to 19 percent in 2010. This increase was driven primarily by much stronger growth in the largest vessel size categories (500 DWT and above), at 43 percent per year over the same 10-year period.

While the number of vessels larger than 50 DWT accounted for only 10 percent of the total number of dry cargo vessels in 2010, they accounted for 60 percent of the river-going fleet's installed carrying capacity (table 3.11 and figure 3.3). By 2010, the 50-plus DWT category's share of total river-going carrying capacity had grown to 85 percent. Similarly, vessels larger than 1,000 DWT, which accounted for just 1.3 percent of the total fleet size in 2010 (by number of vessels), contributed 20 percent of Vietnam's total river-going carrying capacity—up from less than 1 percent of the carrying capacity in 2000. As the transported volumes increased, the capacity share of small vessels (less than 200 DWT) dropped dramatically over the last decade, from 70 percent to 30 percent. This implies that the weighted average age of vessels must have also dropped

Figure 3.2 Vietnam: Number of Vessels by DWT Class as a Share of Total Fleet, 2000–10

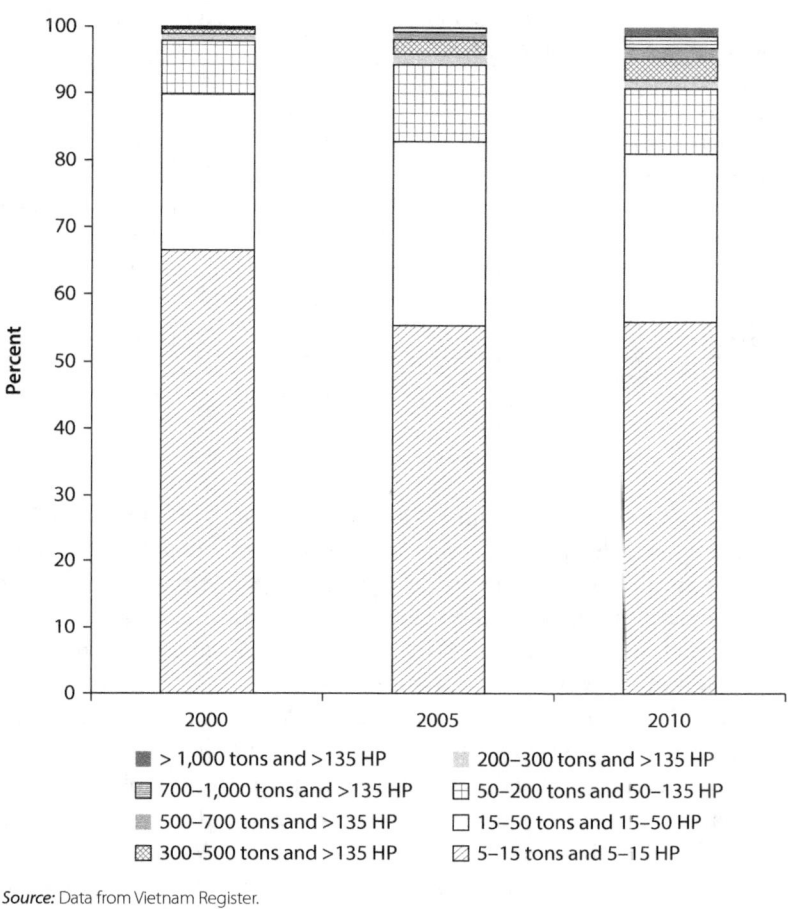

Source: Data from Vietnam Register.
Note: DWT = deadweight tonnage; HP = horsepower.

over the past 10 years (detailed age breakdown data were not available, however, to calculate exact fleet aging numbers). The importance of such "scaling up" of the vessel fleet with regard to fuel efficiency and greenhouse gas (GHG) emissions will be addressed in chapter 4.

Table 3.12 shows that as early as 2002, the share of larger barges had already increased, with the 500-plus DWT barges accounting for almost half of the carrying capacity (table 3.12). This share is most likely much larger at present.

Fleet of Sea-Going Vessels

According to Vinamarine, there are 1,654 ships deployed in coastal and regional trade. Figure 3.4 illustrates the fleet's breakdown by vessel type. Of the total number of vessels, about 68 percent are dry goods vessels and 23 percent are service vessels (e.g., tug boats).

Table 3.11 Vietnam: DWT Carrying Capacity of River-Going Cargo Vessels by Size Class, 2000–10

Size (DWT) class of river-going vessels	Assumed DWT capacity per vessel	DWT capacity 2000	DWT capacity 2005	DWT capacity 2010
5–15 tons and 5–15 HP	7.5	168,983	205,133	399,293
15–50 tons and 15–50 HP	32.5	255,938	440,668	776,815
50–200 tons and 50–135 HP	125	343,625	710,375	1,158,250
200–300 tons and >135 HP	250	85,000	200,500	312,000
300–500 tons and >135 HP	400	95,600	423,600	1,195,600
500–700 tons and >135 HP	600	52,800	346,800	967,800
700–1000 tons and >135 HP	850	28,050	254,150	1,394,850
>1,000 tons and >135 HP	1,300	5,200	78,000	1,596,400
Total cargo vessel fleet	n.a.	1,035,195	2,659,225	7,801,008

Source: Data from Vietnam Register data.
Note: DWT = deadweight tonnage; HP = horsepower; n.a. = not applicable.

From a deployment standpoint, Vinamarine's data reveal that 905 out of 1,654 seagoing vessels operate in coastal routes. Their breakdown into end-use categories is similar to that shown in figure 3.4. Since passenger and service vessels lie beyond the scope of the study, they have been excluded from further analysis. An analysis of DWT size classes shows that most ocean-going vessels are between 500 and 5,000 DWT (see figure 3.5).

There are 38 container vessels registered with Vinamarine. They have an average carrying capacity of 8,633 DWT per vessel and an average age of 16–17 years. The main characteristics of these vessels are summarized in table 3.13.

The smallest and largest container vessels registered are about 4,500 and 16,000 DWT, respectively. Table 3.14 shows typical DWT size classes for container vessels and their corresponding dimensions and 20-foot equivalent unit (TEU) capacity. It appears that all coastal container vessels in Vietnam carry about 400–1,100 TEUs with only a few of them small enough to sail in rivers. A number of sea-river container vessels are probably registered within the IWT vessel fleet by the Vietnam Register.

Fleet of Sea-River Vessels

While Vietnam has integrated sea-river vessels, it does not appear that dedicated vessels of various sizes are used for such movements as is the case in Europe (see box 3.3). In the South region, a number of Mekong Delta river ports are accessible for sea-river ships, reducing the need for IWT between coastal ports and upstream ports for some segments. The importance of this, however, is considered limited.

Class I (Northern and Southern) waterways in Vietnam can currently accommodate self-propelled vessels with a maximum draft of 2.5–3.1 meters, a maximum length of 44–52 meters, and a maximum width of 8.8–10 meters. Sea-river vessels, as presented in box 3.3, would require significant upgrading[7]

Figure 3.3 Vietnam: Carrying Capacity by DWT Class as Share of Total River-Going Cargo Fleet, 2000–10

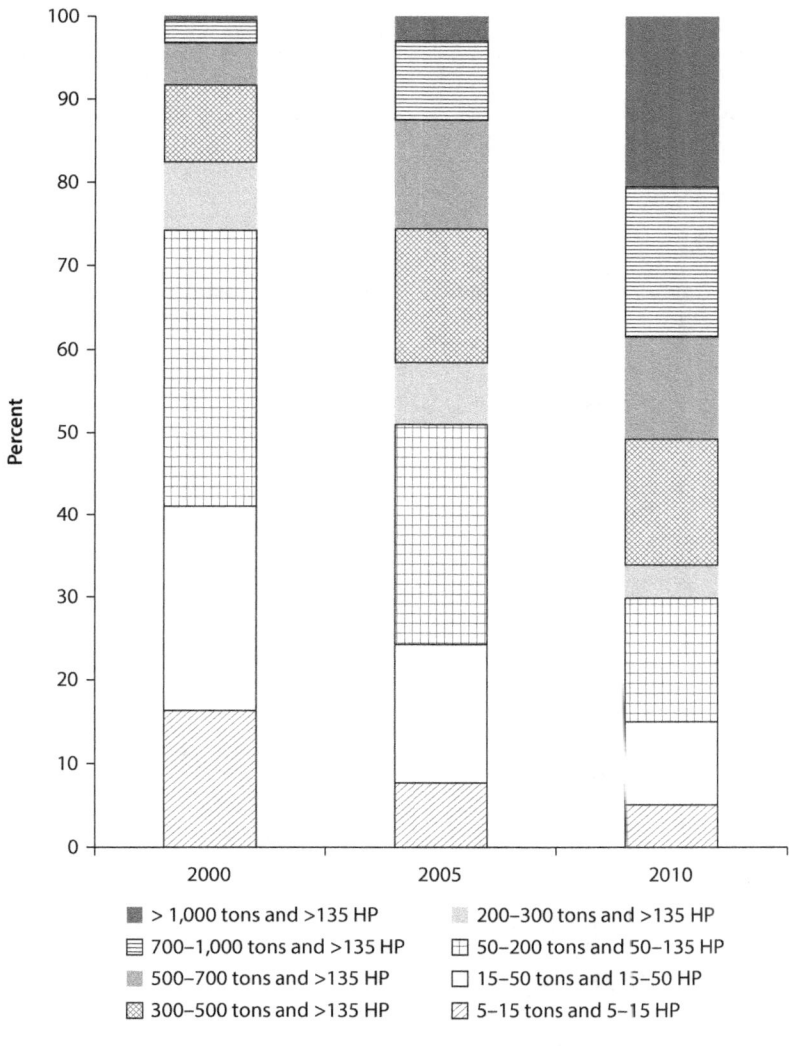

■ > 1,000 tons and >135 HP   200–300 tons and >135 HP
☰ 700–1,000 tons and >135 HP ⊞ 50–200 tons and 50–135 HP
▨ 500–700 tons and >135 HP   □ 15–50 tons and 15–50 HP
▨ 300–500 tons and >135 HP   ▨ 5–15 tons and 5–15 HP

Source: Data from Vietnam Register.
Note: DWT = deadweight tonnage; HP = horsepower.

of the Class I waterways in Vietnam, especially with respect to the length of these vessels.

It should be noted that, according to the *Comprehensive Study on the Sustainable Development of the Transport System in Vietnam* (VITRANSS-2), a basic weakness of Vietnamese flag vessels is the wide gap that separates them from International Maritime Organization (IMO) standards. In interviews with suppliers and owners, the requirement for upgrading the quality standards also was expressed. The situation is confirmed by relatively high detention rates for Vietnamese ships in foreign ports.

Table 3.12 Characteristics of Barge Convoys in the Mekong Delta, 2002

Size class	No. of ships	Share in capacity, %	Average horsepower
0–200 tons	1,101	13	74
200–300 tons	452	14	172
300–500 tons	558	26	240
500–700 tons	415	29	282
>700 tons	200	18	533
Total	2,726	100	n.a.

Source: World Bank 2007.
Note: n.a. = not applicable.

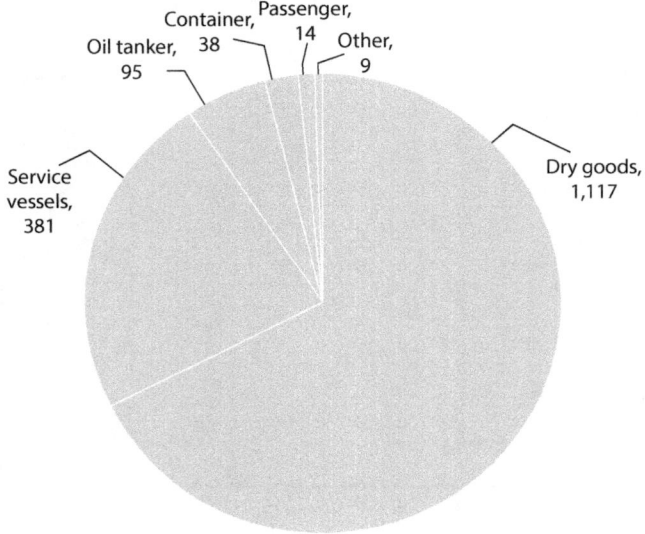

Figure 3.4 Vietnam: Number of Ocean-Going Vessels by Type, 2010

Source: Data from Vinamarine.

Modernization of IWT Fleet

Fleet modernization is a desirable development goal. It is expected to result in (a) an increased share of IWT in total freight movements compared to the business as usual scenario, (b) higher transport cost efficiency in fuel consumption and equipment maintenance, and (c) reduced GHG emissions per ton kilometer (ton-km).

International experience confirms that fleet modernization initiatives typically comprise the following three main activities:

1. Application of modern technologies to existing vessels and their operation (i.e., retrofitting), including:
   - Propulsion engine renewal with significantly lower emission levels
   - Installation of propeller nozzles to improve thrust efficiency
   - Fitting high-efficiency rudder systems for better maneuvering

Figure 3.5 Vietnam: Ocean-Going Vessels by DWT Class, 2010

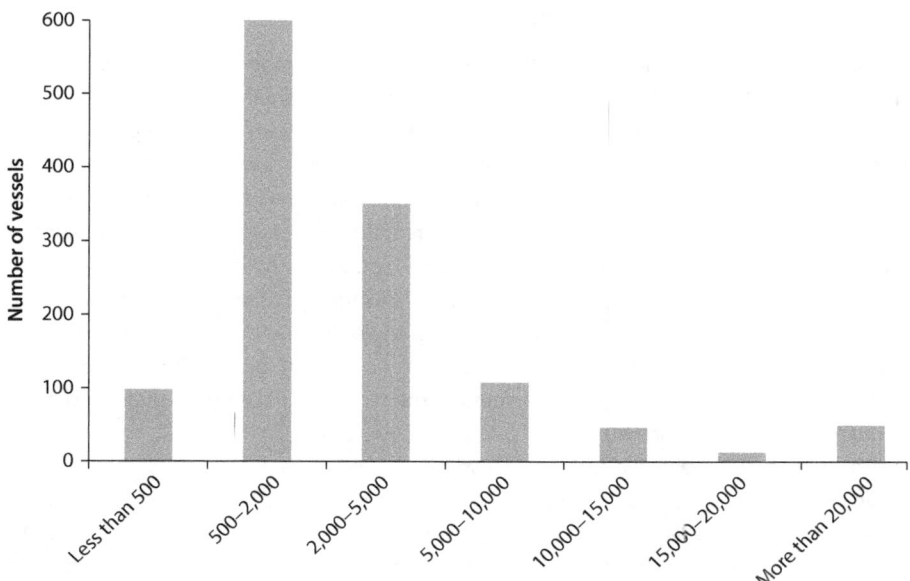

Source: Data from Vinamarine.
Note: Excludes service and passenger vessels. DWT = deadweight tonnage.

Table 3.13 Vietnam: Ocean-Going Container Vessel Fleet Characteristics, 2010

Characteristics	Container vessels
Number of vessels	38
Average DWT capacity	8,633
Total DWT capacity	328,071
Average age in 2010 (years)	16.4
DWT weighted average age in 2010	16.8

Source: Data from Vinamarine.
Note: DWT = deadweight tonnage.

Table 3.14 Typical Container Vessel Characteristics by Size Class, Based on World Fleet

DWT size class	Observations in Lloyd's Register, 2008	TEU	Beam	Draft	LOA
5,000	70	411	18	6.1	105
10,000	754	752	21	7.7	135
15,000	558	1,077	24	8.6	155

Source: Data from Lloyd's Register.
Note: DWT = deadweight tonnage; LOA = length overall; TEU = 20-foot equivalent unit.

Box 3.3 Sea-River Vessels in Europe

A sea-river vessel type, because of its size and constant exposure to the possibility of merging with heavy inland traffic, must have excellent shallow water-steering and propulsion properties—similar to those of modern and powerful self-propelled inland vessels and push boats. In addition, their wheelhouse must be properly laid out for confined water navigation. This is to comply with the convention that "only one person directs and steers the vessel" to avoid delayed reaction and possible misunderstanding, which otherwise may exist between giving and reacting to helm orders. But the most important, and most difficult, requirement to fulfill is for the vessel to cope with shallow water navigation (flat bottom, tunneled stern, preferably twin propeller, high-efficiency rudders, bow steering, and a high payload at shallow draft). Being often incompatible with the requirements for high sea navigation, the tendency in design is that the shallow water properties must prevail.

The development of dedicated sea-river vessels started in the early 1950s and has by now given birth to a variety of vessel types, many of which are designed for special routes only. The most common profile of a highly versatile type is a 2,500 DWT vessel: 87.5 meter long, 11.3 meter beam, 5.4 meter depth, with 4.15 meter maximum draft and either 9.1 or 6.4 meter fixed height. This type of vessel is under construction in series at Thanh Long Shipyard, Haiphong, Vietnam, for Damen Shipyards, the Netherlands.

Source: Ecorys.

- Installation of passive or active bow steering systems to negotiate tight bends
- Installation of articulated barge systems
- Replacement of fixed propeller systems by azimuth drives for better maneuvering
- Installation of state-of-the-art nautical equipment (searchlights, echo-sounders, river radars, rate of turn indicators, gyro compass–controlled steering, communication equipment, GPS, E-Charts) to enable night navigation and optimum use of channel
2. Planning and implementation of new building work on the basis of state-of-the-art concepts to support fleet renewal (see box 3.4)
3. Introduction of new or more efficient waterborne transport systems (e.g., innovative push barge concepts and smooth loading/off-loading equipment).

Average Vessel DWT Capacity Increase

An increase in the national average DWT capacity can be obtained, without improvement of the fairway (channel), by increasing the length, beam, or draft of vessels as far as their area of operation permits. This must be investigated in detail for each area of operation and for each route within that area (see appendix C for general considerations on this topic). The largest existing vessels have

Box 3.4 Fleet Renewal Policies in the Netherlands

The early 1990s saw substantial overcapacity in the IWT fleet in Europe. Many more vessels were in operation than necessary for shipping the available goods. To decrease a structural overcapacity in the market (estimated at 15 percent of the fleet), a European coordination action plan was launched in 1996–98. Yet long before the European Union (EU) took action, the Dutch government had already made efforts toward vessel scrapping to reduce domestic overcapacity in inland waterway transport. This was done by providing financial incentives for scrapping smaller vessels if these were replaced by a smaller number of larger vessels, resulting in lower overall capacity but larger unit sizes—thus helping to increase economies of scale. As a result, the Dutch fleet modernized at an impressively rapid pace. The observed wave of new construction and expansion was mainly triggered by the use of so-called Demolition of Vessels schemes in the 1970s and 1980s, followed by an Old-for-New scheme in the 1990s (see table B3.4.1). The Old-for-New scheme resulted in approximately 50 percent more demolition of vessel DWT than newly added vessel DWT capacity.

Table B3.4.1 Fleet Renewal and Modernization in the Netherlands

Scheme	Number of vessels retired	DWT	Cost (million)
Results of demolition of Dutch inland vessels			
1968	905	163,000	5
1976	517	231,000	9
1977	1,019	481,000	15
1980	157	56,000	2
1986	359	324,00	12
Results of old-for-new arrangement of Dutch inland waterway vessels 1990–97			
Dry bulk vessels	679	586,000	—
Tank vessels	77	84,000	—

Source: Ecorys.
Note: Costs refer to government funds spent on program costs or incentives paid. DWT = deadweight tonnage; — = not available.

---

dimensions that have more or less emerged naturally in relation to limitations in the fairway, as explained in table 3.15.

In addition, economic growth and attractive fiscal regimes provided further incentives to invest in new vessels or improve existing fleet. Tanker vessels also had to deal with the pressure to transition from single to double hull. Until late 2006, the Netherlands was the only country that provided tax advantages to manage national fleets (e.g., use tax owed to invest in a new ship with guaranteed credit).

Fleet renewal and fleet-wide unit capacity increases are long-term processes. Figure 3.6 depicts the historical long-term scaling-up trend of average vessel capacity for the inland shipping sector in Western Europe over the past 50 years.

Table 3.15 Constraints for Vessel DWT Capacity Increases

Parameter	Constraints
Length	Fairway curvature, lock length, fairway width, and vessel maneuverability
Beam	Fairway (bottom) width, lock, and/or bridge passage width
Draft	Water depth, bottom soil type, and acceptable underkeel clearance versus speed

Source: Ecorys.
Note: DWT = deadweight tonnage.

Figure 3.6 Average Increase in Tonnage (DWT) in the Western European (Belgium, Germany, and the Netherlands) IWT Fleet Relative to Vietnam's Position

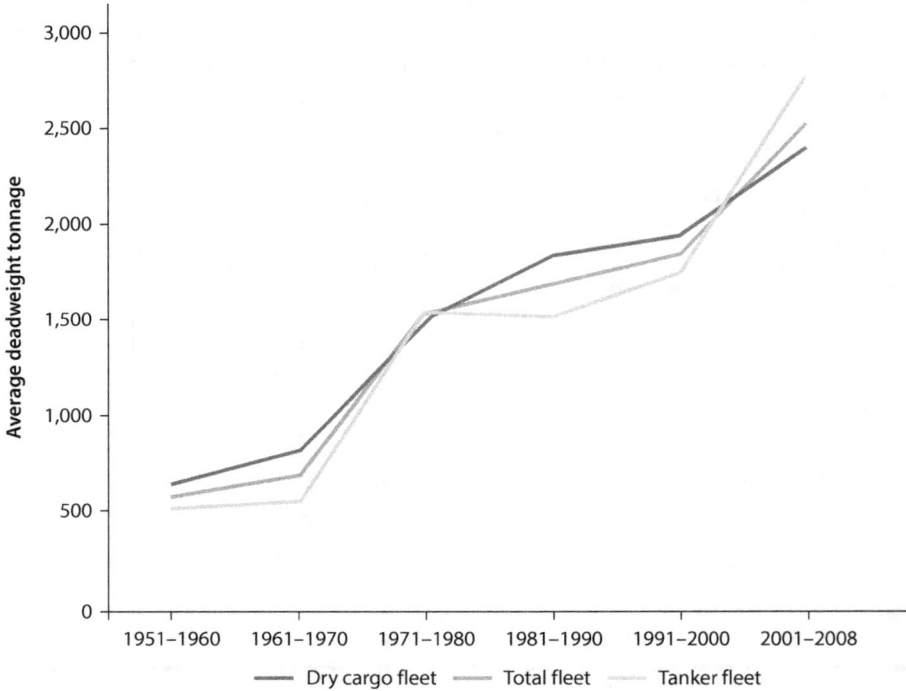

Source: Dutch Inland Shipping Information Agency 2009.
Note: DWT = deadweight tonnage; IWT = inland waterway transport.

Box 3.5 shows the evolution of the IWT vessel fleet in the Netherlands between 2000 and 2008. In Vietnam, a sustained market-driven scaling-up trend in the IWT fleet has taken place over the past 10 years, as discussed earlier. By way of comparison, approximately 4,500 cargo vessels currently operating in the Netherlands have a combined carrying capacity of close to 6 million tons, or about 1,300 DWT per vessel. In Vietnam, there are about 95,000 operational vessels with nearly 8 million tons in aggregate capacity, or only about 80 DWT per vessel. The largest 8,700 vessels in Vietnam have a carrying capacity of about 5.5 million tons, or slightly more than 600 DWT per vessel.

Box 3.5 Dutch IWT Vessel Fleet Evolution, 2000–08

The total number of dry cargo and tanker vessels in the Dutch IWT fleet decreased by 18 percent between 2000 and 2008 (see bottom row of table B3.5.1). But the headline growth rate masks a large dichotomy in the evolution of the fleet by vessel size: while small size classes (less than 1,500 DWT) showed large decreases, the larger classes (1,500 to over 3,000 DWT) showed increases of varying magnitudes.

In contrast with the number of vessels, the total carrying capacity of the Dutch fleet expanded by 4 percent between 2000 and 2008 (see table B3.5.2). Again, a large decrease was observed for the smaller size classes, while capacity from ships over 3,000 DWT grew rapidly.

Table B3.5.1 Vessel Count in the Dutch Inland Waterway Fleet by DWT Category, 2000 vs. 2008

Vessel DWT category	2000			2008			% change 2000–08
	No. of dry cargo vessels	No. of tanker vessels	Total vessels	No. of dry cargo vessels	No. of tanker vessels	Total vessels	
Up to 249	449	232	681	235	222	457	−33%
250–399	532	37	569	302	27	329	−42
400–649	808	81	889	567	58	625	−30
650–999	1,066	70	1,136	761	56	817	−28
1,000–1,499	920	154	1,074	714	100	814	−24
1,500–1,999	315	80	395	331	74	405	3
2,000–2,499	190	75	265	220	82	302	14
2,500–2,999	291	43	334	347	51	398	19
3,000 and more	113	29	142	268	84	352	148
Total	4,684	801	5,485	3,745	754	4,499	−18

Source: Central Commission for Navigation on the Rhine 2009.
Note: DWT = deadweight tonnage.

Table B3.5.2 Tonnage Deployed in the Dutch Inland Waterway Fleet by DWT Category, 2000 vs. 2008
Thousands of tons

Vessel DWT category	2000			2008			% change 2000–08
	Dry cargo vessel tonnage	Tanker vessel tonnage	Total tonnage	Dry cargo vessel tonnage	Tanker vessel tonnage	Total tonnage	
Up to 249	65	24	89	30	23	53	−40%
250–399	173	12	185	101	9	110	−41
400–649	434	40	474	308	29	337	−29
650–999	868	57	925	617	45	662	−28
1,000–1,499	1,115	194	1,309	860	126	986	−25

table continues next page

box continues next page

Box 3.5 Dutch IWT Vessel Fleet Evolution, 2000–08 *(continued)*

Table B3.5.2 Tonnage Deployed in the Dutch Inland Waterway Fleet by DWT Category, 2000 vs. 2008 *(continued)*
Thousands of tons

Vessel DWT category	2000			2008			% change 2000–08
	Dry cargo vessel tonnage	Tanker vessel tonnage	Total tonnage	Dry cargo vessel tonnage	Tanker vessel tonnage	Total tonnage	
1,500–1,999	537	135	672	561	123	684	2
2,000–2,499	426	166	592	495	180	675	14
2,500–2,999	807	119	926	961	140	1,101	19
3,000 and more	412	98	510	990	326	1,316	158
Total	4,837	845	5,682	4,923	1,001	5,924	4

Source: Central Commission for Navigation on the Rhine 2009.
Note: DWT = deadweight tonnage.

While Vietnam has undergone a desirable fleet scaling-up process over the past 10 years, the average vessel carrying capacity remains comparatively low. As such, there is significant potential for further scaling up of the Vietnamese IWT fleet. However, Vietnam is expected to encounter a number of impediments to the use of larger vessels, particularly network infrastructure bottlenecks that limit further up-scaling of the IWT fleet and/or the use of sea-river vessels. Therefore, the scaling-up trend will not realistically hold for all waterway classes.

Scaling up could bring about economies of ship size: the effect by which a 1 percentage point increase in ship size decreases unit shipping costs by more than 1 percent. Not only will fixed costs (labor, capital, insurance) per DWT decrease, but larger ships are also more fuel efficient, resulting in lower fuel costs and a reduction in CO_2 emissions. On the core routes, a scaling-up trend of about 400–500 DWT per decade, starting from 600 DWT in 2010 for the most commercially oriented portion of the national fleet, appears to be a plausible pathway for Vietnam (see chapter 5 for further discussion of potential policy measures). Since Vietnam's fleet scaling-up track record over the past decade did not involve explicit public policy interventions, there is evidence that the sector is flexible enough to accommodate growing demand volumes on its own while driving further modernization and scale increase. Targeted public sector policies, however, may speed up this process while generating attractive economic returns.

Conclusions on Waterways, Ports, and Fleet

Vietnam has an extensive amount of inland waterways, of which 41,900 kilometers are navigable and 15,000 kilometers are under central management. The core sections in the North and South regions (about 4,500 kilometers) are classified as the highest waterways classes. Investment projects have been defined for a few of these core sections, but public funding for improving and maintaining the waterways appears to be insufficient.

Vietnam has 7,000 river ports and landing stages, but only about 30 are of major importance for cargo flows. A large number of the landing stages are neither licensed nor regulated, and while they are convenient to the industries located along the river bank, they also hinder navigation and safety. Vietnam also has 49 seaports, of which the most important ones are located in the North region, around Haiphong, and in the South region, around HCMC.

The number of vessels in Vietnam's 2010 river-going fleet was almost three times the corresponding number in 2000 due to the opening up of the Vietnamese IWT market to private operators in 2000. Vietnam also experienced a scaling-up trend in the IWT fleet over the past 10 years, along the same lines of Western Europe over the past five decades, but of a different magnitude, given the relatively nascent position of the industry in Vietnam. As the transported volumes increased, the capacity share of vessels less than 200 DWT dropped dramatically over the past decade from 70 percent to 30 percent. Vessels larger than 1,000 DWT, for example, contributed 20 percent of Vietnam's total river-going carrying capacity in 2010, up from less than 1 percent of the carrying capacity in 2000.

Despite the large scaling up in Vietnam, the low average carrying capacity per IWT cargo vessel of 80 DWT, compared to 1,300 DWT in the Netherlands, for example, clearly indicates that the potential for further scaling up is large and should indeed be a path to be considered. The level that can be reached will, however, depend on the waterway capacity that can be made available on the most important routes. Vietnam is expected to encounter various impediments to the use of larger vessels because of infrastructure bottlenecks. It is also worth noting that the rapid scaling up in Western Europe and in the Netherlands, in particular, was facilitated by government tax advantages and other financial incentives. While Vietnam has not resorted to any incentives so far in the scaling up of its fleet, which was largely driven by market forces, incentives could speed up the modernization and scaling-up process.

Notes

1. This chapter deals primarily with inland waterways. A brief discussion of coastal waterways is included at the end of the chapter.
2. Some of the main seaports in Vietnam are on rivers. These are administered by Vinamarine.
3. The same wet and dry seasonal patterns apply in the South region as in the North region. In the South region, the water level difference between the two seasons is 5–7 meters (JICA 2009).
4. JICA 2009. From 1994 to 2002, this figure stood at about 3.2 percent of GDP (World Bank 2006).
5. General purpose river ports are ports where multiple types of commodities are handled (e.g., bulk cargo, general cargo, and containers; the facility may also service

passenger itineraries). Freight handling ports do not operate as passenger ports. River-crossing docks are not technically ports; rather, they are the landing points of river-crossing ferries. Nevertheless, while landing stages or improvised berths may not qualify as ports due to their small size and their dedicated use, they typically fulfill some port functions.

6. Data as of end-April 2010.

7. A maximum draft of 4.15 meters is reached only when a vessel is heavily loaded with cargo. Under different load factor circumstances, a typical sea-river vessel could also be operated with a draft of 3.0 meters.

References

Central Commission for Navigation on the Rhine. 2009. *Inland Navigation in Europe: Market Observation*. Report 7. Strasbourg, France: Secretariat of the Central Commission for Navigation on the Rhine.

Dutch Inland Shipping Information Agency (BVB). 2009. *The Power of Inland Navigation 2010–2011*. Rotterdam, the Netherlands: BVB.

ECMT (European Conference of Ministers of Transport). 1992. *Resolution No. 92/2 on New Classification of Inland Waterways*. http://www.internationaltransportforum.org/IntOrg/acquis/wat19922e.pdf.

JICA (Japan International Cooperation Agency). 2009. *The Comprehensive Study on the Sustainable Development of Transport System in Vietnam (VITRANSS-2)*. Hanoi: JICA.

Louis Berger Group and Royal Haskoning. 2006. *Mekong Delta Transport Infrastructure Development Project (MTIDP) Feasibility Study*. World Bank: Washington, DC.

VIWA (Vietnam Inland Waterway Administration). 2007. *National Technical Regulation on Technical Classification of Inland Waterways*. Draft. Hanoi: VIWA.

———. 2009. *The Review on the Master Plan of Inland Waterway Transport Development Up to 2020*. Hanoi: VIWA.

World Bank. 2006. *Transport Strategy, Transition, Reform, and Sustainable Management*. Hanoi: World Bank.

———. 2007. *Mekong Delta Transport Infrastructure Development Project (MDTIDP) Project Appraisal Document*. Washington, DC: World Bank.

———. 2008. *Northern Delta Transport Development Project (NDTDP) Project Appraisal Document*. Washington, DC: World Bank.

CHAPTER 4

Modal Differences in Fuel Efficiency and Greenhouse Gas Emissions

In 2005, Vietnam's carbon dioxide (CO_2) emissions amounted to 81.6 million tons, of which 20.3 million tons—25 percent of the total—were attributed to the transport sector. Within the transport sector, about 92 percent of the CO_2 emissions originated from road transport and about 5 percent from waterborne transport (inland waterways and coastal shipping). However, both of these figures include passenger as well as freight transport. As no data are available for Vietnam for emissions resulting from freight movements by mode, the modal ton-kilometer (ton-km) breakdown from table 2.1 was used as a basis for developing crude estimates of the shares of road freight transport and waterborne freight transport. Assuming that road transport emits 2–3 times as much greenhouse gas (GHG) per ton-km as waterborne transport, and based on a road sector modal share of about 38 percent and a waterborne freight combined share of about 62 percent (ignoring for simplicity the 4 percent share of rail and air freight), road transport's share of GHG emissions, although accounting for a smaller share of ton-km transported, would be between 1.2 and 1.8 times the GHG emissions produced by the inland and coastal waterways. This chapter attempts to refine these crude estimates by giving a better sense of the emissions produced by each subsector.

Relative Carbon Intensity among Transport Modes

Financial prices of transportation services typically do not reflect all social costs and benefits. External costs and benefits include environmental costs due to pollution, GHG emissions, congestion, traffic accidents, and noise, as well as positive impacts (often referred to as Mohring effects).[1] Emissions per ton or ton-km can vary significantly depending on the mode of transport used. Typically, transport by inland or coastal waterways fares better than road transport with respect to GHG emissions, noise, safety, congestion, and Mohring effects.

Mohring or density effects in inland waterway transport (IWT) can generate economic benefits. The Mohring effect for the waterways can be explained as follows: If traffic and transport levels by road increase, congestion increases, resulting in a higher sum of vehicle operation and time costs. However, an increase in transport levels on coastal and inland waterways could have positive effects. An increase in the level of international trade, for example, would enable the use of bigger ships, which results in lower shipping costs and higher frequency of shipping services,[2] which in turn results in lower inventory carrying costs for importers and exporters. This effect also applies to scheduled coastal shipping services, where the strong increase in volume will lead to a combination of lower shipping costs and lower inventory carrying costs (see appendix E for further details).[3]

Transport emissions by road and waterways are significantly influenced by the size and age of the vehicles and vessels deployed. Specifically, the larger the vehicle or vessel, the lower the emissions per unit of service; the older the vehicle or vessel engine, the less fuel efficient it is. The precise outcome in a modal comparison therefore depends on the size of trucks and ships compared and the composition and evolution of the fleet. In addition to size and age, higher levels of congestion result in higher GHG emissions. Moreover, the operational costs of the road network (maintenance costs from wear and tear) are likely to increase with higher traffic intensities and higher truck load factors. While congestion could occur in the waterways, it is typically more of a road phenomenon.

In this section, emission performance data for road and IWT that are taken from the literature are presented. Subsequently, indicative estimates are made for assessing the potential benefits of measures to improve environmental performance of IWT. For the design of the modal split model (see chapter 7 and appendix D), this approach is further detailed using field data gathered and intervention-specific assumptions made.

Figures 4.1, 4.2, and 4.3 present the range of emissions per ton-km transported associated with various transport modes. (Box 4.1 discusses the carbon intensity of the Dutch IWT sector as a key benchmark.) It should be noted that these estimates are for European and Organisation for Economic Co-operation and Development countries, suggesting that higher emission factors (or at least the upper bound within a given range) are more applicable to emerging economies, which typically devote considerably less resources to vehicle and infrastructure maintenance and are prone to less efficient driving/voyage conditions.

Large trucks are up to three times more carbon-intense compared with coastal container vessels. Emissions from coastal container vessels range from 32 to 36 gCO_2 per ton-km, while those for heavy duty trucks range from 51 to 91 gCO_2 per ton-km (see figure 4.1). Figure 4.2 provides estimates that are more relevant to Vietnam's current situation (i.e., reflecting an environment of relatively small and inefficient trucks and inland shipping vessels). Based on figure 4.2, the carbon intensity of trucks (at 90–125 gCO_2 per ton-km) is on average closer to two times that of inland waterway vessels (40–70 gCO_2 per ton-km).

Modal Differences in Fuel Efficiency and Greenhouse Gas Emissions

Figure 4.1 CO$_2$ Intensity of Selected Freight Transport Modes, Log Scale
g/ton-km

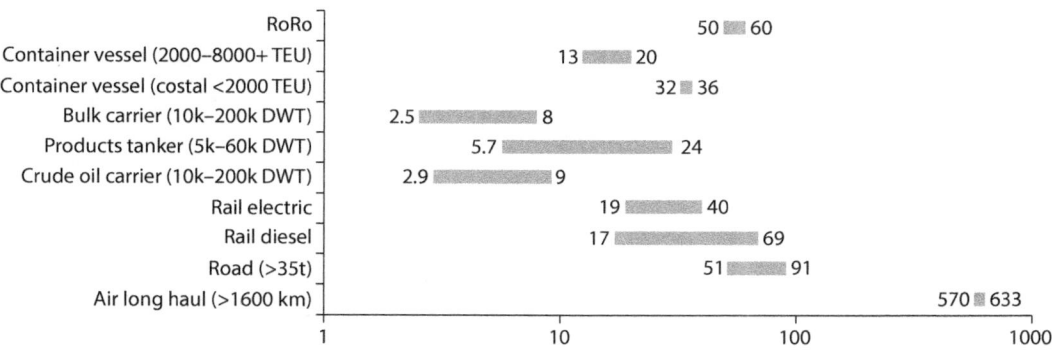

Source: International Transport Forum (ITF) estimates and Buhaug et al. 2008, as shown in Crist 2009.
Note: DWT = deadweight tonnage; RoRo = roll on/roll off; TEU = 20-foot equivalent units.

Figure 4.2 CO$_2$ Emissions, Long Distance (>150 km) Freight Transport, 2010
g/ton-km

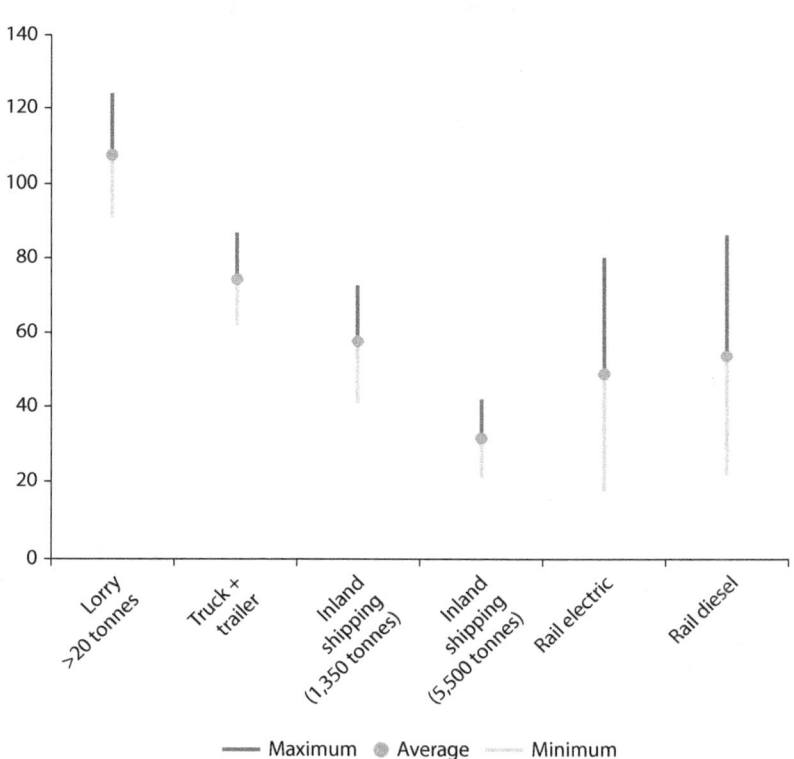

Source: Dutch Inland Shipping Information Agency 2009.

Figure 4.3 CO_2 Emissions for Long Distance Bulk Freight Transport, 2000
g-ton/km

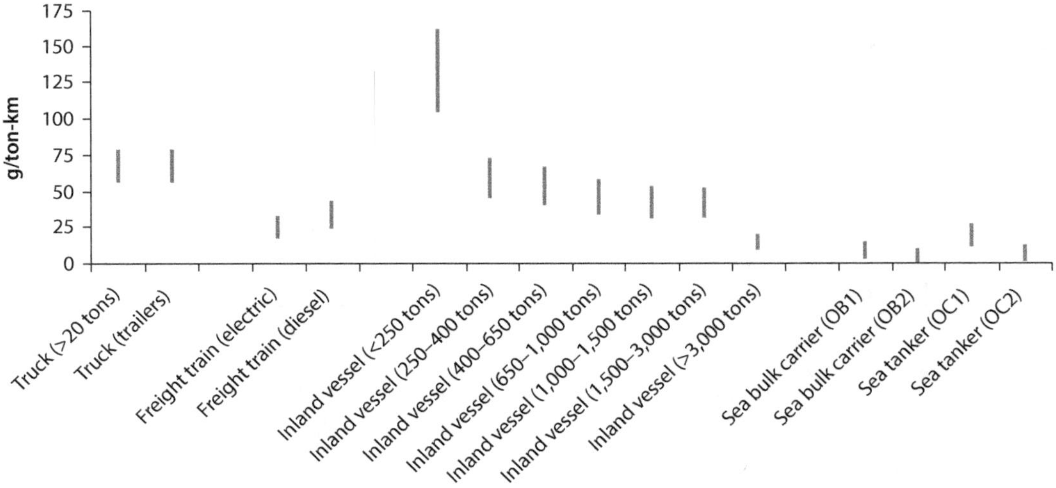

[Bar chart showing g/ton-km ranges on y-axis (0–175) for categories: Truck (>20 tons), Truck (trailers), Freight train (electric), Freight train (diesel), Inland vessel (<250 tons), Inland vessel (250–400 tons), Inland vessel (400–650 tons), Inland vessel (650–1,000 tons), Inland vessel (1,000–1,500 tons), Inland vessel (1,500–3,000 tons), Inland vessel (>3,000 tons), Sea bulk carrier (OB1), Sea bulk carrier (OB2), Sea tanker (OC1), Sea tanker (OC2).]

Source: Van Essen et al. 2003.

Box 4.1 CO_2 Emissions from Inland Shipping in the Netherlands, 1995–2005

In the Netherlands, inland shipping CO_2 emissions per ton-km decreased by about 13 percent in the 10 years between 1995 and 2005 to roughly 40 gCO_2 per ton-km (see figure B4.1.1). On the other hand, CO_2 emissions per vessel-km increased over the same period and at a similar rate. Taken together, these trends confirm that a sustained increase in the scale of inland shipping vessels in the Netherlands has been attained, as more freight is being shipped with fewer vessels, thus increasing fleet efficiency per ton-km.

Figure B4.1.1 Inland Shipping CO_2 Emissions in the Netherlands, 1995–2005

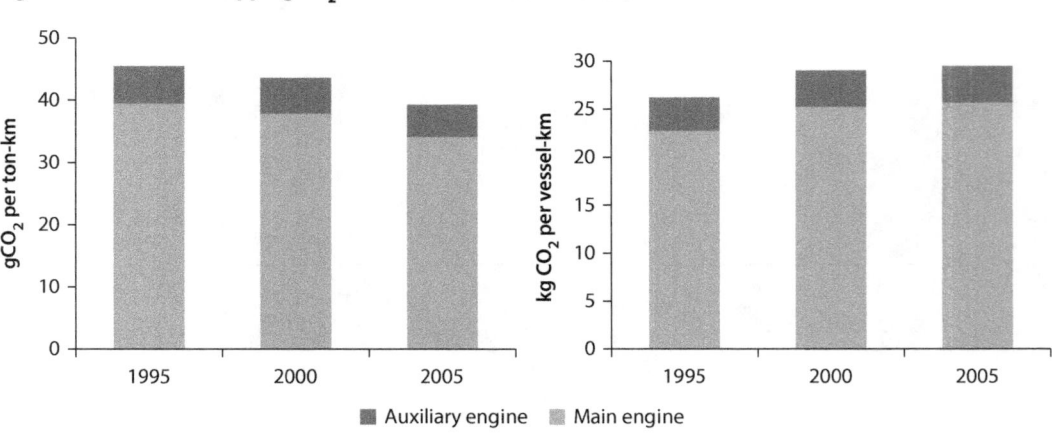

■ Auxiliary engine ■ Main engine

Source: Denier van der Gon and Hulskotte 2010.

Figure 4.3 shows emission ranges that are perhaps the most applicable to Vietnam, as this figure particularly focuses on bulk cargo—the most dominant commodity type for IWT in the country—transported by relatively small inland vessels (less than 250 tons). Road freight emissions are 60–80 gCO_2 per ton-km for trucks and 30–160 gCO_2 per ton-km for inland shipping vessels. One could argue that the smaller trucks used in Vietnam, particularly in the Mekong Delta, are at the higher end of this range. The figure also shows that the most significant efficiency gain in inland shipping is achieved when vessel sizes increase from less than 250 deadweight tonnage (DWT) to vessels larger than 250 DWT. This suggests that as the scaling up of the fleet and the shift toward larger vessels continues, Vietnam would be expected to move toward the lower end of the waterway vessel emissions range.

Indicative Estimates of GHG Emission Reductions

This section further focuses on CO_2 emissions from road and waterway freight transport by estimating, on an indicative basis, potential reductions from fleet modernization and modal shift. Table 4.1 shows different IWT vessel size classes in Vietnam and the corresponding number of vessels by class in 2000 and 2010. The column on emission factors (EFs) shows indicative EFs for Vietnam's vessel DWT classes based on expert judgment and the above-presented literature findings. Weighted by number of vessels,[4] the weighted average fleet EF in Vietnam for 2000 is estimated at 146 gCO_2 per ton-km, improving to 137 gCO_2 per ton-km by 2010. Weighted by carrying capacity,[5] the weighted average fleet EF in Vietnam for 2000 is estimated at 110 gCO_2 per ton-km, improving to 71 gCO_2 per ton-km by 2010.

Table 4.1 Indicative Evolution of Vietnam's Average IWT Vessel Fleet Emissions
CO_2 per ton-km

Carrying capacity (DWT) IWT vessels	EF IWT gCO_2 per ton-km	Number of vessels in 2000	Number of vessels in 2010
5–15 tons and 5–15 HP	160	22,531	53,239
15–50 tons and 15–50 HP	130	7,875	23,902
50–200 tons and 50–135 HP	100	2,749	9,266
200–300 tons and >135 HP	75	340	1,248
300–500 tons and >135 HP	60	239	2,989
500–700 tons and >135 HP	50	88	1,613
700–1,000 tons and >135 HP	45	33	1,641
>1,000 tons and >135 HP	40	4	1,228
Number of ships weighted average EF (gCO_2 per ton-km)	n.a.	146	137
Capacity weighted average EF (gCO_2 per ton-km)	n.a.	110	71

Source: Ecorys.
Note: DWT = deadweight tonnage; EF = emission factor; HP = horsepower; IWT = inland waterway transport; n.a. = not applicable.

The average fleet EFs and traffic volumes were then used to estimate the total CO_2 emissions from IWT in Vietnam (table 4.2). The 2030 columns show two scenarios. The "scaling up and modernization" scenario assumes that Vietnam's fleet EF will improve from 71 to 50 gCO_2 per ton-km between 2010 and 2030. The "frozen EF" (i.e., same as baseline) scenario assumes no further improvement after 2010. The indicative annual emissions savings reach 1 million tons of CO_2 in 2030. Such gain is expected to be in part market-driven and in part attributable to government policies and incentives.

Table 4.3 shows an indicative estimate of the reduction in GHGs as a result of a hypothetical 10 percent modal shift from the roads to the waterways. The table uses indicative EFs for trucks in Vietnam based on expert judgment. The total annual emissions reduction achieved by the modal shift in this example is 0.4 million tons CO_2 in 2030.

By comparing tables 4.2 and 4.3, these initial results suggest that the most critical opportunity for Vietnam to reduce freight transport emissions, all else being equal, is to enable the use of larger vessels and more modern, cleaner engines. In particular, the impact of these practices appears to be significantly larger than the reduction in emissions that could be obtained from modal shift away from the roads, even if a rather optimistic rate of modal shift of 10 percent is assumed (as will be shown later in the report, feasible levels of modal

Table 4.2 Indicative Gain from Fleet Modernization and Upgrading

Vietnam IWT CO_2 emissions	2010	Scaling up and modernization 2030	"Frozen" EF 2030
Average IWT fleet EF (gCO_2/ton-km)	71	50	71
IWT[a] ton-km (billion ton-km)	23	48	48
IWT CO_2 emissions (million tons CO_2)	1.6	2.4	3.4

Source: Ecorys/World Bank analysis.
Note: EF = emission factor; IWT = inland waterway transport.
a. Based on an annual growth rate of 3.7% for IWT between 2008 and 2030 according to JICA 2009.

Table 4.3 Indicative Gain from Modal Shift from Road to Waterway Freight Transport

Vietnam IWT CO_2 emissions	2010	2030
Average truck fleet EF (gCO_2/ton-km)	110	80
Average IWT fleet EF (gCO_2/ton-km)	71	50
Road[a] ton-km (billion ton-km)	30	129
Road CO_2 emissions (million tons CO_2)	3.3	10.3
Road modal share minus 10%: road ton-km (billions)	n.a.	116
Modal shift to IWT: IWT ton-km (billions)	n.a.	13
Road CO_2 (million tons)	n.a.	9.3
IWT CO_2 for freight shifted from road (million tons)	n.a.	0.6
Modal shift case road + IWT (million tons CO_2)	n.a.	9.9
Total CO_2 reduction modal shift case (million tons CO_2)	n.a.	0.4

Source: Ecorys/World Bank analysis.
Note: EF = emission factor; IWT = inland waterway transport; n.a. = not applicable.
a. Based on an annual growth rate of 7.5% for road freight between 2008 and 2030, according to JICA 2009.

shift for Vietnam are estimated to be in the range of 1–3 percentage points in the long run). This should help prioritize policies that address vessel and engine use.

Conclusions

Three conclusions emerge from this chapter:

1. IWT (on vessels larger than 250 DWT) and coastal shipping generate lower CO_2 emissions per ton-km than road freight transport.
2. Mirroring the experience of Western Europe, significant improvements in the national fleet's environmental performance are expected in Vietnam as the country continues to develop and to the extent that larger vessels with more modern engines are adopted by the shipping market.
3. These mode-specific efficiency improvements are expected to have a much larger impact on reducing GHG emissions than any reasonable levels of modal share shift from the roads to the waterways.

While the above conclusions have been obtained on the basis of indicative analysis presented in this chapter, they are formally tested—and confirmed—later in the report with the use of modal split and cost-benefit modeling (see chapter 7 and appendixes D–F).

Notes

1. While the "Mohring effect" originally referred to the positive impact of increasing returns in transit service—where an increase in transit frequencies would result in a decrease in wait times, an increase in demand, and a further increase in transit frequencies—it also applies in other transport settings.
2. It is noted, however, that, initially, larger ships will lead to lower frequency of service, but this will change once volumes further increase.
3. To the extent that larger trucks could be used on the road, therefore reducing the total number of trucks, road transport could also generate some positive Mohring effects.
4. The average fleet EF weighted by number of vessels is calculated as the sum of the products of the average EF by size class and the number of ships per size class divided by the total number of ships.
5. The average fleet EF weighted by the fleet carrying capacity is calculated as the product of (a) the average EF by size class, (b) the average DWT size by DWT size class, and (c) the number of ships per size class divided by the product of the number of ships in each size class and the DWT size in each DWT size class.

References

Buhaug, Ø., James J. Corbett, Øyvind Endresen, Veronika Eyring, Jasper Faber, Shinichi Hanayama, et al. 2008. *Updated Study on Greenhouse Gas Emissions from Ships: Phase I Report*. London International Maritime Organization.

Crist, Philippe. 2009. "Greenhouse Gas Emissions Reduction Potential from International Shipping." Joint Transport Research Center of the OECD and the International Transport Forum, Discussion Paper 2009–11, Organisation for Economic Co-operation and Development, Paris.

Denier van der Gon, H., and Jan Hulskotte. 2010. *Methodologies for Estimating Shipping Emissions in the Netherlands: A Documentation of Currently Used Emission Factors and Related Activity Data*. AH Bilthoven, the Netherlands: Netherlands Environmental Assessment Agency.

Dutch Inland Shipping Information Agency (BVB). 2009. *The Power of Inland Navigation 2010–2011*. Rotterdam, the Netherlands: BVB.

JICA (Japan International Cooperation Agency). 2009. *The Comprehensive Study on the Sustainable Development of Transport System in Vietnam (VITRANSS-2)*. Hanoi: JICA.

Van Essen, H. P., Olivier Bello, Jos Dings, and Robert van den Brink. 2003. *To Shift or Not to Shift, That's the Question*. Delft, the Netherlands: CE Delft.

CHAPTER 5

Main Challenges and Recommendations

The main challenges that could impede the further development of the inland and coastal waterway sectors of Vietnam are summarized under four headings: (a) current planning practice, (b) the institutional/regulatory environment, (c) incidence of physical bottlenecks, and (d) financing bottlenecks. They are discussed in this chapter.

Planning

- *A single-mode focus on transport subsectors adversely affects efficient resource utilization and hinders waterborne transport growth ambitions.* Transport plans are typically prepared with a single-mode focus, with little attention to multimodal operations and the integration of modal services. Moreover, the basis for resource allocation within such plans is seldom clear. The majority of resources for the transport sector go into roads, with expenditures on waterways left at even lower levels than those proposed in the Public Investment Plan. As a result, it is highly unlikely that system improvements are being realized. The single-mode planning also reflects the organization of Vietnam's Ministry of Transport (MoT) (which is similar to that of equivalent ministries in many other countries). While MoT acknowledges the value of integrated transport planning under one department, it recognizes difficulties both at the organizational and at the human resource level in realizing this setup, and for the time being is working on ensuring coordination between the different subsectoral plans as they are being developed as a way of ensuring multimodal planning. Successful examples from the European Union (EU), where a number of programs were set up to support multimodal transport planning, and the success stories thereby publicized could be of value to Vietnam. MoT could benefit from capacity development in this area.

- *The dry port concept in the vicinity of large cities should be further investigated.* Multimodal transport chains rely heavily on logistics service facilities at both ends of the chain. While most manufactured goods' freight flows involve import/export movements, such facilities are required near the main cities and industrial zones in Vietnam—specifically the conurbations of Hanoi and Ho Chi Minh City (HCMC), as these two areas account for about 60 percent of the country's gross domestic product (GDP).

- *Historical focus on bulk flows underestimates containers' potential.* In Vietnam, as in Europe, inland waterways have historically been used for shipping bulk cargo (building materials, minerals, etc.). The bulk sector will continue to grow and will benefit from improvements in the fleet, waterways, and ports. However, strong growth in freight transport is currently associated with a broader group of commodities, most of which are shipped in containers. And since current forecasts are largely based on historical trends, they likely underestimate the true growth potential of new segments. As a result, the shipping routes defined as "core" routes may not be the ones critical for container flows. These freight flows will be strongly focused on the corridors between the main seaport terminals and the large cities/industrial areas.

- *There is a need to rationalize the port planning process.* Market stakeholders indicate a need for proper river port development master planning, clearly indicating future port developments from a long-term perspective. At present, both the Vietnam Inland Waterway Administration (VIWA) and Vietnam Maritime Administration (Vinamarine) are responsible for river port planning, which creates some confusion in their roles. The current port master plan includes too many ports even though the capacity of the current port system is not fully utilized. The port master-planning process needs to be rationalized with clear definitions for the river ports administered by VIWA and those by Vinamarine and their respective roles. The port planning process itself will require strong coordination between Vinamarine and VIWA not only for the river ports but for seaports as well, given the linkages between the two and how river ports can often serve as feeders into the seaports or distribution points for imports. This point is also discussed below under the scattered responsibilities section.

- *Allow for integrated port planning.* It is common for ports to drive, at least partially, facility location decisions of firms and industry clusters. They are also a critical link in numerous production networks. As a result, port authorities are often given the jurisdiction to carry out integrated planning, development, and management of ports (see the Port of Hengelo case in box 3.1). This model can be considered for Vietnam's core ports.

- *Fleet Planning: Supply-demand uncertainty in the investment cycle.* Over the past several years, operators have invested heavily in new vessels on the back of a growing Vietnamese economy, as evidenced by the fleet developments presented in chapter 3. This has contributed to capacity increases as well as higher average vessel sizes. However, such investments (many of which debt financed) appear to have gone beyond true market needs on account of unwarrantedly high optimism—and the 2009–10 economic crisis magnified the risks for investors taking on large debts. This investment wave, which has similarities to fluctuations historically seen in the Netherlands, poses risks that, while not atypical for private sector operators, can severely impact the stability not only of the shipping industry but of the many industries the latter serves. Frequently published and widely accessible information on demand-supply trends and expectations could assist private investors in making capacity and operating decisions and mitigate the impact of adverse economic shocks. Such market information could be made available through a sector organization representing the industry vis-à-vis shippers, suppliers, and the government.

Institutional/Regulatory Environment

- *Scattered and unclear roles and responsibilities in the sector.* This manifests itself in several ways.
  - *Seaports.* The task of port authority is scattered among several authorities: usually Vinamarine (on the maritime side), the port operator (which is often Vinalines but also several other state-owned enterprises [SOEs]), and the local government (on the hinterland side). This causes port developments to be difficult to implement and may result in longer implementation times or unsuccessful investments due to insufficient or late co-investment in the surrounding support infrastructure.
  - *Waterways.* Coastal shipping and river transport near seaports are particularly affected by the fact that these sections are under the jurisdiction of both VIWA and Vinamarine. For example, sea-river vessels can sail up to river ports (the latter sometimes managed by Vinamarine) on river sections managed by VIWA. Conversely, inland waterway vessels can sail to seaports under the jurisdiction of Vinamarine. Most seaports are, in fact, located along rivers rather than directly at the coast, further contributing to administration overlap.
  - *River ports.* While the larger ports are registered and regulated by VIWA, with SOEs in place to operate facilities, smaller ports are often neither registered nor regulated.
  - Each of the involved stakeholders no doubt has a reasonable view on the development of the waterway sector from its own perspective. The main challenge is to reach a shared vision that all stakeholders can agree to. This cannot happen without MoT playing a strong leadership and coordination role. MoT could play a coordinating/moderating role among all stakeholders, including not only regional and local governments but notably also transport operators.

- *Unbalanced playing field for private operators.* Private operators report facing disadvantages compared to SOEs competing in the same sector(s). The enactment of the Law on Enterprises (in 2008) and the abolishment of the Law on SOEs (in 2010) have formally introduced the same market conditions for private firms and SOEs. In practice, however, the latter are believed to still enjoy easier access to finance, where they benefit from longer-term maturities and lower interest rates, as well as implicit state guarantees. In addition, some SOEs have a dominant position in particular markets, greatly reducing competition. For example, the Northern Inland Waterway Transport Corporation (NIWTC) controls 80 percent of the inland waterway transport (IWT) market in the North region. Similarly, Vinalines and the Vietnam Shipbuilding Industry Group (Vinashin) account for substantial portions of the coastal shipping and shipbuilding market, respectively. Irrespective of whether former SOEs receive these benefits, the perception that they do remains strong. This needs to be addressed in a clear and transparent manner to avoid holding up, or slowing down, the development of multimodal logistics and the modernization of the fleet, and to avoid further depriving the sector from the innovation and efficiencies that the private sector brings.

- *Cooperation among the different players in the transport chain requires more attention.* Another field that needs to be further developed is the integration of activities along the transport chain. If shippers cannot easily coordinate itineraries across modes, they tend to continue their historical (silo-based) ways of operation instead of shifting to more integrated (intermodal) operations. Cooperation platforms bringing together shippers, transport companies, and service providers could be set up to overcome this impediment. Moreover, minimizing the number of times for interaction along the supply chain reduces the opportunity for rent seeking and corruption. A recommendation from the 2006 Multimodal Transport Regulatory Review in Vietnam regarding the establishment of a National Logistics Forum to promote consultation between the government, the logistics industry, and customers should be considered. This could also serve to market and promote the sector's services to large shippers.

- *The roles of the public and private sectors in river port ownership, operation, and management need to be clarified.* The actual role of the public and private sectors in port ownership, financing, operation, and management is not made clear by the regulatory framework, nor is there a consensus as to the role each should play. If the private sector is willing to invest in the operation of public ports, then the role of the public sector could be limited to ownership and oversight. This would free up scarce government resources for other activities as well as harness private sector efficiencies and innovation.

- *Separate port authority responsibilities from terminal operations.* In order to modernize river port operations, it is recommended that the operation of major river ports be devolved to private operators under a landlord port arrangement. Competition between ports could incentivize investments in cargo-handling and storage facilities to the benefit of end users. Investments in port modernization can also be undertaken by the private sector.

- *Alliances between container terminal operators and shipping lines have their benefits but could also be problematic.* Over the past 5–10 years, shipping companies have looked to merge with terminal operators to gain control of a larger segment of the supply chain and hence be more competitive. While this argument has some merit, it may end up creating a monopolistic situation, which would disadvantage smaller shippers and reduce competition. Consequently, there is an argument for splitting Vinalines' container terminal operations and shipping activities. The need to do this will finally depend on the extent of competition from other ports and the market share of an alliance/consortium in a given market.

- *Weak capacity at the main sectoral institutions hinders the performance of the sector.* The key government agencies responsible for the planning and regulation of the sector need capacity strengthening:
  - *VIWA* has no survey vessels and its river maps are considered inaccurate by private companies. This requires investment in equipment and capacity building. At the time of writing, two World Bank–supported projects, the Mekong Delta Transport Infrastructure Development Project (MDTIDP) and Northern Delta Transport Development Project (NDTDP), were providing well-targeted capacity development and institutional support to VIWA. Investments in survey vessels could be financed through the proposed Waterway Maintenance Fund (WMF) (see the discussion below on financing).
  - *Vinamarine* staff acknowledges weak capacity to perform their planning and regulatory roles. Holistic capacity development programs need to be developed for Vinamarine staff.
  - The capacity of the *Vietnam Register*, as the quality assurance authority, needs to be strengthened, and the quality standards of Vietnamese flag vessels upgraded and enforced. The Register should be also afforded the capacity to register all vessels. This could later help in generating funds, as discussed under financing below. In addition, the capacity of local shipyards needs to be raised, building on ongoing efforts by a number of development partners (e.g., Norwegian-funded training support to Vinashin, and plans in the Netherlands to develop education support in this area).

- *The warehousing function as a strategic component of the river port business model.* Warehousing services are critical to efficient supply chains. If not efficiently designed, they would result in higher inventory carrying costs and reduce competitiveness. As goods are delivered from factories to ports, the latter become de facto inventory-carrying locations. Located closer to market, port-side warehouses can enhance delivery response times and may allow IWT to carry goods cheaply in large lots while still being able to deliver to customers in small lots and high frequency. It is therefore strategic for IWT ports to examine the potential of the warehousing function as part of their business model, along with the improvement of the more traditional cargo-handling functions.

Physical Bottlenecks

Waterways

The distribution of IWT activity in Vietnam is disproportionately concentrated on a limited number of routes in the North and South regions. Maps 5.1 and 5.2 define the core routes carrying the largest volumes (both for current and projected long-term [2030] freight flows) and the locations of the priority ports to which the bulk of resources and improvement efforts should be directed.

It is expected that, in addition to these routes, the waterways connecting the seaports to the main cities of Hanoi and HCMC will face strong volume growth if international container shipping continues to expand rapidly (as is projected).

Map 5.1 Main Inland Waterways and Ports in the North Region

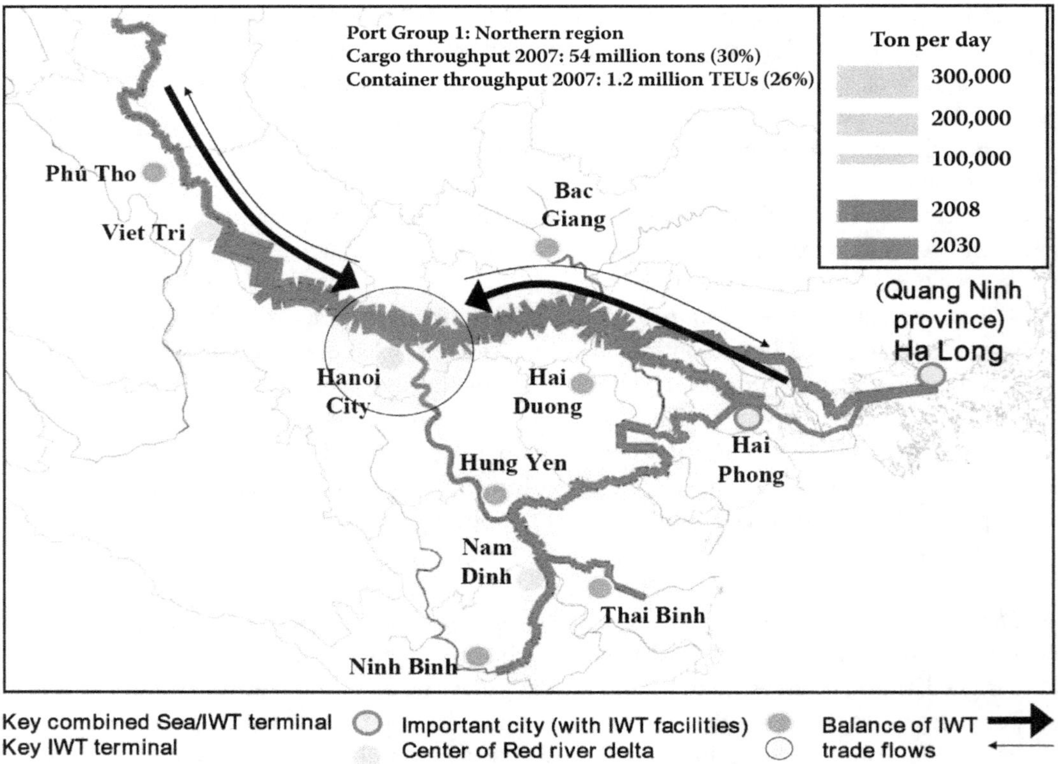

Source: Ecorys with data from JICA 2009.
Note: IWT = inland waterway transport; TEU = 20-foot equivalent unit.

Map 5.2 Main Inland Waterways and Ports in the South Region

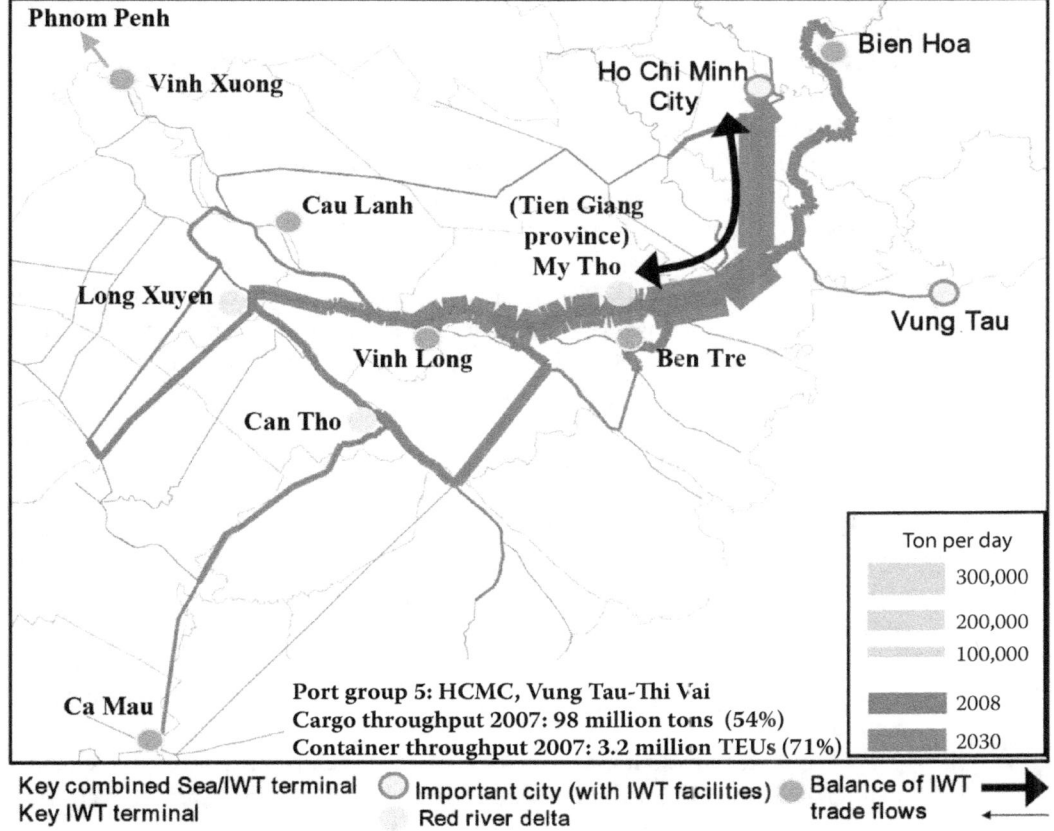

Source: Ecorys with data from JICA 2009.
Note: IWT = inland waterway transport; TEU = 20-foot equivalent unit.

The expected increase in transport volume is already putting pressure on transport infrastructure and fleet requirements. In addition, IWT faces increasingly strong competition from road transport operators. In such an environment, Vietnam requires a competitive inland waterway sector capable of reducing transport costs per unit of service. Such a decrease can be achieved by economies of ship size through the deployment of larger ships, in combination with increased operating efficiency and better logistics services provisions (e.g., IT-based services). This is especially needed for the sector to be able to play a more active role in multimodal transport. Moreover, the overall sustainability of the transport system requires an important role of the inland waterway sector, as this reduces greenhouse gas (GHG) emissions and congestion on roads.

Service needs, however, will vary by shipper type. Among waterway shippers that require higher inland waterway technical standards (e.g., fewer channel depth limitations) are large-scale enterprises that operate their own barges.

Their long-term direction is to shift to bigger vessels and barges to achieve efficiency, but channel limitations and low bridge clearances have decelerated this trend. A strong competitive position for IWT also depends on these shippers' ability to concentrate their operations on a limited number of routes, thereby attaining the required volume aggregation that enables the use of larger ships. Therefore, a focus of investments on these core routes is recommended.

However, in Vietnam's rapid-growth environment, the waterway capacity expansion investments currently underway are likely to sufficiently address demand only through the medium term (e.g., 2020). Additional investments, either to further expand previously upgraded waterways or to address long-neglected bottlenecks such as the Cho Gao Canal, will be needed. Similarly, the issue of underprovision of recurrent expenditures in maintenance (see next subsection) will need to be addressed with comparable priority as that given to capital expenditures in new projects.

Lack of IWT Maintenance Hinders Market Development

Maintenance of the core waterways is of utmost importance. Once routes are selected and the desired capacity/design is defined, maintenance works should be organized such that these design capacities are met, in order to offer reliability and predictability to waterway users. Reliable logistics networks and competitive delivery times are required for IWT to become a more competitive transport option for manufactured goods, which have a higher value density than bulk cargo. This can be realized only if sufficient maintenance of fairways is conducted.

IWT maintenance suffers from lack of funds. Currently, funds for channel maintenance, mainly for dredging and bank protection works, are derived from state funds and fall short of needs. Although there is no firm estimate on what is the minimum amount necessary for maintenance, the consensus is that only 50–60 percent of that minimum is nowadays being made available.

VIWA estimates that they would need $2,000 per kilometer of fairway for proper maintenance, while they receive only $1,000 per kilometer from the central budget. There are not sufficient resources for regular surveys. Thus, the conformity of existing waterways to the technical standards of their respective classes cannot be ascertained. Another consequence of insufficient maintenance funds is the inability to publish up-to-date navigational charts to guide vessels. Siltation levels are poorly defined or tracked as a planning tool for maintenance dredging programs, which cannot be implemented rigorously and regularly due to lack of funds.

Maintenance needs to be given priority. The benefits of upgraded channels can be realized only if it induces the use of bigger and more efficient IWT vessels. Investment in these vessels is expensive, so if there is a risk that channel standards cannot be guaranteed by regular maintenance, then operators will not invest in better vessels. Investment in channel development and upgrading will become ineffective unless standards are maintained. The ability of IWT to be competitive, even on selected corridors only, will be impaired if waterways cannot be maintained. One of the actions needed to address this problem is to strengthen funding for IWT maintenance.

Ports

Vietnam should develop a network of sea and river ports with hinterland connections by focusing on the key needs of different cargo types: (a) *main seaports and connections to river ports for bulk transport*—focus on potential river ports (within industrial areas and firms that primarily use IWT) that can make use of inland waterways that are accessible by large vessels and (b) *main seaports and connections to river ports for containerized transport*—focus on potential river container terminals (with logistics areas and companies that import and/or export in the container trade) that can grow and have excellent hinterland connections by IWT, road, and rail.

Efforts in the North region should focus on the development of the Haiphong-area seaports and IWT ports, complemented with IWT terminals in Nam Dinh, Hanoi, and Viet Tri (see map 5.1). This would provide a core triangular network along the most intensive trade routes (per projected growth rates to 2030). Efforts in the South region should prioritize the development of the combined seaport and IWT ports at Vung Tau and HCMC, complemented with terminal development in My Tho, Can Tho, and Long Xuyen (see map 5.2). Such interventions would not only support the existing intensive use of the IWT route between HCMC and My Tho/Ben Tre, but also support the development of the Southwest and Southeast Mekong Delta and cross-border IWT trade.

River ports. The future role envisaged for river ports as freight transfer centers needs to be clarified to guide investment strategies in ports. Tier 1 river ports should not be regarded only as loading and unloading points for barges, but also as points for intermodal services linking IWT to roads (and rail where available) and for activities such as stuffing and stripping of containers, customs clearance, and other support services. Priority should thus be given to port developments at the core nodes identified. It is important to ensure that these port facilities—which may be privately operated—are accessible to all possible users. Viet Tri Port, which is being improved under NDTDP, would serve as an excellent example of a freight transfer point as it is served by waterways, roads, and rail.

While it is expected that much of the port activity will be in industrial ports, where some of the infrastructure provision falls under the responsibility of the port users themselves, public ports still have an important role to play for large-scale shippers. These goods are first brought in bulk by inland waterway vessels to a port for distribution and shipped in small lots by trucks (intermodal transport). It is strategic for the subsector to continue to be competitive in this service, not just for its viability, but also to discourage the use of highway alternatives, which would contribute to road congestion.

The inherent disadvantage of inland waterway transportation is the unavoidable double handling of cargo; but this can be countered if the subsector can offer better interface with other modes, particularly trucking.

Seaport investments and transport linkages. The plans for the expansion of the ports of Saigon/greater HCMC, Da Nang, and Haiphong are under implementation. Hence, the focus should now shift to improving the connectivity of ports to roads, railways, and inland waterways. Such connecting infrastructure is vital to the success and viability of the new deep-water seaports. For example, the Lach Huyen Port complex will need a 2.4-kilometer bridge to connect it to the mainland of Haiphong.

In the South region, expressway access should be provided, in time, for the full operation of Cai Mep-Thi Vai. The same can be said about channel dredging of the Soai Rap channel to coincide with the completion of terminals in the Hiep Huoc area or the navigation channel to Lach Huyen. Linkages to the ports of Can Tho and My Tho also require improvements—especially with the completion of the Quang Chanh Bo channel.

Container terminals: limited container-handling capacity at river ports. Several private operators perceive potentially attractive opportunities in the development of container services between seaports and river ports, where truck drayage and/or transloading services can be arranged for delivery to regional customers. That, however, would require the availability of publicly accessible, efficiently run container terminals. Some of the larger private IWT operators suggest that it could be more efficient for them to own and operate their own river terminal facilities rather than seeking better negotiated terms with public port operators. Even if that were the case, the development of public-use container terminals is critical for smaller IWT operators as multimodal centers located at or near ports become consolidation stations arranging for the pooling of small consignments into larger shipments.

Fleet

Impressive modernization of the inland waterway fleet in Vietnam has been taking place since about 2000 with little government intervention. Before that time, the commercial fleet was smaller in number as well as size, but as of that year the fleet size and capacity have risen remarkably. While investments have been made in small vessels, a significant amount of larger vessels has been added to the fleet. And although the fleet modernization over the past decade has taken place with little government intervention, which could argue for continuing along the same path, experience from Europe indicates that financial incentives have accelerated the pace of modernization. Generally the trend in Europe could be characterized as "doing more with fewer vessels," while in Vietnam, small vessels continue to account for the bulk of the vessel counts in the national fleet. Vietnam could further focus on building of new, larger vessel sizes while discouraging smaller vessel sizes. From a policy intervention perspective, focus could be directed toward stimulating clean engine technologies and fuel-efficient operations, coupled with sustainable shipbuilding practices. This is particularly important given that GHG emission reductions resulting from fleet modernization are expected to be much higher than those resulting from modal shift from roads to waterways (see chapter 4).

Financing

Options for Enhancing the Sector's Financing

While capital investments in the waterways have historically been funded through government budget allocations and Official Development Assistance (ODA), ensuring sustainable financing for waterway maintenance has proven challenging. One way to safeguard the funds required for adequate IWT maintenance is through the creation of a WMF. Revenues for such a fund would originate from annual budgetary support as well as contributions from waterway users (primarily shipping carriers, but also industrial users and waterfront real estate owners). Several options for this fund are discussed below. The fund could be governed and managed by VIWA, under the overall guidance of a supervisory council that includes members of the various stakeholder groups.

Pricing to unlock additional funds: Ideally, prices of transport services should reflect the true economic and social cost of the provided services so that each mode reflects its true cost to the economy, and users are able to choose freely in response to market signals. This would level the playing field across modes; encourage competition, consistency, and predictability in the application of rules; and allow inefficient enterprises (private and public) to exit the market as may be the case. To the extent feasible, the full life-cycle cost of transportation infrastructure should be recovered from its direct beneficiaries. Where this is not possible, a mechanism for covering the shortfall should be instituted.

However, it is important to recognize that additional fees charged by the sector may affect its competitive position if competing modes are not treated similarly. Furthermore from a political economy perspective the implementation of levies or charges may be sensitive and difficult if other measures to improve the sector's position are not undertaken simultaneously. The following four types of fees could be considered:

- Channel usage fee
- Registration fee
- Fuel levy
- Frontage fee

Channel fee: One obvious source is a channel fee, which is much like a toll road fee. This can be collected at key points of the waterway. Although conceptually appealing for its ability to target direct beneficiaries, a fee scheme of that sort would not be without operational risks. A program to collect user fees for channel maintenance was piloted in Vietnam three years ago, but failed. By studying the reasons for failure, a more sustainable system could be introduced.

Registration fee: An annual levy for vessel registration could be imposed on vessel owners. In principle, this source offers a huge potential. With an estimated fleet of 7.8 million registered tons (see table 3.11) at, say, Vietnamese dong (VND) 20,000 per registered ton, the WMF could receive VND 150 billion ($7.5 million) a year, sufficient to cover the current maintenance financing shortfall for the core network. However, this would require an effective vessel registry system. The registration system could also be used as an incentive/disincentive mechanism to promote fleet renewal and modernization. Establishing a special financing facility for domestic fleet expansion could lead to greater competition and efficiency in domestic coastal shipping services.

Fuel levy: Another option is a fuel levy, a portion going to roads and a portion to IWT. The road sector has estimated that VND 2.5 trillion ($125 million) can be generated for the road fund. If only 5 percent of this is given to IWT, then VND 125 billion ($6.25 million) can be added to WMF every year, which would cover nearly all annual core maintenance needs (beyond what is already being provided through the existing budgetary process).

Frontage fee: A fourth source of funds for maintenance is a kind of frontage fee. Businesses locate along riverbanks because there is value to the location. At VND 50,000 per meter per year, and assuming only 1,000 kilometers of riverbank fronts are eligible, funds raised could reach VND 50 billion ($2.5 million). Given that there is no property tax in Vietnam, such a frontage fee would not constitute double taxation.

One or more of the above funding mechanisms have been utilized with reasonable success in other countries, notably the United States. While it seems feasible to raise the necessary funds to close the funding gap for waterway maintenance in Vietnam, strong political leadership and an active engagement of the private sector by the relevant public sector agencies will undoubtedly be required.

Reference

JICA (Japan International Cooperation Agency). 2009. *The Comprehensive Study on the Sustainable Development of Transport System in Vietnam (VITRANSS-2)*. Hanoi: JICA.

CHAPTER 6

Strategy and Action Plan

Based on the analysis of the waterway sectoral demand and supply, the sector's potential, and the current institutional and financial impediments identified, key challenges and recommendations were summarized in a proposed inland waterway transport (IWT) and coastal shipping strategy (see figure 6.1). The strategy brings in demand-supply considerations, sets out objectives, and outlines approaches and measures to achieve them.

Enabling further growth of IWT and coastal shipping requires that actions be taken in the areas of waterway, port, fleet, and logistics services and infrastructure development. In order to realize these, and given the increasing limitations in public budgets facing Vietnam, it is recommended that interested parties take the following steps:

- Focus waterway and port investments on the core network.
- Ensure continuous maintenance of these priority waterways to provide reliable navigation conditions to the market.
- Promote IWT and coastal shipping as transport options for shippers.
- Support the development of multimodal logistics services.

When it comes to fleet modernization, while autonomous (i.e., market-driven) developments with little government intervention have proven viable in the past, government support could speed up the pace of transformation. Coastal waterways are natural waterways not requiring specific upgrading measures, except for the maintenance of port access channels, particularly in the North region. The development of intermodal facilities is another area where public and private sectors could collaborate.

In order to achieve the objective of sustainable growth in IWT and coastal shipping, actions are identified in four areas:

- Secure stable funding.
- Enhance financing options.
- Improve the competitive position of IWT and coastal shipping.
- Strengthen the institutional framework.

Figure 6.1 Schematic of the Proposed IWT and Coastal Shipping Strategy

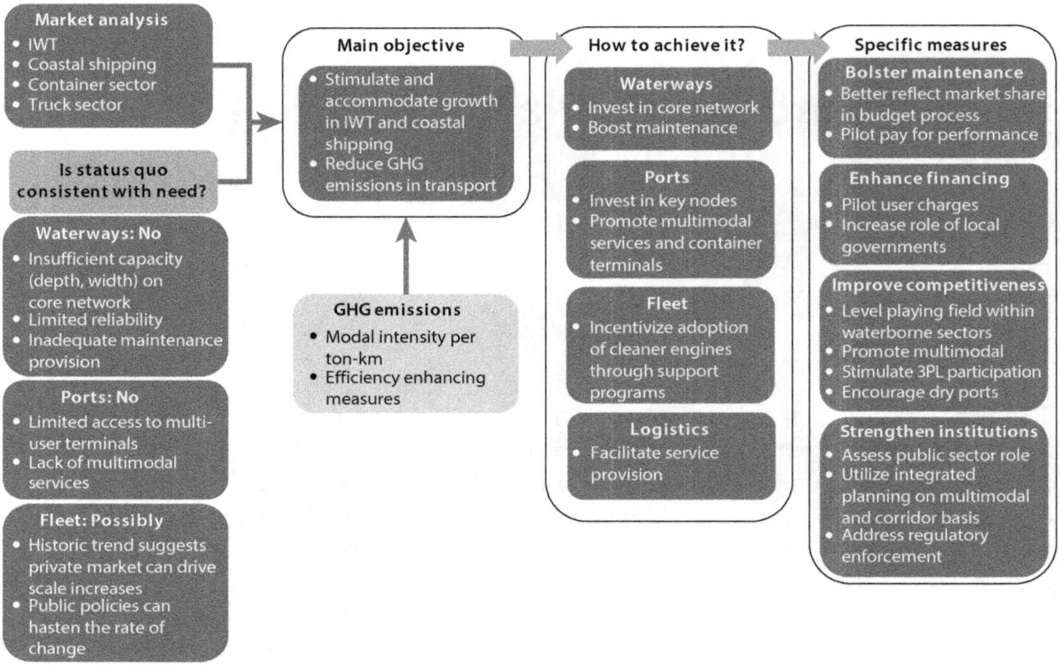

Market analysis
- IWT
- Coastal shipping
- Container sector
- Truck sector

Is status quo consistent with need?

Waterways: No
- Insufficient capacity (depth, width) on core network
- Limited reliability
- Inadequate maintenance provision

Ports: No
- Limited access to multi-user terminals
- Lack of multimodal services

Fleet: Possibly
- Historic trend suggests private market can drive scale increases
- Public policies can hasten the rate of change

Main objective
- Stimulate and accommodate growth in IWT and coastal shipping
- Reduce GHG emissions in transport

GHG emissions
- Modal intensity per ton-km
- Efficiency enhancing measures

How to achieve it?

Waterways
- Invest in core network
- Boost maintenance

Ports
- Invest in key nodes
- Promote multimodal services and container terminals

Fleet
- Incentivize adoption of cleaner engines through support programs

Logistics
- Facilitate service provision

Specific measures

Bolster maintenance
- Better reflect market share in budget process
- Pilot pay for performance

Enhance financing
- Pilot user charges
- Increase role of local governments

Improve competitiveness
- Level playing field within waterborne sectors
- Promote multimodal
- Stimulate 3PL participation
- Encourage dry ports

Strengthen institutions
- Assess public sector role
- Utilize integrated planning on multimodal and corridor basis
- Address regulatory enforcement

Source: Ecorys/World Bank analysis.
Note: 3PL = third-party logisitics; GHG = greenhouse gas; IWT = inland waterway transport.

Based on the overall strategy, a list of actions has been developed (see table 6.1), indicating the following:

- Description of the action
- Suggested timeframe for execution (for illustrative purposes only)
- Ideal stakeholder responsibility allocation
- Potential financing options
- Remarks, if any

The next chapter assesses the economic attractiveness of selected public sector interventions.

Table 6.1 Recommended Actions for IWT and Coastal Shipping Development in Vietnam

Type of intervention/strategy	Strategy component	Description	Execution	Stakeholders responsible	Way to finance	Remarks
Alleviating physical bottlenecks	Waterways	Invest in core network	2013–20	VIWA	GoV, ODA	Corridor 1 of the Red River Delta and Corridor 1 of the Mekong River Delta, which attract the highest levels of traffic, should be given priority
		Provide adequate maintenance by fully funding maintenance needs in collaboration with carriers and end users	Continuous	VIWA	WMF	To be concentrated on core network
	Ports	Invest in core sea and river ports	2013–20	Regions in their capacity of port authority (see institutional component)	Regional government, GoV, ODA	This concerns public infrastructure only (e.g., better hinterland access); suprastructure investments are to be made by private operators
	Fleet	Introduce a stimulation program for engine efficiency	2013–20	GoV	GoV	Relevant both for IWT and coastal fleet
Planning reforms	Introduce multimodal planning practices (including dry ports)	Ensure coordination among different subsectoral administrations for effective multimodal planning	2013–14	MoT/DoT		
		Launch demonstration program and promotion council	2013–20	GoV and private sector	GoV and private sector participation	Examples of promotion councils are found throughout Europe (European Intermodal Association, various national member organizations, best practices applied)
	Rationalize the port planning process, and update port master plan	MoT to coordinate between Vinamarine and VIWA and update master plan	2012–13	VIWA and port authorities	GoV, ODA	

table continues next page

Table 6.1 Recommended Actions for IWT and Coastal Shipping Development in Vietnam *(continued)*

Type of intervention/ strategy	Strategy component	Description	Execution	Stakeholders responsible	Way to finance	Remarks
Financing strategy	Increase funds for IWT and coastal shipping	Safeguard investment in waterways and ports	2012–20	MoT with MPI/MoF	GoV/ODA	
	Fund maintenance through WMF	Establish waterway maintenance fund by mix of government contributions, fuel levy, and revenues from user charges such as channel fees, registration fees, or frontage fees	2013 onwards	MoT and VIWA and private sector	GoV and user fees	Relates to maintenance action above
Institutional/regulatory reform	Strengthen the regulatory framework for port management	Introduce landlord principles in river ports and seaports with increased role for local government (compare Hengelo case)	2012 onwards	Concerted effort of all stakeholders involved: municipalities, regions, GoV, MoT, private sector, and IFIs	Mixed	
	Unify vision for the sector	Alignment of vision on development of the water transport sector	2012–13	VIWA, Vinamarine, MoT		
	Promote a level playing field in market access and competition	Same treatment for all enterprises (including access to new capital)	2012 onwards	SOEs, GoV, banking system	Private	
	Fair treatment of all users in ports		2012 onwards	GoV, port authorities		
	Minimize rent seeking	Strict enforcement of regulation, and acting upon malpractices	2012 onwards	GoV	GoV	

Source: Ecorys/World Bank analysis.

Note: DoT = Department of Transport; GoV = government of Vietnam; IFI = international financial institutions; IWT = Inland waterway transport; MoF = Ministry of Finance; MoT = Ministry of Transport; MPI = Ministry of Planning and Investment; ODA = official development assistance; Vinamarine = Vietnam Maritime Authority; VIWA = Vietnam Inland Waterway Administration; WMF = Waterway Maintenance Fund.

CHAPTER 7

Estimated Impact of Public Sector Interventions in IWT and Coastal Shipping

Translating the IWT/Coastal Shipping Strategy into Tangible Interventions

The stock-taking exercise of the previous chapters has shown that inland waterway transport (IWT) activity in Vietnam is disproportionately concentrated on primary routes and key nodes in both the North and South regions. It was on this basis that chapter 6 recommended that policy makers focus available investment budgets on a limited number of ports and core sections of the network. Long-term forecasts of transport volumes indicate that today's main routes will retain this status through 2030. This was confirmed by the report's stakeholder interviews, where views on freight volumes, routes, infrastructure provision, fleet, and cost structures were discussed (see appendix A for the list of interviewees).

Based on the above, this chapter will consider infrastructure investments that comply with two key criteria: (a) they belong in the core waterway and/or port network and (b) they are strictly incremental to any existing or ongoing investments (where the latter are considered part of a "business-as-usual" baseline).

In addition to infrastructure-based interventions, other performance-enhancing policies in IWT and coastal shipping have been identified. These relate to waterway maintenance management, engine and fleet modernization incentives, awareness and behavioral change incentives for users, and measures to stimulate a more intense use of coastal shipping.

Nine individual interventions are proposed, summarized in table 7.1 (interventions are listed in no particular order; a detailed description of each is provided in appendix E). It is relevant to assess the desirability of a variety of interventions because international experience (e.g., in Europe and elsewhere) has shown that successful outcomes in IWT often require multipronged approaches, where a combination of interventions can target improvements in sector competitiveness from several angles simultaneously.

Table 7.1 Proposed Interventions to Enhance Performance

No.	Intervention name	Intervention summary	Implementation time frame	Estimated costs ($)
1	Upgrade waterway Corridor 1 of the Red River Delta	Raises Corridor 1 (Quang Ninh–Haiphong–Pha Lai–Hanoi–Viet Tri) **from waterway Class II to Class I**	2016–20	150–250 million
2	Upgrade waterway Corridor 2 of the Red River Delta	Raises Corridor 2 (Haiphong–Ninh Binh) **from waterway Class III to Class II**	2014–16	150–300 million
3	Upgrade waterway Corridor 3 of the Red River Delta	Raises Corridor 3 (Hanoi–Day/Lach Giang) **from waterway Class III to Class II**	2013–15	100–200 million
4	Enable extended gateway facility in the Red River Delta to serve the Hanoi market	Development of an inland waterway and cargo-handling facility near Hanoi to serve (mostly import/export) container flows between Haiphong and Hanoi	2014	10 million
5	Upgrade waterway Corridor 1 of the Mekong Delta	Raises Corridor 1 (HCMC–Ben Tre–My Tho–Vinh Long) **from waterway Class III to Class II**	2013–16	150–250 million
6	Upgrade a coastal shipping container terminal in Northern Vietnam	Modernization of a container terminal in Haiphong dedicated to domestic container shipping services	2014–15	40 million
7	Introduce user charges to fund waterway maintenance	Imposition of user charges on IWT vessel operators to cover the existing waterway maintenance financing gap	2014–ongoing	0.0003 (VND 6) per ton-km
8	Promote engine and fleet modernization in IWT	Provision of public subsidies to (with private sector matching) for engine improvement	2014[a]	20 million
9	Showcase IWT as an enabler of efficient logistics	Promotion campaign on the use of inland water transport and demonstration projects to illustrate its attractiveness	2014–23[a]	30 million

Source: Ecorys/World Bank analysis.
Note: HCMC = Ho Chi Minh City; IWT = Inland waterway transport.
a. Or until funds are fully disbursed.

Methodology: Translating Interventions into Impacts

The proposed interventions were evaluated to assess their desirability. The economic evaluation methodology was based on two modeling techniques:

1. *Modal split model.* This model translates interventions into modal share impacts. The rationale is as follows. Actual modal choices between two modes—in this case, road versus waterborne transport—respond to mode-specific service attributes (e.g., cost), which typically vary depending on origin-destination (O-D) pair. Policy and infrastructure interventions may lead to a different set of attributes, which would in turn affect shippers' modal decision making. For the purposes of this report, the key modal attribute of interest will be integrated transport costs per ton-kilometer (ton-km). These costs will generally be expected to fall for waterborne transport as a result of purposefully designed interventions relative to those of road transport, prompting shippers and logistics decision makers to shift some of their freight flows from higher cost modes (in this case, the roads) to lower cost modes (barges or

coastal shipping). Given estimated changes in integrated transport costs, the modal split model estimates the magnitude of the freight flows that are shifted as a result of a change in the relative cost of transport across modes. When this is done for all relevant O-D pairs, the model in effect generates new modal share between the roads sector and IWT/coastal shipping. The underlying data for developing the model parameters and independent variables (e.g., O-D freight flows and transport costs) were derived from JICA (2009), expert industry knowledge, and testimonies gathered from interviews with transport sector stakeholders in Vietnam (see appendix E for a detailed description of the modal split methodology).

2. *Cost-Benefit Analysis (CBA)*. Whether by inducing modal shift or by impacting existing (i.e., mode-specific) volumes, interventions generate economic impacts to the broader economy. These must be compared with the economic costs associated with implementation to determine whether particular interventions add or subtract economic value. For example, ton-kilometers may shift from roads to IWT/coastal shipping, generating environmental (e.g., fewer emissions), economic (e.g., transport cost savings), and other societal benefits (e.g., fewer trucks on the road, fewer accidents—deaths, injuries—and less congestion and noise). The CBA framework takes the outcomes of the modal split model as a starting point and calculates the value of these benefits according to Vietnam-specific parameters. Comparing these benefits with the initial investment costs leads to net present value, economic internal rate of return, and benefit-cost ratio calculations. Figure 7.1 illustrates the relationships between the analytical tools used by this report.

Figure 7.1 Analytical Tools and Assessment Outputs

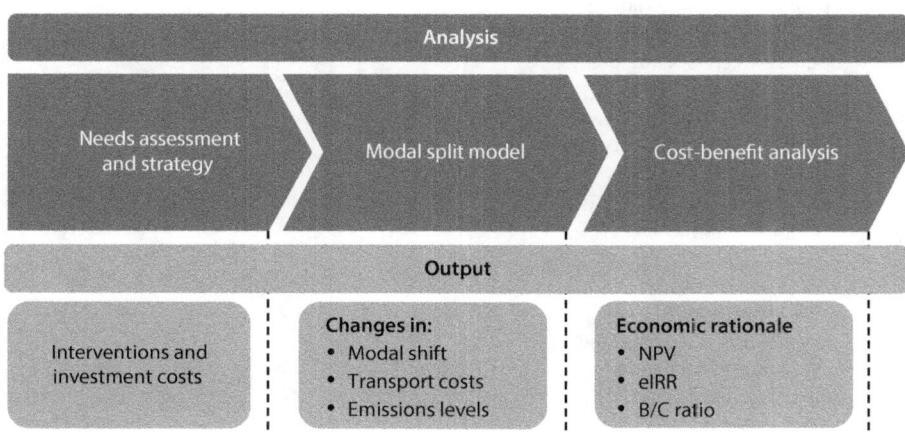

Source: Ecorys/World Bank analysis.
Note: B/C ratio = benefit/cost ratio; eIRR = economic internal rate of return; NPV = net present value.

Modal Shift and Emissions Impact of the Proposed Interventions

The proposed policy and infrastructure interventions were translated into inputs to the modal split model. Table 7.2 summarizes the estimated intervention impacts in terms of long-term modal shift (in tons and relative share) and carbon dioxide (CO_2) reductions (see appendix F for full details on these calculations). Intervention 9 has not been included in the CBA but assessed separately under a break-even analysis framework (see assessment below). The modal split model output suggests that the proposed interventions would result in modest modal shift impacts.

Evaluating Intervention 9 to Promote Waterborne Transport

The proposed promotion and demonstration program differs from the rest of the proposed interventions in that it will not improve the performance or efficiency of the IWT and coastal shipping sectors as such. Rather, it will aim to demonstrate that waterborne transport may offer attractive operational economics to many shippers. As seen elsewhere, notably in Europe, many cargo owners are simply unaware of the advantages of waterborne transport or have the perception that the sector is inherently unattractive and unable to deliver on their needs (including common views that IWT service is "slow," "inflexible," and "inconsistent with just in time," etc.). However, on many routes IWT can provide a

Table 7.2 Long-Term Emission Reduction and Modal Share Impacts of Proposed Interventions

No.	Intervention name	Change in IWT/ coastal volume (tons per day)	Modal share increase (percentage points)	CO_2 emissions reduction tons per day (%Δ)
1	Upgrade waterway Corridor 1 of the Red River Delta	3,623	0.6	414 (11)
2	Upgrade waterway Corridor 2 of the Red River Delta	1,497	1.1	202 (18)
3	Upgrade waterway Corridor 3 of the Red River Delta	543	0.5	55 (11)
4	Introduce an extended gateway facility in the Red River Delta to serve the Hanoi market	681	3.0	−0.7 (−0.5)
5	Upgrade waterway Corridor 1 of the Mekong Delta	7,167	1.8	785 (18)
6	Upgrade a coastal shipping container terminal in Northern Vietnam	2,153	2.9	128 (4.1)
7	Introduce user charges to fund waterway maintenance	225	0.0	159 (1.5)
8	Promote engine and fleet modernization in IWT	106	0.0	71 (0.8)

Source: Ecorys/World Bank analysis; see appendix F for details.
Note: IWT = inland waterway transport.

competitive offer in terms of costs per ton transported even after the cost of additional handling of goods is taken into account.

To evaluate a waterborne transport promotion program, a budget of $30 million was assumed. This includes $10 million in promotion expenses over a 10-year period (i.e., $1 million per year) and $20 million for one or several demonstration projects to showcase the advantages of IWT. For simplicity, it was assumed that the full $30 million budget will disburse over 10 years at a rate of $3 million per year.

Based on the data from the modal split model on transport costs by IWT relative to road transport on all corridors assessed, it was found that IWT has an average cost advantage of about $0.17 per ton-km. This implies that the promotion program would be attractive if about 18 million ton-km were shifted from the roads to IWT (calculated as the expected annual implementation cost of $3 million divided by the expected transport savings of $0.17 per ton-km). Total road transport volume on the five corridors assessed is approximately 3.3 billion ton-km, which implies that at a shift of only 0.5 percent from roads to IWT would justify the promotion program in terms of transport cost savings for shippers. Such a modest shift would appear realistic given the levels of shift associated with the infrastructure-based interventions shown in table 7.2.

CBA Results

The modal shift and environmental impacts of the proposed interventions, as calculated through the modal split model, were subsequently used as inputs to a standard cost-benefit framework. Table 7.3 presents the CBA results (net present values, economic internal rate of returns, and benefit/cost ratios) for each intervention. Economically viable interventions (those with an economic internal rate of return at or above 10 percent) are highlighted in bold. The assumptions and detailed methodology behind this analysis are presented in appendix F. Table 7.4 provides the breakdown of economic benefits associated with each intervention by source: transport cost savings, emission reductions, and safety improvements.

The following key conclusions emerge from the modal split modeling and CBA findings:

- Investments in the waterways can deliver attractive economic returns, but these are heavily dependent on the expected intensity of future traffic.

- Among all main inland waterway corridors in Vietnam's two river delta networks, the upgrading of Corridor 1 of the Mekong Delta (Intervention 5)—including the 29-kilometer Cho Gao Canal, the most pressing bottleneck in the Mekong Delta network for flows to and from Ho Chi Minh City (HCMC)—yields the most attractive economic returns to infrastructure improvements and should be seen as a development priority. The upgrading of Corridor 1 of

Table 7.3 CBA Results for the Proposed Interventions

No.	Intervention name	Implementation time frame	Financial cost ($ million)	Net present value at 10% ($ million)	eIRR	B/C ratio
1	**Upgrade Waterway Corridor 1 of the Red River Delta**	2016–20	$200	$0.6	10%	1.0
2	Upgrade Waterway Corridor 2 of the Red River Delta	2014–16	225	−83	6	0.5
3	Upgrade Waterway Corridor 3 of the Red River Delta	2013–15	150	−102	2	0.2
4	Introduce an Extended Gateway Facility in the Red River Delta to serve the Hanoi market	2014	10	−2.3	8	0.7
5	**Upgrade Waterway Corridor 1 of the Mekong Delta**	2013–16	200	209	16	2.3
6	**Upgrade a coastal shipping container terminal in Northern Vietnam**	2014	40	22.7	13	1.7
7	Introduce user charges to fund waterway maintenance	From 2014	n.a.	32	n.a.	n.a.
8	**Promote engine and fleet modernization in IWT**	From 2014	20	0.6	10	1.0

Source: Ecorys/World Bank analysis; see appendix D for operational assumptions for trucks and vessels, and appendix F for CBA parameter assumptions.
Note: B/C = benefit/cost; CBA = cost-benefit analysis; eIRR = economic internal rate of return; IWT = inland waterway transport; n.a. = not applicable. Economically viable interventions shown in boldface.

Table 7.4 Sources of Economic Benefits by Intervention

No.	Intervention name	Transport costs savings	Emission reductions	Safety improvements	IWT modal share gain by 2030 (percentage points)
		Benefit source (%)			
1	**Upgrade Waterway Corridor 1 of the Red River Delta**	75.5	27.1	0.4	0.6
2	Upgrade Waterway Corridor 2 of the Red River Delta	76.1	23.5	0.4	1.1
3	Upgrade Waterway Corridor 3 of the Red River Delta	75.5	23.8	0.7	0.5
4	Introduce an Extended Gateway Facility in the Red River Delta to serve the Hanoi market	99.6	−1.5	1.9	3.0
5	**Upgrade Waterway Corridor 1 of the Mekong Delta**	75.3	24.1	0.6	1.8
6	**Upgrade a coastal shipping container terminal in Northern Vietnam**	71.7	26.8	1.4	2.9
7	Introduce user charges to fund waterway maintenance	33.9	65.4	0.8	0.0
8	**Promote engine and fleet modernization in IWT**	31.8	68.1	0.1	0.0

Source: Ecorys/World Bank analysis; see appendix D for operational assumptions for trucks and vessels and appendix F for CBA parameter assumptions.
Note: IWT = inland waterway transport. Economically viable interventions shown in boldface.

the Red River Delta (Intervention 1) is also economically viable, albeit yielding slightly lower economic returns than its Mekong Delta counterpart.

- Even though upgrading Corridor 2 of the Red River Delta (Intervention 2) may appear economically unattractive at a 6 percent economic internal rate of return, it may still be desirable for Vietnam to pursue this investment once other criteria are taken into consideration. For example, from a network resiliency perspective, Corridor 2 provides a key north-south alternative route to coastal shipping during portions of the year when ocean conditions are unsafe for coastal navigation.

- Upgrading Corridor 3 of the Red River Delta (Intervention 3) and providing an extended container-handling gateway to Haiphong port in the vicinity of Hanoi (Intervention 4) are found to produce economic returns below the economic cost of capital—particularly in the case of the former intervention. The primary reasons for this are low overall volumes in the case of Corridor 3, and low containerized volumes at the target corridor in the case of the extended gateway project.

- Left to market forces, the potential for modal shift from roads to waterways in Vietnam is limited (to within 1–3 percentage points over the long term). The main reason for this is that the waterway network offers limited and largely east-west geographical coverage, which critically limits waterway lengths of haul. As a result, the average length of haul for waterway transport in Vietnam (112 kilometers) is shorter than that of road transport (143 kilometers). Trucks are inherently more flexible in servicing short-haul itineraries, particularly for containerized shipments that may require extra handling at ports when containers are moved via barges. For shipments of nonbulk commodities, experience in North America and Western Europe shows that waterway transport can become economical only at much longer lengths of haul than Vietnam's average. As for bulk commodities, which account for over 75 percent of Vietnam's freight mix, many such products (e.g., construction materials, coal, and fertilizer) are substantially captured by the waterways already, leaving limited room for further gains away from trucks.

- This being the case, the majority of benefits associated with waterway infrastructure upgrading (e.g., Interventions 1 through 6) stem from within-mode (i.e., IWT-specific) transport cost efficiency improvements, as larger ship sizes enable lower transport costs—including environmental externalities—for commodities already captured by the waterways. For most of the proposed infrastructure upgrading interventions, 25–30 percent of economic benefits are generated through emission reductions, making environmental sustainability considerations a key driver of the economic viability of these investments. Indeed, long-term CO_2 emission reductions are projected to reach up to 18 percent, depending on the intervention. Projected safety gains are modest, owing to the modest expected modal shift.

- Two key factors prevent emission reductions associated with the proposed infrastructure upgrading interventions from being even higher: (a) the constrained window of viability for modal shift away from trucks and (b) the fact that emission performance per ton-km of IWT in Vietnam is not as strong relative to road transport as it is in more developed markets (e.g., Western Europe) because of the still small average scale of Vietnam barges.

- Even at moderate shift levels, it is not surprising that the intervention that would lead to the largest modal shift is the coastal shipping project (Intervention 6), since this corridor is by far the most open to modal competition between roads and waterways owing to the much longer lengths of haul involved. Building on this effect, and the fact that terminal handling charges account for a significant share of coastal shipping costs between Haiphong and HCMC, the results suggest that it is economically desirable to upgrade the container-handling infrastructure at the port of Haiphong to reduce the cost of North-South coastal shipping.

- It is noteworthy that Intervention 4, the extended gateway linking Hanoi and Haiphong, would be expected to increase rather than reduce emissions (i.e., the contribution of changes in emissions volumes to the project's benefits pool is negative). The reason for this is that the waterway route between Hanoi and Haiphong (142 kilometers) is longer than the road route (105 kilometers). The impact of a longer route, as suggested by the above analysis, in the end offsets the modest gains in emissions per ton-km from the induced modal shift. This exemplifies the many complexities that characterize modal policy and the need to consider the underlying demand-supply and economic geography features of each case.

- The main source of benefits for the non-infrastructure-based interventions (Interventions 7 and 8), on the other hand, is the reduction of emissions. In the case of maintenance charges, this is because such charges would actually increase IWT transport costs, although these cost increases are expected to be more than offset by the benefits of better maintained waterways. Meanwhile, emissions are reduced as network availability improves, allowing carriers to better deploy larger vessels at segments that may be unable to handle such equipment year-round with insufficient maintenance coverage. In the case of the engine modernization program, new engines are expected to provide significantly better emissions performance compared with current equipment. While some modest transport cost savings will be obtained via fuel efficiency gains, the larger impact of newer engines is expected to originate from lower emission levels per ton-km transported.

- Better maintenance pays for itself. Those parties responsible for waterway maintenance often do not fully account for the negative implications of lagging maintenance expenditures, many of which are borne by society. And given that the majority of benefits expected to be obtained from a more complete funding of waterway maintenance manifest themselves, as suggested by the above results, in the form of lower emissions—the value of which is not captured in transport rates or public sector revenues—it is not surprising that maintenance of the waterway network is underfunded. But the above analysis suggests that fully funding maintenance would be expected to generate transport cost savings above and beyond the value to society of reduced emissions, thereby more than offsetting the cost impact of a maintenance charge.

Sensitivity tests were carried out for each intervention to test the robustness of the CBA results. Several key assumptions made were tested by recalculating outcomes under higher or lower cost scenarios and varying levels of benefit realization rates. The results are presented in table 7.5.

From the sensitivity tests the following conclusions can be drawn:

- Intervention 1 (Red River Delta Corridor 1 upgrade) falls below the economic internal rate of return (eIRR) threshold of 10 percent if investment costs turn out to be higher than assumed, while its viability solidifies considerably if investment costs are lower than projected. This implies that a more careful estimation of these costs would be critical to more accurately determine this intervention's economic viability (e.g., via a detailed feasibility study distinguishing various specific measures relevant to the corridor).
- While the economic returns to Projects 2 and 3 (upgrade of Corridors 2 and 3 of the Red River Delta) remain below the 10 percent level under all sensitivity assumptions, the eIRR for upgrading Corridor 2 reaches 8.3 percent under a scenario of lower investment costs, which would bolster the economic rationale for the project.
- Intervention 4 (extended gateway at Hanoi) remains unfeasible under all scenarios, suggesting that better road and rail connectivity is the most effective way of boosting hinterland logistics performance at Haiphong ports.
- Intervention 5 (upgrade of Corridor 1 of the Mekong Delta) is confirmed as an economically robust infrastructure improvement project. Specifically, the project remains economically viable even when increasing construction costs by 25 percent or reducing benefits to an 80 percent realization rate. The benefits associated with increasing capacity at this critical and congested corridor are substantial.
- The economic viability of developing a dedicated container terminal for coastal shipping at Haiphong (Intervention 6) is robust to a 25 percent increase in investment cost, but sensitive to the level of terminal handling savings assumptions. The latter should therefore be more carefully estimated in the future.
- Charging for maintenance, as a project (Intervention 7), is sensitive to the fee level charged to waterway users. This suggest that user charges should be set to

Table 7.5 Sensitivity Analysis

No.	Intervention name	Net present value at 10% ($ million)	eIRR	B/C ratio
1	Red River Delta Corridor 1 upgrade	$0.6	10.0%	1.0
	Investment costs increase by 25% (high-cost case)	−30.1	8.5	0.8
	Investment costs decrease by 25% (low-cost case)	31.3	12.2	1.4
	Maximum obtainable level of benefits set at 80%	−21.2	8.7	0.8
2	Red River Delta Corridor 2 upgrade	−83.4	5.8	0.5
	Investment costs increase by 33% (high-cost case)	−141.6	4.2	0.4
	Investment costs decrease by 33% (low-cost case)	−25.3	8.3	0.8
	Maximum obtainable level of benefits set at 120%	−66.2	6.9	0.6
3	Red River Delta Corridor 3 upgrade	−101.9	1.6	0.2
	Investment costs increase by 33% (high-cost case)	−145.2	0.3	0.2
	Investment costs decrease by 33% (low-cost case)	−58.7	3.6	0.3
	Maximum obtainable level of benefits set at 120%	−96.7	2.5	0.3
4	Red River Delta extended gateway	−2.3	8.4	0.7
	Investment costs doubled	−11.0	5.2	0.4
	Maximum obtainable level of benefits set at 120%	−1.1	9.3	0.9
5	Mekong Delta Corridor 1 upgrade	208.6	15.7	2.3
	Investment costs increase by 25% (high-cost case)	165.7	13.9	1.8
	Investment costs decrease by 25% (low-cost case)	251.5	18.1	3.1
	Maximum obtainable level of benefits set at 80%	138.5	14.1	1.8
6	Coastal shipping container terminal development	22.7	13.2	1.7
	Investment costs increase by 25%	14.0	11.7	1.3
	Only 2.5% realized savings in handling charges (rather than the 5% originally assumed)	−6.3	8.8	0.8
7	Charging for maintenance	31.6	n.a.	n.a.
	Increase charge from VND 6 to VND 10 per ton-km	−2.6	n.a.	n.a.
	5% (instead of 10%) benefits of a class upgrade	−9.9	n.a.	n.a.
8	Engine and fleet modernization	0.6	10.4	1.0
	Investment costs increase by 25%	−3.6	7.8	0.8
	50% higher volume capture	9.1	16.2	1.6

Source: Ecorys/World Bank analysis; see appendix F for details.
Note: B/C = benefit/cost; eIRR = economic internal rate of return; n.a. = not applicable.

match the magnitude of the maintenance funding shortfall (as assumed in the base case), but no higher.
- The engine modernization project (Intervention 8) appears to be sensitive to higher levels of investment. The economic viability of this project is substantially strengthened if higher levers of freight capture by participating vessels are assumed.

Conclusions

Overall, the CBA results yield positive outcomes for numerous infrastructure and policy-based interventions in the IWT and coastal shipping sectors. The evidence suggests that upgrading Corridor 1 of the Mekong Delta should be seen as the most immediate priority for the national inland waterway network. Increasing coastal shipping container-handling capacity at Haiphong would also appear to be an economically robust investment priority. Returns to investments in portions of the Northern Delta network outside of Corridor 1 are comparatively less attractive, as the current and expected volume of cargo transported along these corridors is insufficient to generate enough economic benefits to offset the associated investment costs.

The economic impact of most interventions is primarily associated with internal IWT/coastal shipping features—notably transport cost savings due to increases in vessel sizes and operating efficiencies—whereas modal shift impacts remain relatively modest. A fuller provision of maintenance funding through user charges and public support for engine modernization appear to be promising policy measures to improve performance in the waterway sector.

Reference

JICA (Japan International Cooperation Agency). 2009. *The Comprehensive Study on the Sustainable Development of Transport System in Vietnam (VITRANSS-2)*. Hanoi: JICA.

APPENDIX A

List of Stakeholders Interviewed

Private Sector Stakeholders Interviewed (2010–12)

ANC Co., Ltd., international forwarding and logistics, Ms. Doan Thi Bich Thuy, Finance and Administrative Division, and Ms. Bui Ngoc Thuy Tien, Transport Division.

Bao Tin Shipbuilding Company Ltd., shipbuilding, Mr. Ho Tuan Chi, Deputy Director.

Binh Minh JSC/Sunrise Shipping and Trading JSC, IWT, marine shipping and freight forwarding, Mr. Truong Manh Hung, General Director; Mr. Le Huy Hoang, Marketing Department; Mr. Tu, Director; and Mr. Hoang, Operations Manager.

Dai Viet Company Ltd., shipping and freight forwarding, Mr. Nguyen Van Truong, Trading Deputy Director.

Hanoi Transport Corporation (Transerco), transport operator, Mr. Truonng, Deputy Director; Ms. Huong, Chief Administrator; and Mr. Nam, Manager.

International Labour and Services Stock Company (INLACO), transport operator, Mr. Nguyen Ba Hai, Shipping Department.

Nhat Hai Dang JSC (Lighthouse), ocean shipping company, Mr. Nguyen Ba Hai, Deputy Director.

PETROLIMEX Joint Stock Tankers (PJTACO), petroleum tankers, oil import/export, Mr. Lam Duc Qui, Vice Manager of Marine Department, and Mr. Pham Van Toan, Manager of River Department.

Quang Dung Company Ltd., IWT shipping company, Mr. Tran Van Khoi, Director.

Sai Gon Shipbuilding and Marine Industries (SHIPMARINE), shipbuilding company under Vinashin, Mr. Le Van Giang, Trading and Planning Manager.

Schenker Vietnam, international freight forwarder, Ms. Doan Thi Diem Hang, Ocean Freight Manager.

Shiptranco, container shipping company under Shipmarin, Vinashin, Ms. Le Thu Hien, Deputy Director.

Song Sinh Company Ltd. (SIFFCO), logistics company in coastal transport, Mr. Le Hung, Director.

Song Thanh Company, multimodal transportation company and freight forwarder, Ms. Nguyen Thu Hang.

Truong Giang Shipping Company, Mr. Truong, Director, and Mr. Xuan, Worldwide Broker.

Vietnam Freight Forwarders Association (VIFFAS), trade association with members in freight forwarding, logistics, warehousing, transport, and customs brokerage services, Mr. Nguyen Hung, Chief of Secretariat.

Multimodal Transport Holding Company (VIETRANSTIMEX), major heavy equipment transportation services provider, Mr. Tran Nguyen Giap, Vice Director, and Mr. Bui Ngoc Dung, Sales Manager.

Vinalink Logistics, third-party logistics service provider, Mr. Dinh Quang Ngoc, Director.

Public Sector Stakeholders Interviewed (2010–12)

Hanoi Port, state-owned port, Mr. Pham Ngoc Dich, Hanoi Port Director and Vice Director of Northern Inland Waterway Transportation Corporation.

Ministry of Transport (MoT), Ms. Hang, Deputy Director Planning and Investment Department; Ms. Hong Anh, Planning and Investment Department; Mr. Bang, Department of Transportation; Mr. Thanh, Department of Environment; Ms. Thanh, Project Management Unit.

Northern Waterway Transportation Corporation (NWTC), state-owned enterprise in waterway transport, mechanical equipment production, and port services, Mr. Le Khanh Bong, Vice Director, and Mr. Nguyen Van Son, Sales Manager.

Transport Development and Strategy Institute (TDSI), Mr. Viet and Mr. Cuong.

Vietnam Inland Waterway Administration (VIWA), policy and planning agency under the Ministry of Transport, Mr. Tran Van Cuu, Deputy Director; Mr. Toan, Deputy Director; Mr. Vu Manh Hung, Director of Science, Technology, International Cooperation and Environmental Department; Mr. Doanh, Science, Technology International Cooperation and Environmental Department; Mr. Thong, Project Management Unit; Ms. Thanh, Project Management Unit; Mr. Hoang Van Hung, Director of VIWA in the South; Mr. Dong Huu Phong, Deputy Director of VIWA in the South; and Mr. Sang, Manager, Technical Department of VIWA in the South.

Vietnam Maritime Administration (Vinamarine), policy and planning agency under the Ministry of Transport, Mr. Pham Hung Toan, Vice Director of Service Transportation Department; Mr. Do Hung Cuong, Service Transportation Department; Ms. Thuong, Service Transportation Department; and Mr. Khuc Truong Minh, Department of International Relations.

Vietnam National Shipping Lines (Vinalines), state-owned enterprise involved in ocean-going and coastal shipping services (14 shipping companies), port and terminal operations (18 port and terminal companies), and marine services (43 companies), Mr, Le Ahn Son, Vice President; Mr, Le Quang Trung, Deputy Director of Logistics and Business Development Department;

Mr. Dung, Logistics; Mr. Cuong, Logistics; Mr. Ha, Port Department; and Mr. Long, Business and International Cooperation Department.

Vietnam Railways, Mr. Tuyen, Manager of Business and Transport Department, and Mr. Nguyen Manh Hien, International Cooperation Department.

Vietnam Register, nonprofit state body for the promotion of safety and environmental protection across all transport modes, Mr. Pham Hai Bang, Vice Director of Seagoing Ship Classification and Register Department, and Mr. Do Trung Hoc, Director of River Going Ship Classification and Register Department.

APPENDIX B

Major Waterway Routes in the Northern and Southern Regions

Table B.1 Major Routes in the North Region

Route		Location			Critical dimensions						
From	To	River/canal	Province	Length (km)	Depth (m)	Width (m)	Radius (m)	Obstacles	River bed	Navigation aid	Dredging works
Cua Day	Ninh Binh	Day River	Nihn Binh	72.0	2.4	40	350	—	S	B	+
Lach Giang	Ha Noi	Hong River, Ninh Co River	Ha Noi, Hung Yen, Thai Binh, Nam Dinh	186.5	2.4	40	—	B	S	B	+
Quang Ninh (canal)	Ninh Binh	Ba Mom Channel, Cai Trap Channel, Bach Dang River, Dinh Vu Canal, Cam River, Dao River, LachTray River, Van Uc River, Khe Canal, Luoc River, Hong River, Day River	Quang Ninh, Haiphong, Thai Binh, Hai Duong, Nam Dinh, Ninh Binh	251.2	1.5	30	—	B	S	B	+
Quang Ninh (Lach Tray)	Ninh Binh	—	—	—	—	—	—	—	—	—	—
Haiphong	Hanoi	Cam River, Han River, Kinh Thay. Thay Binh River, Duong River, Hong River	Haiphong, Hai Duong, Bac Ninh, Ha Noi	150.5	1.5	30	—	B	S	B	+
Haiphong	Hanoi	Cam River, Kinh Mon River, Kinh Thay. Thai Binh River, Duong River, Hong River	Haiphong, Hai Duong, Bac Ninh, Ha Noi	152.0	1.5	30	—	B	S	B	+
Quang Ninh	Pha Lai	Ba Mom Channel, Chang River, Da Bach River, Phi Liet River, KinhThay River, Thai Binh River	Quang Ninh, Hai Duong	127.5	1.5	30	—	B	S	B	—

table continues next page

Table B.1 **Major Routes in the North Region** (continued)

Route		Location		Length (km)	Critical dimensions			Obstacles	River bed	Navigation aid	Dredging works
From	To	River/canal	Province		Depth (m)	Width (m)	Radius (m)				
Hanoi (Viet Tri)	Lao Cai	Hong River, Thao River	Ha Noi, Ha Tay, Phu Tho, Yen Bai, Lao Cai	362.0	<1	30	300	B	S/R	—	—
Hong Da Confluence	Hoa Binh Port	Da River	Hoa Binh	53.0	2.0	30	—	—	S/R	—	—
Viet Tri	Tuyen Quang	Lo River	Phu Tho, Tuyen Quang	106.0	1.2	30	—	—	S/R	—	—
Pha Lai	Da Phuc	Cau River, Cong River	Bac Ninh, Bac Giang, Thai Nguyen	88.0	1.4	20	—	—	S	—	—
Pha Lai	A Lu	Thoung River	Bac Giang	33.0	1.5	30	180	—	S	—	—
Ninh Binh	Thanh Hoa	—	—	72.0	—	—	—	—	—	—	—

Source: JICA 2009.

Note: Obstacles: B means existence of bridge(s). River bed: S means sandy bed; R means rocky bed. Navigation aid: B means existence of buoy(s). Dredging: "+" means implementation of dredging works from 2002 to 2005. — = not available.

Table B.2 Major Routes in the South Region

Route			Location	Length (km)	Critical dimensions			Obstacles
From	To	Via	River/canal		Depth (m)	Width (m)	Radius (m)	
Cua Tieu	Hong Ngu	—	Tien River	227.0	4.0	90	—	B
Dinh An Estuary	Tan Chau	—	Hau River	235.0	—	3	80	B
Sai Gon	Ca Mau	Xa No Canal	Doi Canal, Ong Lon Canal, Cay Kho Canal, Can Giuoc River, Nuoc Man Canal, Vam Co River, Rach La Canal, Cho Gao Canal, Ky Hon Canal, Tien River, Cho Lach Canal, Co Chien Canal, Mang Thit River, Tra On Canal, Hau River, Can Tho Canal, Xa No Canal, Cai Nhat Canal, Cai Tu Canal, Tat Cay Tram Canal, Nga Ba Dinh Canal, Trem River, Ong Doc River, Tat Thu River, Ganh Hao River	341.0	2.7	20	—	B
Sai Gon	Kien Luong	Lap Vo Canel	Doi Canal, Ong Lon Canal, Cay Kho Canal, Can Giuoc River, Nuoc Man Canal, Vam Co River, Rach La Canal, Cho Gao Canal, Ky Hon Canal, Tien River, Sa Dac Canal, Lap Vo Canal, Hau River, Rach Soi Canal, (-Hau Giang), Vanh Dai Canal, Rach Gia Canal (-Ha Tien), Ba Hon Canal,	319.0	2.2	22	—	B
Sai Gon	Ben Suc	Sai Gon River	Sai Gon River	132.5	1.0	35	250	B
Sai Gon	Ben Keo	Vam Co Dong River	Sai Gon River, Nha Be River, Soai Rap River, Can Giuoc River, Nuoc Man Canal, Vam Co River, Vam Co Dong River	154.7	6.1	80	205	B
Sao Gon	Moc Hoa	Vam Co Tay River	Sai Gon River, Nha Be River, Soai Rap River, Can Giuoc River, Nuoc Man Canal, Vam Co River, Vam Co Tay River	129.7	3.7	80	250	B
Sai Gon	Ca Mau	Coastal	—	380.4	1.0	16	—	B
Sai Gon	Kien Luong	Dong Thap Muoi Province	Te Ca. Doi Canal, Ben Luc River, Vam Co Dong River, Thu Thua Canal, Vam Co Tay River, Thap Muoi Canal, Lagrange Canal, Dong Tien Canal, Tien River, Vam Nao River, Hau River, Tri Ton Canal (-Hau Giang) Rach Gia Canal (Ha Tien)	337.2	1.9	20	—	B

table continues next page

Table B.2 Major Routes in the South Region *(continued)*

Route			Location		Length (km)	Critical dimensions			Obstacles
From	To	Via	River/canal			Depth (m)	Width (m)	Radius (m)	
Moc Hoa	Ha Tien	—	Vam Co Tay River, Hong Ngu-Vinh Hung Channel, Vinh An Channel, Vinh Te Canal,		183.5	—	—	—	—
Sai Gon	Hieu Liem	Dong Nai River	Dong Nai River, Sai Gon River		98.8	0.6	18	220	B
Phuoc Xuyen Canal	Canal 28	—	Phuoc Xuyen Canal 4 Bis, Tu Moi Canal 28		91.5	1.2	20	—	—
Rach Gia	Ca Mau	—	—		91.4	2.3	30	400	B
Mekong River Delta	Vung Tau, Thi Vai	A	—		60.5	1.6	40	150	B
Mekong River Delta	Vung Tau, Thi Vai	B	—		58.2	—	—	—	—

Source: JICA 2009.
Note: Obstacle: B means existence of bridge(s). n.a. = not available.

Reference

JICA (Japan International Cooperation Agency). 2009. *The Comprehensive Study on the Sustainable Development of Transport System in Vietnam (VITRANSS-2)*. Hanoi: JICA.

APPENDIX C

General Considerations on DWT Capacity Increases in the National IWT Fleet

Length Increase

Among the three parameters that drive vessel scale—length, beam, and draft—without any fairway improvements, the most readily implementable and effective means of capacity increase is length increase. Length increase can be achieved by (a) building a new and longer vessel or (b) adding a section to an existing hull. Irrespective of the option chosen, attention must be paid to allowing sufficient longitudinal strength, characterized by the ratio of length to draft, which should not exceed a value of 20–25, depending on the method of (un)loading (i.e., in one pass or distributed) and on the penalty of a heavy construction with less payload.

Typically, however, vessels in operation have already reached what is considered the maximum length, in which case the above options (and insofar as not determined by the length of a lock in the fairway) may be applicable only with an increase in maneuverability (bow steering), so that the longer vessel can still negotiate the bends. Another effective and nearly always applicable solution is adding a barge to an existing self-propelled vessel. This might require some additional propulsive power, but not as much as one would imagine on the basis of the increased deadweight tonnage (DWT), because of the much improved hydraulic performance. The principal addition required would be some means of bow steering for this longer vessel combination, or even an articulated barge system (ABS).

Beam Increase

This option is generally reserved for new building of vessels and may be principally subject to width limitations of civil structures and/or the bottom width of the fairway, whether or not at natural passage obstructions. Without these, there is hardly a limit, other than of an engineering/construction nature, to beam increase. For example, in Western Europe the traditional beams of vessels were determined by the width of the locks to pass through (or the reverse), ranging from 6 to 10 meters. The first pushed barges on the Rhine were 9.5 meters wide, but soon increased to 11.4 meters so they could still pass through the 12 meter locks in the lateral canals. For those vessels that do not have to pass through these locks or canals, beams are applied up to 16 meters and even up to about double the standard barge size, up to 24 meters. But these are exceptions. Normally, a double width is achieved by lashing two standard barges side by side, where the fairway permits, and where not, the barges are simply untied and pass one by one. The drawback of this is a reduction in hydraulic performance (see below).

Draft Increase

For existing vessels a draft increase may be achieved by minimizing the freeboard. However, this may undermine safety of navigation. Nevertheless, when certain rules are taken into account, the freeboard for navigation in sheltered waters may effectively be driven to zero. This would require adjustments to hold access, and possibly watertight hatches and openings into hull compartments provided with watertight covers above a certain minimum height.

The more critical question, however, is whether the depth of the fairway (at low tide) would permit such an action. Apart from compulsory maximum drafts that aim at safety of navigation, protection of lock sills, and reduction of erosion caused by the screw race, there is the increase of bottom drag, which costs more energy—resulting in the carrying capacity gain to be largely lost against higher fuel costs.

Hydraulic Impact

For vessel lengthening, the ratio change of length to beam determines the impact on vessels' resistance in such a way that the higher the ratio, the more efficient the propulsion. In other words, a longer vessel carries more cargo and sails more efficiently in terms of energy use. For vessel widening, the opposite is true.

However, when two wide-beam barges are coupled in tandem, the length-to-beam value suddenly doubles, and this effect becomes larger when more barges are added in length. This is the reason why a long snake of small barges, as can be seen on the canals in the Mekong Delta, is moved by a relatively small tug.

For vessel deepening, the determinant phenomena for bottom drag are characterized by the ratio of water depth to draft, keel clearance, blockage coefficient, and installed power. It must be noted, however, that in the case of installed power, in some situations the speed remains low regardless of the power installed. This happens when sailing in narrow canals (high blockage coefficient), with little under-keel clearance. Thus increasing the draft, if it were possible, does not seem to be a good solution for capacity increases.

APPENDIX D

Cargo Data and Modal Split Model

The VITRANSS-2 Dataset Structure

The information on cargo flows used as the basis of this report was obtained from JICA (2009), a comprehensive transportation study widely referred to as VITRANSS-2. The data concern cargo flows shipped between 64 provinces, broken down by 13 commodity types and five modes of transport (road, rail, IWT, coastal shipping, and air) for the base year 2008 and target years 2020 and 2030.

Detailed tables of cargo flows for 2008 and 2030 were made available through the Ministry of Transport's Transport Development and Strategy Institute. Data for 2020 were available at an aggregated level only, as published in VITRANSS-2. The data provided for 2008 and 2030 are for two tables: a table of cargo flows between 64 provinces by type of cargo and a table of cargo flows between 64 provinces by mode of transport. No table of interprovincial cargo flows by both type of cargo and mode of transport was available for this study. Consequently, the modal split models tested are unable to distinguish between commodity types.

The VITRANSS-2 cargo flow data are based on daily traffic count surveys conducted in 2008. Domestic cargo carried by coastal ships cannot be captured adequately by traffic counts because these do not distinguish between stopovers of international shipping routes and purely domestic services. Therefore, an alternative approach has been applied based on statistics of ships engaged in coastal container shipping during 2007. These data were obtained from Vinalines.

Reference Scenario

For all analyses, a "business as usual" scenario was the basis for comparison. "Business as usual" implies that ongoing works will be completed, but no additional measures will be taken.

It is essential that the reference scenario establishes projections of the most plausible development of all transport sectors without new policies or interventions. For example, because of large increases in road transport, both freight trucks and cars competing for the same infrastructure capacity will likely result in congestion, higher emissions of both greenhouse gases (GHGs) and local pollutants, and damage to the road surface, requiring additional maintenance and rehabilitation investments. This study did not develop projections of future freight flows by mode. Instead, the report uses the reference scenario data as defined in VITRANSS-2 (see box D.1).

Under the report's Do Nothing scenario it is further assumed that the following apply:

(a) All works under the ongoing Northern Delta Transport Development Project (NDTDP) are completed by mid-2015, resulting in the Northern Corridor 1 being upgraded to Class II, and
(b) All works under the ongoing Mekong Delta Transport Infrastructure Development Project (MDTIDP) are completed by 2013, resulting in the Southern Corridors II and III being upgraded to Class III.

In other words, it was assumed that ongoing inland waterway transport (IWT) projects are completed, and that no further projects are subsequently conducted.

It is thus assumed that the Do Nothing forecast reflects both the 2008 transportation network and the two network upgrades listed above. For maintenance

---

Box D.1 VITRANSS-2 Scenarios

VITRANSS-2 forecasts freight traffic levels for the years 2010, 2020, and 2030, using 2008 as base year. National population growth rates were taken from the National Committee for Population and Family Planning (NCPFP) forecast, whereas for each region regional development directions were taken into account. For Vietnam as a whole, annual population growth rates of 1.4 percent between 2005 and 2010, 1.3 percent between 2010 and 2020, and 1.2 percent between 2020 and 2030 are assumed. Urban population in particular is expected to grow faster: 4.1 percent between 2005 and 2010, 3.6 percent between 2010 and 2020, and 3.0 percent between 2020 and 2030. Three gross domestic product (GDP) growth scenarios are considered through 2030: a high-growth scenario, with an average annual growth rate of 7.2 percent; a medium-growth scenario, with an average annual growth rate of 6.4 percent; and a low-growth scenario, with an average annual growth rate of 5.6 percent. Only one freight transport volume scenario was available in sufficient analytical detail for this study, however, and this corresponds to the medium-growth GDP scenario. VITRANSS-2 adopts three policy scenarios for its transport demand forecasts by mode:

1. A "Do Nothing" scenario, where the 2008 transportation network was applied
2. Scenario 1: Assuming an improved railway network (up to 100 kilometers/hour) and all planned expressways completed, excluding the Ho Chi Minh route
3. Scenario 2: The Scenario 1 assumption plus high-speed rail at 300 kilometers/hour. As the additional investment concerns passenger transport only, this scenario is not relevant for this study.

This report utilizes the VITRANSS-2 "Do Nothing" scenario as baseline.

Source: JICA 2009 and Ecorys/World Bank analysis.

of the waterways, it is noted that current maintenance levels are underfunded (it is estimated that only up to 60 percent of maintenance needs are covered). It has been assumed that in the baseline (i.e., Do Nothing) scenario future maintenance remains at current levels, and that investments in expanding waterway capacity will be accompanied by similar maintenance levels as are currently observed. The reason for the latter is that improved maintenance will be addressed as a separate policy intervention from waterway upgrading works (see appendix E).

Development of Cargo Flows in the Main Waterway Transport Regions

The report uses forecasts of cargo flows by commodity type and transport mode as provided by JICA (2009) for the base year 2008 and target years 2020 and 2030. For 2008 and 2030, detailed data are available for 13 commodity types, 4 transport modes (excluding aviation), and 64 provinces. Tables D.1–D.22 present detailed VITRANSS-2 cargo flow data.

Cargo Data and Other Inputs Used from the VITRANSS-2 Database

Table D.1 VITRANSS Zones: Vietnamese Provinces

Provinces of Vietnam			
Ha Noi	Yen Bai	Da Nang	Dong Nai
Vinh Phuc	Thai Nguyen	Quang Nam	Ba Ria-Vung Tau
Bac Ninh	Lang Son	Quang Ngai	HCM
Ha Tay	Quang Ninh	Binh Dinh	Long An
Hai Duong	Bac Giang	Phu Yen	Tien Giang
Hai Phong	Phu Tho	Khanh Hoa	Ben Tre
Hung Yen	Dien Bien Phu	Kon Tum	Tra Vinh
Thai Binh	Lai Chau	Gia Lai	Vinh Long
Ha Nam	Son La	Dak Lak	Dong Thap
Nam Dinh	Hoa Binh	Dak Nong	An Giang
Ninh Binh	Thanh Hoa	Lam Dong	Kien Giang
Ha Giang	Nghe An	Ninh Thuan	Can Tho
Cao Bang	Ha Tinh	Binh Thuan	Hau Giang
Bac Kan	Quang Binh	Binh Phuoc	Soc Trang
Tuyen Quang	Quang Tri	Tay Ninh	Bac Lieu
Lao Cai	Thua Thien Hue	Binh Duong	Ca Mau

Source: Data from JICA 2009.

Table D.2 VITRANSS-2 Commodity Groupings

Commodities	
Rice	Coal
Sugar cane/sugar	Petroleum
Wood	Industrial crops
Steel	Manufactured goods
Construction materials	Fishery products
Cement	Animal meats and others
Fertilizer	

Source: Data from JICA 2009.

Point-to-Point Distances

Table D.3 Road Distances from Northern and Southern Provinces to the Northern Provinces
Kilometers

									Destination									
		1	2	3	4	5	6	7	8	9	10	11	12	13	14	15	16	17	18
Origin		Hanoi	Vinh Phuc	Bac Ninh	Ha Tay	Hai Duong	Haiphong	Hung Yen	Thai Binh	Ha Nam	Nam Dinh	Ninh Binh	Bac Kan	Tuyen Quang	Yen Bai	Quang Ninh	Bac Giang	Phu Tho	Hoa Binh
1	Hanoi	n.a.	43	23	5	54	105	56	108	66	95	98	148	127	152	137	45	65	66
2	Vinh Phuc	43	n.a.	56	48	98	149	99	151	106	135	138	120	84	115	170	79	22	77
3	Bac Ninh	23	56	n.a.	28	60	107	66	119	87	116	119	141	140	171	118	22	78	88
4	Ha Tay	5	48	28	n.a.	59	110	60	112	61	91	93	153	132	157	142	50	70	63
5	Hai Duong	54	98	60	59	n.a.	51	64	91	77	107	109	187	181	207	97	58	120	120
6	Haiphong	105	149	107	110	51	n.a.	108	77	125	103	119	235	232	258	55	106	171	171
7	Hung Yen	56	99	66	60	64	108	n.a.	52	30	60	63	195	183	208	154	89	121	111
8	Thai Binh	108	151	119	112	91	77	52	n.a.	52	26	53	247	235	260	124	141	173	156
9	Ha Nam	66	106	87	61	77	125	30	52	n.a.	30	32	213	189	213	171	109	127	104
10	Nam Dinh	95	135	116	91	107	103	60	26	30	n.a.	31	243	219	243	149	139	157	134
11	Ninh Binh	98	138	119	93	110	119	63	53	32	31	n.a.	246	222	245	165	141	160	134
12	Bac Kan	148	120	141	153	187	235	195	247	213	243	246	n.a.	149	211	245	141	142	196
13	Tuyen Quang	127	84	140	132	181	232	183	235	189	219	222	149	n.a.	62	252	147	78	158
14	Yen Bai	152	115	171	157	207	258	208	260	213	243	245	211	62	n.a.	285	193	93	169
15	Quang Ninh	137	170	118	142	97	54	154	123	171	149	165	245	251	285	n.a.	117	192	203
16	Bac Giang	45	79	22	50	58	106	89	141	109	139	141	141	147	193	117	n.a.	100	111
17	Phu Tho	65	22	78	70	120	170	121	173	127	157	160	142	78	93	192	100	n.a.	89
18	Hoa Binh	66	77	88	63	120	171	111	156	104	134	134	196	158	169	203	111	89	n.a.
19	Binh Duong	1,572	1,612	1,593	1,567	1,584	1,593	1,537	1,527	1,507	1,506	1,474	1,720	1,696	1,719	1,639	1,616	1,634	1,579
20	Dong Nai	1,598	1,638	1,619	1,593	1,609	1,618	1,563	1,553	1,532	1,531	1,500	1,745	1,722	1,745	1,664	1,641	1,660	1,605

table continues next page

Table D.3 Road Distances from Northern and Southern Provinces to the Northern Provinces (continued)
Kilometers

											Destination								
		1	2	3	4	5	6	7	8	9	10	11	12	13	14	15	16	17	18
Origin		Hanoi	Vinh Phuc	Bac Ninh	Ha Tay	Hai Duong	Haiphong	Hung Yen	Thai Binh	Ha Nam	Nam Dinh	Ninh Binh	Bac Kan	Tuyen Quang	Yen Bai	Quang Ninh	Bac Giang	Phu Tho	Hoa Binh
21	Ba Ria-Vung Tau	1,647	1,687	1,668	1,642	1,659	1,668	1,612	1,603	1,582	1,581	1,549	1,795	1,771	1,795	1,714	1,691	1,709	1,654
22	HCM	1,589	1,629	1,610	1,584	1,600	1,609	1,553	1,544	1,523	1,522	1,491	1,736	1,712	1,736	1,655	1,632	1,650	1,596
23	Long An	1,644	1,684	1,665	1,639	1,655	1,664	1,608	1,599	1,578	1,577	1,546	1,791	1,767	1,791	1,710	1,687	1,706	1,651
24	Tien Giang	1,668	1,708	1,689	1,663	1,679	1,688	1,632	1,623	1,602	1,601	1,570	1,815	1,791	1,815	1,734	1,711	1,729	1,675
25	Ben Tre	1,680	1,720	1,701	1,675	1,692	1,701	1,645	1,635	1,615	1,614	1,582	1,828	1,804	1,827	1,747	1,724	1,742	1,687
26	Tra Vinh	1,733	1,773	1,754	1,728	1,745	1,754	1,698	1,689	1,668	1,667	1,635	1,881	1,857	1,881	1,800	1,777	1,795	1,740
27	Vinh Long	1,706	1,746	1,727	1,701	1,717	1,726	1,670	1,661	1,640	1,639	1,608	1,853	1,829	1,853	1,772	1,749	1,768	1,713
28	Dong Thap	1,735	1,775	1,756	1,730	1,746	1,755	1,699	1,690	1,669	1,668	1,637	1,882	1,858	1,882	1,801	1,778	1,797	1,742
29	An Giang/Kien Giang	1,795	1,835	1,817	1,791	1,807	1,816	1,760	1,751	1,730	1,729	1,697	1,943	1,919	1,943	1,862	1,839	1,857	1,802
30	Can Tho	1,742	1,782	1,763	1,737	1,753	1,762	1,706	1,697	1,676	1,675	1,644	1,889	1,865	1,889	1,808	1,785	1,803	1,749
31	Hau Giang	1,800	1,840	1,821	1,795	1,812	1,821	1,765	1,756	1,735	1,734	1,702	1,948	1,924	1,948	1,867	1,844	1,862	1,807
32	Soc Trang	1,789	1,829	1,810	1,784	1,800	1,809	1,753	1,744	1,723	1,722	1,691	1,936	1,912	1,936	1,855	1,832	1,850	1,796
33	Bac Lieu/Ca Mau	1,837	1,877	1,858	1,832	1,848	1,858	1,802	1,792	1,771	1,770	1,739	1,985	1,961	1,984	1,903	1,880	1,899	1,844

Source: From JICA 2009.
Note: n.a. = not applicable.

Table D.4 Road Distances from Northern and Southern Provinces to the Southern Provinces
Kilometers

		Destination													
		1	2	3	4	5	6	7	8	9	10	11	12	13	14	15
Origin		Binh Duong	Dong Nai	Ba Ria-Vung Tau	HCM	Long An	Tien Giang	Ben Tre	Tra Vinh	Vinh Long	Dong Thap	An Giang/ Kien Giang	Can Tho	Hau Giang	Soc Trang	Bac Lieu/ Ca Mau
1	Hanoi	1,572	1,598	1,647	1,589	1,644	1,668	1,680	1,733	1,706	1,735	1,795	1,742	1,800	1,789	1,837
2	Vinh Phuc	1,612	1,638	1,687	1,629	1,684	1,708	1,720	1,773	1,746	1,775	1,835	1,782	1,840	1,829	1,877
3	Bac Ninh	1,593	1,619	1,668	1,610	1,665	1,689	1,701	1,754	1,727	1,756	1,817	1,763	1,821	1,810	1,858
4	Ha Tay	1,567	1,593	1,642	1,584	1,639	1,663	1,675	1,728	1,701	1,730	1,791	1,737	1,795	1,784	1,832
5	Hai Duong	1,584	1,609	1,659	1,600	1,655	1,679	1,692	1,745	1,717	1,746	1,807	1,753	1,812	1,800	1,848
6	Haiphong	1,593	1,618	1,668	1,609	1,664	1,688	1,701	1,754	1,726	1,755	1,816	1,762	1,821	1,809	1,858
7	Hung Yen	1,537	1,563	1,612	1,553	1,608	1,632	1,645	1,698	1,670	1,699	1,760	1,706	1,765	1,753	1,802
8	Thai Binh	1,527	1,553	1,603	1,544	1,599	1,623	1,635	1,689	1,661	1,690	1,751	1,697	1,756	1,744	1,792
9	Ha Nam	1,507	1,532	1,582	1,523	1,578	1,602	1,615	1,668	1,640	1,669	1,730	1,676	1,735	1,723	1,771
10	Nam Dinh	1,506	1,531	1,581	1,522	1,577	1,601	1,614	1,667	1,639	1,668	1,729	1,675	1,734	1,722	1,770
11	Ninh Binh	1,474	1,500	1,549	1,491	1,546	1,570	1,582	1,635	1,608	1,637	1,697	1,644	1,702	1,691	1,739
12	Bac Kan	1,720	1,745	1,795	1,736	1,791	1,815	1,828	1,881	1,853	1,882	1,943	1,889	1,948	1,936	1,985
13	Tuyen Quang	1,696	1,722	1,771	1,712	1,767	1,791	1,804	1,857	1,829	1,858	1,919	1,865	1,924	1,912	1,961
14	Yen Bai	1,719	1,745	1,795	1,736	1,791	1,815	1,827	1,881	1,853	1,882	1,943	1,889	1,948	1,936	1,984
15	Quang Ninh	1,639	1,664	1,714	1,655	1,710	1,734	1,747	1,800	1,772	1,801	1,862	1,808	1,867	1,855	1,903
16	Bac Giang	1,616	1,641	1,691	1,632	1,687	1,711	1,724	1,777	1,749	1,778	1,839	1,785	1,844	1,832	1,880
17	Phu Tho	1,634	1,660	1,709	1,650	1,706	1,729	1,742	1,795	1,768	1,797	1,857	1,803	1,862	1,850	1,899
18	Hoa Binh	1,579	1,605	1,654	1,596	1,651	1,675	1,687	1,740	1,713	1,742	1,802	1,749	1,807	1,796	1,844
19	Binh Duong	n.a.	30	102	20	75	99	112	165	142	171	232	173	232	220	268
20	Dong Nai	30	n.a.	84	16	71	95	108	161	140	169	229	169	228	216	265

table continues next page

Table D.4 Road Distances from Northern and Southern Provinces to the Southern Provinces (continued)
Kilometers

							Destination								
		1	2	3	4	5	6	7	8	9	10	11	12	13	14	15
Origin		Binh Duong	Dong Nai	Ba Ria-Vung Tau	HCM	Long An	Tien Giang	Ben Tre	Tra Vinh	Vinh Long	Dong Thap	An Giang/ Kien Giang	Can Tho	Hau Giang	Soc Trang	Bac Lieu/ Ca Mau
21	Ba Ria-Vung Tau	102	84	n.a.	82	127	151	164	217	198	230	288	225	284	272	320
22	HCM	20	16	82	n.a.	55	79	92	145	123	152	213	153	212	200	248
23	Long An	75	71	127	55	n.a.	27	40	93	74	111	163	101	160	148	196
24	Tien Giang	99	95	151	79	27	n.a.	13	66	47	89	137	74	133	121	169
25	Ben Tre	112	108	164	92	40	13	n.a.	53	34	76	124	61	120	108	157
26	Tra Vinh	165	161	217	145	93	66	53	n.a.	58	100	148	85	144	63	111
27	Vinh Long	142	140	198	123	74	47	34	58	n.a.	42	90	39	98	100	148
28	Dong Thap	171	169	230	152	111	89	76	100	42	n.a.	131	81	140	142	190
29	An Giang/Kien Giang	232	229	288	213	163	137	124	148	90	131	n.a.	86	86	88	133
30	Can Tho	173	169	225	153	101	74	61	85	39	81	86	n.a.	59	61	109
31	Hau Giang	232	228	284	212	160	133	120	144	98	140	88	59	n.a.	89	138
32	Soc Trang	220	216	272	200	148	121	108	63	100	142	133	61	89	n.a.	48
33	Bac Lieu/Ca Mau	268	265	320	248	196	169	157	111	148	190	141	109	138	48	n.a.

Source: Data from JICA 2009.
Note: HCM = Ho Chi Minh; n.a. = not applicable.

IWT Distances

Table D.5 IWT Distances between Northern Provinces
Kilometers

Origin		1 Hanoi	2 Vinh Phuc	3 Bac Ninh	4 Ha Tay	5 Hai Duong	6 Haiphong	7 Hung Yen	8 Thai Binh	9 Ha Nam	10 Nam Dinh	11 Ninh Binh	12 Bac Kan	13 Tuyen Quang	14 Yen Bai	15 Quang Ninh	16 Bac Giang	17 Phu Tho	18 Hoa Binh
1	Hanoi	n.a.	44	111	—	105	142	55	108	55	95	150	—	—	—	182	—	72	—
2	Vinh Phuc	44	n.a.	133	—	127	164	—	—	—	—	—	—	—	—	204	—	28	—
3	Bac Ninh	111	133	n.a.	—	70	105	—	—	—	—	—	—	—	—	147	—	161	—
4	Ha Tay	—	—	—	n.a.	—	—	—	—	—	—	—	—	—	—	—	—	—	—
5	Hai Duong	105	127	70	—	n.a.	101	—	—	—	—	—	—	—	—	141	—	155	—
6	Haiphong	142	164	105	—	101	n.a.	—	180	149	167	222	—	—	—	40	—	192	—
7	Hung Yen	55	—	—	—	—	—	n.a.	53	—	40	95	—	—	—	220	—	—	—
8	Thai Binh	108	—	—	—	—	180	53	n.a.	53	43	98	—	—	—	220	—	—	—
9	Ha Nam	55	—	—	—	—	149	—	53	n.a.	40	95	—	—	—	189	—	—	—
10	Nam Dinh	95	—	—	—	—	167	40	43	40	n.a.	55	—	—	—	207	—	—	—
11	Ninh Binh	150	—	—	—	—	222	95	98	95	55	n.a.	—	—	—	262	—	—	—
12	Bac Kan	—	—	—	—	—	—	—	—	—	—	—	n.a.	—	—	—	—	—	—
13	Tuyen Quang	—	—	—	—	—	—	—	—	—	—	—	—	n.a.	—	—	—	—	—
14	Yen Bai	—	—	—	—	—	—	—	—	—	—	—	—	—	n.a.	—	—	—	—
15	Quang Ninh	182	204	147	—	141	40	—	220	189	207	262	—	—	—	n.a.	—	232	—
16	Bac Giang	—	—	—	—	—	—	—	—	—	—	—	—	—	—	—	n.a.	—	—
17	Phu Tho	72	28	161	—	155	192	—	—	—	—	—	—	—	—	232	—	n.a.	—
18	Hoa Binh	—	—	—	—	—	—	—	—	—	—	—	—	—	—	—	—	—	n.a.

Source: Data from JICA 2009.
Note: IWT = inland waterway transport; — = not available; n.a. = not applicable.

Table D.6 IWT Distances between Southern Provinces
Kilometers

		Destination														
		1	2	3	4	5	6	7	8	9	10	11	12	13	14	15
Origin		Binh Duong	Dong Nai	Ba Ria-Vung Tau	HCM	Long An	Tien Giang	Ben Tre	Tra Vinh	Vinh Long	Dong Thap	An Giang/ Kien Giang	Can Tho	Hau Giang	Soc Trang	Bac Lieu/ Ca Mau
1	Binh Duong	n.a.	—	—	—	—	—	—	—	—	—	—	—	—	—	—
2	Dong Nai	—	n.a.	—	—	—	—	—	—	—	—	—	—	—	—	—
3	Ba Ria-Vung Tau	—	—	n.a.	—	—	—	—	—	—	—	—	—	—	—	—
4	HCM	—	—	—	n.a.	—	85	102	146	143	201	218	193	225	221	277
5	Long An	—	—	—	—	n.a.	—	—	—	—	—	—	—	—	—	—
6	Tien Giang	—	—	—	85	—	n.a.	25	69	58	116	133	108	140	144	200
7	Ben Tre	—	—	—	102	—	25	n.a.	44	83	146	163	137	137	119	175
8	Tra Vinh	—	—	—	146	—	69	44	n.a.	127	150	167	93	93	75	136
9	Vinh Long	—	—	—	143	—	58	83	127	n.a.	68	85	109	141	177	238
10	Dong Thap	—	—	—	201	—	116	146	150	68	n.a.	17	57	89	125	181
11	An Giang/Kien Giang	—	—	—	218	—	133	163	167	85	17	n.a.	74	106	142	198
12	Can Tho	—	—	—	193	—	108	137	93	109	57	74	n.a.	32	68	124
13	Hau Giang	—	—	—	225	—	140	137	93	141	89	106	32	n.a.	68	124
14	Soc Trang	—	—	—	221	—	144	119	75	127	125	142	68	68	n.a.	66
15	Bac Lieu/Ca Mau	—	—	—	277	—	200	175	136	238	181	198	124	124	66	n.a.

Note: IWT = inland waterway transport; HCM = Ho Chi Minh; n.a. = not applicable; — = not available.

Cargo Flows

Cargo Flows for Northern Provinces: Road Transport in Tons per Day

Table D.7 Northern Provinces: Road Cargo Flows in 2008

Tons per day

Origin		1 Hanoi	2 Vinh Phuc	3 Bac Ninh	4 Ha Tay	5 Hai Duong	6 Haiphong	7 Hung Yen	8 Thai Binh	9 Ha Nam	10 Nam Dinh	11 Ninh Binh	12 Bac Kan	13 Tuyen Quang	14 Yen Bai	15 Quang Ninh	16 Bac Giang	17 Phu Tho	18 Hoa Binh	Total
1	Hanoi	0	2,564	10,835	20,574	2,071	2,200	5,257	54	232	215	88	71	4	449	109	3,014	214	42	47,993
2	Vinh Phuc	7,674	0	35	648	65	1,591	7	2	0	10	963	0	98	58	151	74	535	9	11,920
3	Bac Ninh	5,215	16	0	400	3	126	213	88	4	3	10	0	0	81	60	8,364	30	30	14,643
4	Ha Tay	14,483	2,432	77	0	19	363	3,132	22	4,988	15	214	16	5	6	235	46	653	2,501	29,207
5	Hai Duong	1,810	873	964	19	0	7,606	0	61	435	68	0	0	0	10	830	1,736	255	14	14,681
6	Haiphong	17,462	218	452	687	10,034	0	4,107	4,789	11	1,475	531	0	0	0	1,055	99	365	0	41,285
7	Hung Yen	22,426	2	926	972	0	232	0	272	26	33	0	1	0	1	64	49	17	726	25,747
8	Thai Binh	51	3	0	5	36	1,308	248	0	0	75	0	0	0	8	127	3	20	1	1,885
9	Ha Nam	706	294	4	12,424	0	210	2,818	6	0	78	0	0	0	0	9	10	0	76	16,635
10	Nam Dinh	34	0	11	88	0	444	0	0	20	0	0	0	0	0	57	0	10	2	666
11	Ninh Binh	346	0	0	2	0	105	3	248	0	0	0	0	0	0	0	28	0	0	732
12	Bac Kan	292	0	0	0	1	0	5	0	0	0	0	0	0	0	0	0	0	0	298
13	Tuyen Quang	12	203	0	0	27	135	4,018	0	0	0	0	0	0	0	0	0	0	0	4,395
14	Yen Bai	711	312	756	60	3,953	11	1,170	4	0	0	0	0	0	0	220	0	0	0	7,197
15	Quang Ninh	376	220	106	20	2,695	5,910	403	0	0	73	0	0	20	0	0	199	0	0	10,022
16	Bac Giang	1,976	15	8,791	0	1,178	141	23	178	4	4	1	0	24	0	219	0	0	0	12,554
17	Phu Tho	72	4,818	812	2,256	3	756	30	193	240	6	0	0	0	0	0	58	0	4	9,248
18	Hoa Binh	1,707	0	15	3,873	17	426	944	5	49	1	0	0	0	0	8	50	0	0	7,095
	Total	75,353	11,970	23,784	42,028	20,102	21,564	22,378	5,922	6,009	2,056	1,807	88	151	613	3,144	13,730	2,099	3,405	256,203

Source: Data from JICA 2009.

Table D.8 Northern Provinces: Road Cargo Flows in 2020
Tons per day

										Destination										
	Origin	1 Hanoi	2 Vinh Phuc	3 Bac Ninh	4 Ha Tay	5 Hai Duong	6 Haiphong	7 Hung Yen	8 Thai Binh	9 Ha Nam	10 Nam Dinh	11 Ninh Binh	12 Bac Kan	13 Tuyen Quang	14 Yen Bai	15 Quang Ninh	16 Bac Giang	17 Phu Tho	18 Hoa Binh	Total
1	Hanoi	0	9,309	21,103	37,403	4,713	5,364	6,503	821	529	1,564	347	265	808	1,958	1,822	6,085	668	256	99,519
2	Vinh Phuc	14,134	0	256	747	1,981	2,510	15	106	2	27	5,134	3	409	138	503	97	1,210	45	27,315
3	Bac Ninh	13,544	247	0	1,064	113	153	361	1,013	14	11	14	3	79	149	94	10,908	102	207	28,076
4	Ha Tay	29,893	3,441	266	0	68	475	5,078	137	7,235	89	401	19	64	15	824	50	946	4,155	53,154
5	Hai Duong	3,453	1,017	1,295	25	0	10,377	7	116	482	900	5	7	48	32	2,658	2,113	283	490	23,307
6	Haiphong	31,643	1,144	516	794	12,341	0	4,448	6,590	12	2,606	729	282	2,666	22	2,049	211	840	196	67,089
7	Hung Yen	31,032	40	1,204	1,066	63	281	0	395	175	68	44	28	290	2	83	58	52	1,000	35,878
8	Thai Binh	410	208	100	44	794	2,685	280	0	21	491	51	12	88	73	382	4	340	22	6,003
9	Ha Nam	994	310	7	14,369	31	263	3,896	21	0	241	1	2	29	1	10	11	1	169	20,354
10	Nam Dinh	479	47	44	265	253	1,013	1	109	53	0	37	5	79	5	67	2	85	19	2,562
11	Ninh Binh	1,648	213	140	94	2,030	253	7	640	1	127	0	43	508	15	11	54	8	102	5,891
12	Bac Kan	553	1	3	1	57	178	8	6	1	3	11	0	80	15	1	4	33	32	986
13	Tuyen Quang	364	232	14	2	344	1,170	4,230	30	3	11	23	31	0	167	7	40	159	75	6,900
14	Yen Bai	1,222	1,046	1,096	69	4,332	132	3,514	49	30	20	39	58	171	0	155	7	59	56	12,653
15	Quang Ninh	583	1,826	173	23	3,429	6,920	444	7	0	317	2	1	55	2	0	211	2	2	13,997
16	Bac Giang	2,687	19	9,589	2	1,539	652	24	233	7	7	3	1	46	1	232	0	1	2	15,043
17	Phu Tho	278	6,376	905	2,631	17	881	34	239	503	14	15	26	61	6	3	73	0	15	12,076
18	Hoa Binh	5,711	83	344	5,525	225	786	2,253	45	78	22	21	16	135	11	117	147	5	0	15,524
	Total	138,626	25,558	37,053	64,122	32,327	34,092	31,105	10,554	9,145	6,519	6,876	801	5,615	2,612	9,615	20,074	4,794	6,842	446,329

Source: Data from JICA 2009.

Table D.9 Northern Provinces: Road Cargo Flows in 2030
Tons per day

	Origin	1 Hanoi	2 Vinh Phuc	3 Bac Ninh	4 Ha Tay	5 Hai Duong	6 Haiphong	7 Hung Yen	8 Thai Binh	9 Ha Nam	10 Nam Dinh	11 Ninh Binh	12 Bac Kan	13 Tuyen Quang	14 Yen Bai	15 Quang Ninh	16 Bac Giang	17 Phu Tho	18 Hoa Binh	Total
1	Hanoi	0	14,930	29,660	51,427	6,915	8,000	7,542	1,461	776	2,689	562	426	1,478	3,216	3,249	8,645	1,047	434	142,457
2	Vinh Phuc	19,518	0	440	829	3,578	3,275	21	192	3	42	8,610	5	668	205	796	116	1,772	75	40,145
3	Bac Ninh	20,484	440	0	1,618	204	176	485	1,783	23	17	18	6	145	205	123	13,028	162	354	39,271
4	Ha Tay	42,734	4,281	423	0	108	569	6,700	232	9,108	151	556	22	113	22	1,314	53	1,190	5,534	73,110
5	Hai Duong	4,822	1,137	1,570	30	0	12,686	13	161	521	1,594	9	12	88	51	4,181	2,428	307	886	30,496
6	Haiphong	43,461	1,915	569	883	14,264	0	4,733	8,090	13	3,549	894	517	4,888	40	2,877	305	1,235	360	88,593
7	Hung Yen	38,203	71	1,435	1,145	115	321	0	497	299	97	81	51	531	2	98	65	82	1,228	44,321
8	Thai Binh	709	379	183	76	1,425	3,832	307	0	38	837	94	22	162	127	594	4	606	39	9,434
9	Ha Nam	1,234	324	10	15,989	56	307	4,795	33	0	376	1	4	53	2	11	11	1	247	23,454
10	Nam Dinh	849	86	72	412	463	1,487	2	199	80	0	68	10	144	10	75	4	148	33	4,142
11	Ninh Binh	2,733	390	256	170	3,721	377	11	966	1	232	0	78	931	28	20	75	15	187	10,191
12	Bac Kan	770	2	6	1	104	326	10	11	2	6	20	0	146	27	1	8	61	59	1,560
13	Tuyen Quang	657	256	25	3	608	2,032	4,407	55	5	21	42	56	0	306	13	73	291	137	8,987
14	Yen Bai	1,647	1,657	1,379	77	4,647	233	5,467	86	55	36	71	106	314	0	1,201	12	108	103	17,199
15	Quang Ninh	756	3,164	228	25	4,040	7,762	479	13	0	521	4	2	84	3	0	221	4	3	17,309
16	Bac Giang	3,279	23	10,254	3	1,839	1,078	24	279	10	9	4	2	65	2	243	0	1	3	17,118
17	Phu Tho	449	7,674	982	2,944	29	985	37	278	723	21	27	47	111	11	5	85	0	25	14,433
18	Hoa Binh	9,048	153	618	6,901	398	1,086	3,344	78	102	40	39	29	248	20	207	227	10	0	22,548
	Total	191,353	36,882	48,110	82,533	42,514	44,532	38,377	14,414	11,759	10,238	11,100	1,395	10,169	4,277	15,008	25,360	7,040	9,707	604,768

Source: Data from JICA 2009.

Cargo Flows for Northern Provinces: IWT in Tons per Day

Table D.10 Northern Provinces: IWT Cargo Flows in 2008
Tons per day

		1	2	3	4	5	6	7	8	9	10	11	12	13	14	15	16	17	18	
	Origin	Hanoi	Vinh Phuc	Bac Ninh	Ha Tay	Hai Duong	Haiphong	Hung Yen	Thai Binh	Ha Nam	Nam Dinh	Ninh Binh	Bac Kan	Tuyen Quang	Yen Bai	Quang Ninh	Bac Giang	Phu Tho	Hoa Binh	Total
1	Hanoi	0	100	0	0	300	5,640	0	0	0	0	0	0	300	0	880	0	3,040	0	10,260
2	Vinh Phuc	1,430	0	0	0	0	0	1,600	2,054	850	600	0	0	0	0	590	0	30	0	7,154
3	Bac Ninh	1,200	0	0	0	0	0	0	0	0	0	0	0	0	0	0	0	0	0	1,200
4	Ha Tay	0	0	0	0	0	0	0	0	0	0	0	0	0	0	0	0	120	0	120
5	Hai Duong	49,880	0	0	5,200	0	0	2,110	3,000	0	0	550	0	0	0	7,605	0	5,860	0	74,205
6	Haiphong	4,500	0	0	350	0	0	5,950	4,426	280	0	200	0	0	0	4,050	0	5,200	738	25,694
7	Hung Yen	0	0	0	0	0	0	0	0	0	0	0	0	0	0	0	0	0	0	0
8	Thai Binh	0	0	0	0	0	0	0	0	0	500	600	0	0	0	0	0	0	0	1,100
9	Ha Nam	1,600	0	0	0	0	0	0	2,000	0	800	0	0	0	0	0	0	0	0	4,400
10	Nam Dinh	3,340	0	0	0	500	1,500	900	900	0	0	400	0	0	0	800	0	0	0	8,340
11	Ninh Binh	800	0	0	0	1,250	5,800	800	5,000	0	2,250	0	0	0	0	0	0	0	0	15,900
12	Bac Kan	0	0	0	0	0	0	0	0	0	0	0	0	0	0	0	0	0	0	0
13	Tuyen Quang	16,900	0	0	1,762	0	0	1,374	1,540	0	600	0	0	0	160	0	0	0	0	22,336
14	Yen Bai	0	0	0	0	0	0	0	0	0	0	0	0	0	0	0	0	0	0	0
15	Quang Ninh	17,400	150	14,720	4,835	15,477	560	2,980	11,060	300	11,920	8,830	0	0	0	0	2,897	14,280	0	105,409
16	Bac Giang	0	0	0	0	0	12,460	0	0	0	0	0	0	0	0	1,000	0	0	0	13,460
17	Phu Tho	11,400	300	3,010	2,570	6,319	44,110	2,100	3,488	980	1,866	0	0	50	0	7,640	0	0	0	83,833
18	Hoa Binh	0	0	0	0	0	805	0	0	0	0	0	0	0	0	400	0	0	0	1,205
	Total	108,450	550	17,730	14,717	23,846	70,875	17,814	33,468	2,410	18,536	10,580	0	350	160	22,965	2,897	28,530	738	374,616

Source: Data from JICA 2009.
Note: IWT = inland waterway transport.

Table D.11 Northern Provinces: IWT Cargo Flows in 2020
Tons per day

		1	2	3	4	5	6	7	8	9	10	11	12	13	14	15	16	17	18	
						Hai		Hung	Thai	Ha	Nam	Ninh	Bac	Tuyen	Yen	Quang	Bac	Phu	Hoa	
Origin		Hanoi	Vinh Phuc	Bac Ninh	Ha Tay	Duong	Haiphong	Yen	Binh	Nam	Dinh	Binh	Kan	Quang	Bai	Ninh	Giang	Tho	Binh	Total
1	Hanoi	0	2,226	0	6	432	23,206	15	120	4	28	99	0	333	124	708	50	4,159	43	31,553
2	Vinh Phuc	2,231	0	0	0	0	0	2,167	2,452	950	845	0	0	0	0	590	0	32	0	9,268
3	Bac Ninh	1,300	0	0	0	0	0	0	0	0	0	0	0	0	0	0	0	0	0	1,300
4	Ha Tay	214	0	0	0	3	18	1	2	1	2	3	0	0	13	195	1	123	10	584
5	Hai Duong	63,340	0	0	5,678	0	5	2,210	3,382	1	7	644	0	0	8	8,167	1	6,194	2	89,640
6	Haiphong	21,179	0	0	396	10	0	6,224	4,720	281	5	356	0	0	499	5,171	42	9,429	1,520	49,833
7	Hung Yen	89	0	0	1	17	13	0	5	2	3	21	0	0	1	14	0	1	32	196
8	Thai Binh	123	0	0	1	20	26	0	0	7	1,029	1,740	0	0	29	4	0	9	25	3,012
9	Ha Nam	3,329	0	0	0	15	4	1	2,130	0	1,023	0	0	0	2	1	0	1	6	6,511
10	Nam Dinh	5,005	0	0	3	2,938	2,677	1,533	1,168	1	0	3,030	0	0	8	817	1	6	7	17,194
11	Ninh Binh	836	0	0	0	2,319	6,936	2,037	8,070	26	6,386	0	0	0	43	20	0	12	51	26,735
12	Bac Kan	0	0	0	0	0	0	0	0	0	0	0	0	0	0	0	0	0	0	0
13	Tuyen Quang	40,128	0	0	2,241	0	0	2,490	2,169	0	1,174	0	0	0	283	0	0	0	0	48,485
14	Yen Bai	98	0	0	5	23	388	3	34	25	24	40	0	0	0	34	15	60	95	845
15	Quang Ninh	20,874	220	15,421	5,207	16,596	652	3,343	11,933	544	12,719	9,621	0	0	2	0	3,140	15,231	3	115,506
16	Bac Giang	22	0	0	1	5	14,364	0	7	1	3	2	0	0	2	1,020	0	0	1	15,426
17	Phu Tho	13,983	509	3,305	2,754	8,532	52,184	2,375	3,756	1,053	2,125	1	0	51	16	8,839	2	0	27	99,512
18	Hoa Binh	96	0	0	2	10	2,138	10	25	5	11	12	0	0	19	427	0	6	0	2,761
	Total	172,847	2,955	18,727	16,294	30,921	102,611	22,408	39,974	2,900	25,383	15,569	0	384	1,048	26,008	3,251	35,261	1,821	518,361

Source: Data from JICA 2009.
Note: IWT = inland waterway transport.

Table D.12 Northern Provinces: IWT Cargo Flows in 2030
Tons per day

		1	2	3	4	5	6	7	8	9	10	11	12	13	14	15	16	17	18	
										Destination										
	Origin	Hanoi	Vinh Phuc	Bac Ninh	Ha Tay	Hai Duong	Haiphong	Hung Yen	Thai Binh	Ha Nam	Nam Dinh	Ninh Binh	Bac Kan	Tuyen Quang	Yen Bai	Quang Ninh	Bac Giang	Phu Tho	Hoa Binh	Total
1	Hanoi	0	3,997	0	11	542	37,845	27	220	8	52	182	0	361	227	564	92	5,091	78	49,297
2	Vinh Phuc	2,898	0	0	0	0	0	2,640	2,784	1,034	1,050	0	0	0	0	590	0	34	0	11,030
3	Bac Ninh	1,384	0	0	0	0	0	0	0	0	0	0	0	0	0	0	0	0	0	1,384
4	Ha Tay	392	0	0	0	5	33	1	4	1	3	5	0	0	23	358	1	125	19	970
5	Hai Duong	74,557	0	0	6,077	0	9	2,294	3,700	1	12	723	0	0	15	8,635	2	6,473	4	102,502
6	Haiphong	35,078	0	0	435	19	0	6,452	4,965	281	9	486	0	0	915	6,106	77	12,953	2,172	69,948
7	Hung Yen	164	0	0	1	31	23	0	9	3	5	38	0	0	1	26	0	1	58	360
8	Thai Binh	226	0	0	1	36	47	0	0	13	1,469	2,690	0	0	54	8	0	16	45	4,605
9	Ha Nam	4,770	0	0	0	27	8	1	2,239	0	1,208	0	0	0	3	2	0	1	11	8,270
10	Nam Dinh	6,393	0	0	6	4,970	3,658	2,060	1,392	1	0	5,221	0	0	15	831	1	11	13	24,572
11	Ninh Binh	866	0	0	0	3,210	7,882	3,067	10,628	47	9,833	0	0	0	79	37	0	22	93	35,764
12	Bac Kan	0	0	0	0	0	0	0	0	0	0	0	0	0	0	0	0	0	0	0
13	Tuyen Quang	59,484	0	0	2,640	0	0	3,420	2,694	0	1,652	0	0	0	386	0	0	0	0	70,276
14	Yen Bai	179	0	0	9	43	712	5	63	46	44	74	0	0	0	63	21	110	175	1,550
15	Quang Ninh	23,769	278	16,006	5,517	17,529	728	3,646	12,660	748	13,385	10,280	0	0	4	0	3,343	16,023	5	123,921
16	Bac Giang	41	0	0	1	9	15,950	0	13	2	5	3	0	0	3	1,036	0	0	2	17,065
17	Phu Tho	16,135	684	3,551	2,907	10,377	58,913	2,604	3,979	1,114	2,340	2	0	52	29	9,838	3	0	49	112,577
18	Hoa Binh	176	0	0	3	18	3,249	19	46	9	21	22	0	0	34	450	0	11	0	4,058
	Total	226,512	4,959	19,557	17,608	36,816	129,057	26,236	45,396	3,308	31,088	19,726	0	413	1,788	28,544	3,546	40,871	2,724	638,149

Source: Data from JICA 2009.
Note: IWT = inland waterway transport.

Cargo Flows for Southern Provinces: Road Transport in Tons per Day

Table D.13 Southern Provinces: Road Cargo Flows in 2008

Tons per day

		Destination															
		1	2	3	4	5	6	7	8	9	10	11	12	13	14	15	
Origin		Binh Duong	Dong Nai	Ba Ria-Vung Tau	HCM	Long An	Tien Giang	Ben Tre	Tra Vinh	Vinh Long	Dong Thap	An Giang/ Kien Giang	Can Tho	Hau Giang	Soc Trang	Bac Lieu/ Ca Mau	Total
1	Binh Duong	0	10,986	21	10,470	24	149	56	91	68	121	24	1,351	375	55	72	23,863
2	Dong Nai	8,995	0	22,064	32,833	246	685	203	0	5	9	1,547	1,810	4,968	0	0	73,365
3	Ba Ria-Vung Tau	1,753	10,376	0	9,208	0	153	799	0	0	0	243	0	0	0	0	22,532
4	HCM	2,954	30,623	8,828	0	4,530	916	122	80	102	179	757	350	48	28	86	49,603
5	Long An	30	592	3	2,718	0	2,182	19	0	0	0	0	0	149	20	0	5,713
6	Tien Giang	2	473	73	717	3,972	0	0	0	0	0	0	23	14	128	0	5,402
7	Ben Tre	80	72	0	206	0	0	0	0	0	0	3	0	0	0	32	393
8	Tra Vinh	0	0	0	59	0	0	0	0	0	0	0	0	0	0	0	59
9	Vinh Long	342	270	0	177	45	0	0	0	0	0	0	574	80	45	134	1,667
10	Dong Thap	81	675	0	354	0	0	0	0	0	0	9	16	45	0	0	1,180
11	An Giang/Kien Giang	134	969	10	1,126	0	2	0	0	0	0	872	3,144	56	135	0	6,448
12	Can Tho	9	0	0	168	12	242	0	40	1,087	0	3,253	0	5,424	627	349	11,211
13	Hau Giang	0	460	0	69	0	0	0	0	15	10	0	2,707	0	0	0	3,261
14	Soc Trang	0	0	0	31	396	0	0	0	0	0	0	55	39	0	0	521
15	Bac Lieu/Ca Mau	0	2	0	100	0	110	0	0	0	0	10	221	0	0	0	443
	Total	14,380	55,498	30,999	58,236	9,225	4,439	1,199	211	1,277	319	6,718	10,251	11,198	1,038	673	205,661

Source: Data from JICA 2009.
Note: HCM = Ho Chi Minh.

Table D.14 Southern Provinces: Road Cargo Flows in 2020
Tons per day

		Destination															
		1	2	3	4	5	6	7	8	9	10	11	12	13	14	15	
Origin		Binh Duong	Dong Nai	Ba Ria-Vung Tau	HCM	Long An	Tien Giang	Ben Tre	Tra Vinh	Vinh Long	Dong Thap	An Giang/Kien Giang	Can Tho	Hau Giang	Soc Trang	Bac Lieu/Ca Mau	Total
1	Binh Duong	0	13,276	192	36,241	54	135	69	469	81	195	59	1,447	375	91	51	52,734
2	Dong Nai	14,891	0	36,815	91,192	464	2,509	570	63	119	184	3,248	3,433	6,626	169	122	160,405
3	Ba Ria-Vung Tau	2,800	11,635	0	27,592	428	267	1,009	61	3	102	314	39	10	80	49	44,388
4	HCM	19,013	76,897	26,463	0	8,919	4,865	900	1,378	471	3,019	5,176	1,947	183	743	4,197	154,170
5	Long An	50	1,434	205	7,917	0	2,806	154	18	4	38	51	20	181	53	23	12,953
6	Tien Giang	9	535	885	5,035	5,936	0	52	28	7	21	767	33	37	194	13	13,552
7	Ben Tre	83	711	55	1,988	6	35	0	45	4	14	305	7	0	58	37	3,348
8	Tra Vinh	26	10	156	1,239	17	22	130	0	12	28	54	2	59	142	81	1,978
9	Vinh Long	508	297	50	506	174	67	65	35	0	87	189	949	113	233	367	3,640
10	Dong Thap	85	763	70	1,427	22	8	3	6	11	0	265	19	48	21	14	2,763
11	An Giang/Kien Giang	366	1,235	115	3,141	13	41	31	52	25	47	2,094	5,462	112	352	36	13,121
12	Can Tho	16	5	27	1,356	40	352	26	121	1,506	11	5,088	0	7,002	1,013	617	17,180
13	Hau Giang	2	463	22	605	0	7	2	8	62	32	22	3,399	0	41	16	4,681
14	Soc Trang	22	16	158	713	632	62	111	106	15	50	197	221	121	0	180	2,604
15	Bac Lieu/Ca Mau	3	11	109	1,952	5	349	22	22	8	38	23	128	2	89	0	2,761
	Total	37,873	107,289	65,321	180,905	16,710	11,525	3,144	2,414	2,327	3,866	17,851	17,106	14,868	3,279	5,802	490,279

Source: Data from JICA 2009.

Table D.15 Southern Provinces: Road Cargo Flows in 2030
Tons per day

		Destination															
		1	2	3	4	5	6	7	8	9	10	11	12	13	14	15	
Origin		Binh Duong	Dong Nai	Ba Ria-Vung Tau	HCM	Long An	Tien Giang	Ben Tre	Tra Vinh	Vinh Long	Dong Thap	An Giang/Kien Giang	Can Tho	Hau Giang	Soc Trang	Bac Lieu/Ca Mau	Total
1	Binh Duong	0	15,184	335	57,716	79	124	79	784	92	256	88	1,527	375	121	33	76,793
2	Dong Nai	19,805	0	49,107	139,825	646	4,029	875	116	214	330	4,666	4,786	8,007	310	223	232,939
3	Ba Ria-Vung Tau	3,672	12,685	0	42,912	784	362	1,184	112	6	187	373	71	18	146	90	62,602
4	HCM	32,396	115,458	41,159	0	12,576	8,156	1,549	2,460	778	5,385	8,858	3,278	296	1,339	7,622	241,310
5	Long An	67	2,135	373	12,250	0	3,326	266	33	7	69	93	37	208	80	42	18,986
6	Tien Giang	14	586	1,561	8,634	7,573	0	95	52	12	39	1,406	42	56	249	24	20,343
7	Ben Tre	85	1,244	100	3,473	11	65	0	83	7	26	556	13	0	107	41	5,811
8	Tra Vinh	47	18	286	2,223	32	40	238	0	22	52	99	4	108	260	149	3,578
9	Vinh Long	647	320	91	780	281	123	119	64	0	160	346	1,261	141	389	562	5,284
10	Dong Thap	88	837	129	2,322	41	14	6	11	21	0	478	21	50	39	25	4,082
11	An Giang/Kien Giang	559	1,457	203	4,820	24	73	57	96	45	86	3,112	7,393	158	532	66	18,681
12	Can Tho	21	9	49	2,346	63	444	48	189	1,856	20	6,618	0	8,317	1,335	840	22,155
13	Hau Giang	3	466	40	1,051	0	12	3	15	101	51	41	3,975	0	76	30	5,864
14	Soc Trang	41	30	290	1,282	828	113	204	194	27	91	361	360	189	0	330	4,340
15	Bac Lieu/Ca Mau	6	19	200	3,495	9	549	41	40	14	70	33	51	3	163	0	4,693
	Total	57,451	150,448	93,923	283,129	22,947	17,430	4,764	4,249	3,202	6,822	27,128	22,819	17,926	5,146	10,077	727,461

Source: Data from JICA 2009.
Note: HCM = Ho Chi Minh.

Cargo Flows for Southern Provinces: IWT in Tons per Day

Table D.16 Southern Provinces: IWT Cargo Flows in 2008

Tons per day

	Origin	1 Binh Duong	2 Dong Nai	3 Ba Ria-Vung Tau	4 HCM	5 Long An	6 Tien Giang	7 Ben Tre	8 Tra Vinh	9 Vinh Long	10 Dong Thap	11 An Giang/ Kien Giang	12 Can Tho	13 Hau Giang	14 Soc Trang	15 Bac Lieu/ Ca Mau	Total
1	Binh Duong	0	0	0	0	4,800	4,800	1,500	0	0	0	0	0	0	0	0	11,100
2	Dong Nai	0	0	0	0	4,200	13,600	19,320	0	3,300	10,200	3,600	0	2,500	0	0	56,720
3	Ba Ria-Vung Tau	0	0	0	0	0	0	0	0	0	0	834	0	0	0	0	834
4	HCM	0	0	0	0	6,150	4,100	1,380	0	3,005	100	8,935	27,820	0	465	0	51,955
5	Long An	0	1,200	0	3,320	0	0	6,810	0	240	0	0	0	750	0	0	12,320
6	Tien Giang	0	0	0	1,650	0	0	569	0	0	0	108	325	250	0	15	2,917
7	Ben Tre	2,800	5,000	0	12,463	504	1,500	0	0	0	5	63	0	0	0	0	22,335
8	Tra Vinh	0	0	0	0	375	27	73	0	4	0	0	0	100	0	0	579
9	Vinh Long	0	5,952	0	15,135	0	54	284	0	0	0	56	0	5	525	0	22,011
10	Dong Thap	0	0	0	3,300	0	0	2,198	0	0	0	3,378	1,210	0	0	13	10,099
11	An Giang/Kien Giang	0	685	0	6,673	468	702	3,465	240	176	1,349	9,423	7,915	2,801	0	425	34,322
12	Can Tho	0	640	0	500	0	55	70	1,000	0	0	22,720	0	2,123	0	3,840	30,878
13	Hau Giang	0	0	0	250	1,450	225	0	0	0	0	890	0	0	0	0	2,885
14	Soc Trang	0	0	0	0	0	210	1,000	0	25	0	20	0	0	0	0	1,255
15	Bac Lieu/Ca Mau	0	0	0	0	0	0	0	0	0	0	451	2	0	0	0	453
	Total	2,800	13,477	0	43,291	17,947	25,273	36,669	1,240	6,750	11,654	50,478	37,272	8,529	990	4,293	260,663

Source: Data from JICA 2009.

Note: HCM = Ho Chi Minh; IWT = inland waterway transport.

Table D.17 Southern Provinces: IWT Cargo Flows in 2020
Tons per day

Origin		1 Binh Duong	2 Dong Nai	3 Ba Ria-Vung Tau	4 HCM	5 Long An	6 Tien Giang	7 Ben Tre	8 Tra Vinh	9 Vinh Long	10 Dong Thap	11 An Giang/Kien Giang	12 Can Tho	13 Hau Giang	14 Soc Trang	15 Bac Lieu/Ca Mau	Total
1	Binh Duong	0	11	261	131	4,863	4,823	1,645	35	8	49	159	46	0	43	74	12,148
2	Dong Nai	8	0	9,365	183	4,265	14,597	19,783	42	4,124	12,321	4,025	76	2,737	134	136	71,795
3	Ba Ria-Vung Tau	63	88	0	9,551	349	439	333	648	28	1,340	1,430	181	80	595	474	15,599
4	HCM	123	17	12,050	0	13,185	5,967	4,667	873	6,816	1,907	32,575	38,411	201	4,207	370	121,370
5	Long An	2	1,260	395	6,276	0	6	8,483	20	765	33	68	10	819	29	32	18,199
6	Tien Giang	4	3	403	5,116	1	0	1,155	12	3	30	369	363	291	43	46	7,837
7	Ben Tre	3,202	5,146	280	14,112	608	2,911	0	10	2	18	103	4	0	38	29	26,462
8	Tra Vinh	46	13	1,049	723	468	109	118	0	12	51	137	2	498	68	95	3,388
9	Vinh Long	2	8,132	99	28,620	53	81	425	37	0	18	177	14	5	751	11	38,424
10	Dong Thap	5	8	172	9,686	9	14	2,222	17	2	0	4,901	1,213	1	32	64	18,346
11	An Giang/Kien Giang	9	717	377	41,872	513	1,363	3,929	449	193	3,344	12,258	9,211	3,271	153	397	78,057
12	Can Tho	4	656	149	5,077	21	77	23	1,346	2	10	24,163	0	2,566	13	1,803	35,910
13	Hau Giang	3	3	118	1,391	2,101	1,595	103	8	4	18	901	1	0	15	21	6,283
14	Soc Trang	54	41	1,137	975	41	1,159	1,203	58	48	92	226	13	53	0	103	5,203
15	Bac Lieu/Ca Mau	9	28	385	1,688	13	25	22	25	9	79	257	10	2	35	0	2,586
	Total	3,534	16,124	26,242	125,402	26,488	33,165	44,111	3,581	12,015	19,308	81,748	49,554	10,525	6,155	3,655	461,606

Source: Data from JICA 2009.
Note: HCM = Ho Chi Minh; IWT = inland waterway transport.

Table D.18 Southern Provinces: IWT Cargo Flows in 2030
Tons per day

Origin		1 Binh Duong	2 Dong Nai	3 Ba Ria-Vung Tau	4 HCM	5 Long An	6 Tien Giang	7 Ben Tre	8 Tra Vinh	9 Vinh Long	10 Dong Thap	11 An Giang/ Kien Giang	12 Can Tho	13 Hau Giang	14 Soc Trang	15 Bac Lieu/ Ca Mau	Total
1	Binh Duong	0	21	479	240	4,915	4,843	1,766	64	15	89	291	85	0	78	136	13,022
2	Dong Nai	14	0	17,169	336	4,319	15,427	20,168	77	4,811	14,089	4,379	139	2,935	245	250	84,358
3	Ba Ria-Vung Tau	116	162	0	17,511	640	805	610	1,188	51	2,456	1,926	331	147	1,091	869	27,903
4	HCM	226	32	22,092	0	19,048	7,522	7,407	1,601	9,991	3,412	52,275	47,237	368	7,325	679	179,215
5	Long An	4	1,310	725	8,739	0	11	9,877	36	1,202	61	125	19	877	53	59	23,098
6	Tien Giang	7	6	738	8,004	1	0	1,643	22	5	55	587	395	325	78	71	11,937
7	Ben Tre	3,537	5,267	514	15,486	694	4,087	0	19	3	28	137	7	0	70	53	29,902
8	Tra Vinh	84	24	1,923	1,325	545	177	155	0	18	93	251	4	830	125	174	5,728
9	Vinh Long	3	9,948	182	39,857	97	103	542	68	0	33	277	26	5	940	21	52,102
10	Dong Thap	10	15	315	15,008	16	25	2,242	31	4	0	6,170	1,215	2	58	107	25,218
11	An Giang/Kien Giang	16	743	692	71,205	551	1,914	4,316	623	207	5,007	14,620	10,291	3,663	281	373	114,502
12	Can Tho	8	669	274	8,892	38	96	42	1,635	3	18	25,365	0	2,935	23	105	40,103
13	Hau Giang	5	6	217	2,342	2,643	2,737	130	15	8	33	911	1	0	28	38	9,114
14	Soc Trang	99	76	2,085	1,787	75	1,949	1,373	107	68	168	397	23	98	0	188	8,493
15	Bac Lieu/Ca Mau	16	51	705	3,095	24	45	41	46	17	145	95	16	3	65	0	4,364
	Total	4,145	18,330	48,110	193,827	33,606	39,741	50,312	5,532	16,403	25,687	107,806	59,789	12,188	10,460	3,123	629,059

Source: Data from JICA 2009.
Note: HCM = Ho Chi Minh; IWT = inland waterway transport.

Commodity In and Out Tables

Table D.19 Outgoing Commodities for the North Region

Tons per day

		1	2	3	4	5	6	7	8	9	10	11	12	13	
Origin		Rice	Sugar	Wood	Steel	Construction materials	Cement	Fertilizer	Coal	Petroleum	Industrial crops	Manufactured goods	Fishery products	Meats/ other	Total
1	Hanoi	5,408	3	733	1,877	26,304	3,799	1,447	4,385	2,121	81	12,734	16	9,133	68,041
2	Vinh Phuc	264	0	615	2,243	12,873	1,120	28	0	0	7	2,227	0	966	20,343
3	Bac Ninh	2,159	0	540	2,452	4,993	1,920	0	391	329	0	3,191	0	714	16,689
4	Ha Tay	4,853	130	945	1,211	13,423	2,535	212	1,266	1,324	60	3,671	60	2,145	31,835
5	Hai Duong	2,078	0	5,414	529	43,512	31,443	483	290	1,849	0	4,069	51	472	90,190
6	Haiphong	5,164	0	607	18,254	8,956	22,084	1,101	1,397	7,438	332	15,382	132	3,157	84,004
7	Hung Yen	2,884	0	133	6,373	163	0	0	230	31	0	12,465	51	6,297	28,627
8	Thai Binh	165	0	23	85	1,626	205	74	130	33	0	467	63	808	3,679
9	Ha Nam	318	0	22	1	13,534	6,611	27	748	48	0	948	0	490	22,747
10	Nam Dinh	446	0	1	28	4,348	3,500	0	560	0	0	351	20	214	9,468
11	Ninh Binh	107	0	5	32	8,226	9,091	371	1,476	56	0	166	0	344	19,874
12	Bac Kan	68	0	32	200	0	0	0	0	0	0	1	0	5	306
13	Tuyen Quang	4,157	27	136	0	22,336	0	0	0	0	0	45	0	67	26,768
14	Yen Bai	5,266	0	291	1,170	666	757	0	0	0	0	343	3	24	8,520
15	Quang Ninh	243	0	972	105	19,357	5,376	48	99,867	553	14	2,563	60	1,369	130,527
16	Bac Giang	714	0	727	222	24,068	1,046	1,814	428	33	4	1,368	0	870	31,294
17	Phu Tho	188	0	1,557	143	83,209	2,160	4,059	977	651	0	1,345	3	731	95,023
18	Hoa Binh	1,124	491	1,225	0	4,639	180	0	0	4	0	139	0	498	8,300
	Total	35,606	651	13,978	34,925	292,233	91,827	9,664	112,145	14,470	498	61,475	459	28,304	696,235

Source: Data from JICA 2009.

Table D.20 Incoming Commodities for the North Region
Tons per day

	Destination	1 Rice	2 Sugar	3 Wood	4 Steel	5 Construction materials	6 Cement	7 Fertilizer	8 Coal	9 Petroleum	10 Industrial crops	11 Manufactured goods	12 Fishery products	13 Meats/ other	Total
1	Hanoi	8,974	0	1,280	17,698	81,470	32,171	360	16,377	5,430	142	22,546	142	10,049	196,639
2	Vinh Phuc	261	0	173	154	942	4,134	2,950	835	438	30	2,223	70	1,683	13,893
3	Bac Ninh	2,730	11	800	724	30,658	2,392	653	879	312	16	3,784	0	889	43,848
4	Ha Tay	6,107	422	568	1,302	31,471	6,018	232	4,979	198	17	5,009	14	2,940	59,277
5	Hai Duong	4,460	67	191	3,477	8,049	7,474	355	16,113	692	0	2,937	70	802	44,687
6	Haiphong	4,523	13	1,308	2,331	68,922	6,537	868	3,471	2,504	45	13,669	153	3,407	107,751
7	Hung Yen	8,353	2	10	4,864	9,602	8,818	339	3,572	492	0	4,155	0	5,577	45,784
8	Thai Binh	602	5	208	1,209	18,784	7,005	275	12,476	599	20	973	0	651	42,807
9	Ha Nam	354	3	63	4	6,973	918	192	281	37	55	698	0	82	9,660
10	Nam Dinh	402	1	27	690	9,206	3,332	345	11,920	42	106	388	77	140	26,676
11	Ninh Binh	209	0	154	373	2,027	799	31	11,103	206	0	1,128	0	659	16,689
12	Bac Kan	0	0	29	0	0	38	0	15	0	0	7	0	1	90
13	Tuyen Quang	101	0	0	0	0	20	0	350	0	0	1	0	29	501
14	Yen Bai	105	0	1	0	469	85	15	80	17	4	110	4	164	1,054
15	Quang Ninh	4,580	0	8,165	18	9,927	4,619	960	71	53	271	2,175	204	935	31,978
16	Bac Giang	2,525	50	747	1,239	4,346	1,420	105	3,705	856	7	1,841	0	751	17,592
17	Phu Tho	143	0	1,082	213	12,526	2,719	694	15,473	244	8	1,058	28	304	34,492
18	Hoa Binh	1,222	130	45	0	145	773	4	1,053	351	0	56	4	366	4,149
	Total	45,651	704	14,851	34,296	295,517	89,272	8,378	102,753	12,471	721	62,758	766	29,429	697,567

Source: Data from JICA 2009.

Table D.21 Outgoing Commodities for the South Region
Tons per day

	Origin	Commodities													Total
		1 Rice	2 Sugar	3 Wood	4 Steel	5 Construction materials	6 Cement	7 Fertilizer	8 Coal	9 Petroleum	10 Industrial crops	11 Manufactured goods	12 Fishery products	13 Meats/other	
1	Binh Duong	2,240	2	1,258	121	13,858	0	4,803	1	18	212	23,521	13	2,000	48,047
2	Dong Nai	17,242	1,340	1,581	118	45,946	132	6,001	91	6,476	76	48,507	3,210	2,808	133,528
3	Ba Ria-Vung Tau	2,132	0	110	44	6,588	742	10	409	3,305	459	15,130	283	977	30,189
4	HCM	9,406	464	1,355	3,651	34,055	1,628	16,160	769	15,207	169	25,009	8,853	15,950	132,676
5	Long An	5,545	0	1,506	422	7,263	31	600	2	32	32	1,286	1,296	1,077	19,092
6	Tien Giang	9,130	0	340	559	904	900	23	19	586	0	457	679	1,305	14,902
7	Ben Tre	9,323	0	99	0	9,705	14	0	0	0	13	303	43	3,312	22,812
8	Tra Vinh	29	0	0	0	523	0	0	0	0	0	14	45	27	638
9	Vinh Long	1,713	3,880	250	30	16,378	0	405	26	245	0	764	98	159	23,948
10	Dong Thap	3,554	45	50	140	3,736	4	1,608	1	0	1,748	208	23	300	11,417
11	An Giang/Kien Giang	5,205	13	987	41	24,876	3,368	173	470	1,943	819	914	1,991	1,396	42,196
12	Can Tho	3,011	274	195	576	29,125	368	88	272	545	0	1,857	14	6,732	43,057
13	Hau Giang	1,339	0	0	0	995	0	0	0	0	0	645	1,542	1,757	6,278
14	Soc Trang	385	0	0	0	1,235	0	0	20	0	0	6	0	130	1,776
15	Bac Lieu/ Ca Mau	434	0	26	7	0	0	0	0	220	0	20	135	81	923
	Total	70,688	6,018	7,757	5,709	195,187	7,187	29,871	2,080	28,577	3,528	118,641	18,225	38,011	531,479

Source: Data from JICA 2009.
Note: HCM = Ho Chi Minh.

Table D.22 Incoming Commodities for the South Region

Tons per day

	Destination	1 Rice	2 Sugar	3 Wood	4 Steel	5 Construction materials	6 Cement	7 Fertilizer	8 Coal	9 Petroleum	10 Industrial crops	11 Manufactured goods	12 Fishery products	13 Meats/other	Total
1	Binh Duong	724	517	773	1,255	3,731	21	511	2	48	110	8,693	0	3,765	20,150
2	Dong Nai	4,335	1,139	2,017	1,462	21,308	592	2	1,584	3,718	81	30,660	3,654	4,267	74,819
3	Ba Ria-Vung Tau	256	450	78	0	341	273	0	91	6,213	86	15,608	114	8,073	31,583
4	HCM	23,525	4,027	522	856	38,188	5,878	1,438	3,354	4,535	3,014	34,614	734	8,343	129,028
5	Long An	3,282	0	529	1,222	12,712	1,066	1,578	3	2,349	32	2,953	354	1,689	27,769
6	Tien Giang	11,081	14	140	193	7,778	112	8,578	331	234	300	729	71	728	30,289
7	Ben Tre	3,072	0	1,692	5	24,477	507	7,000	0	222	0	746	62	101	37,884
8	Tra Vinh	91	0	0	40	1,000	270	0	0	40	0	10	0	0	1,451
9	Vinh Long	5,513	900	189	210	788	0	0	0	16	160	640	0	0	8,416
10	Dong Thap	1,021	12	3	33	10,227	0	109	10	4	182	165	136	75	11,977
11	An Giang/Kien Giang	5,129	54	102	652	28,835	1,364	3,198	882	272	974	2,718	7,536	5,750	57,466
12	Can Tho	2,553	1	9	93	26,294	1,903	5,976	763	587	164	4,068	4,236	3,486	50,133
13	Hau Giang	1,609	265	0	531	9,579	220	59	0	338	0	5,934	0	1,381	19,916
14	Soc Trang	134	0	0	0	489	0	405	0	135	0	189	52	642	2,046
15	Bac Lieu/Ca Mau	322	0	46	10	4,292	133	0	0	0	0	116	9	298	5,226
	Total	62,647	7,379	6,100	6,562	190,039	12,339	28,854	7,020	18,711	5,103	107,843	16,958	38,598	508,153

Source: Data from JICA 2009.
Note: HCM = Ho Chi Minh.

For 2020, detailed data was only available broken down by commodity type, but not by transport mode or by province. Therefore, these data were obtained by interpolation of the more granular 2008 and 2030 data.

The main waterway transport regions addressed by the report are the Red River Delta, the Mekong River Delta, and the North-South axis. Cargo flows concern 18 provinces in the Red River Delta and 15 provinces in the Mekong River Delta. Within these provinces' freight transport mix the modal shares of road transport and IWT overwhelmingly dominate, such that the incidence of other transport modes (coastal shipping, air, and rail transport) can be safely disregarded for analytical purposes. Information about the breakdown of transported cargo by commodity type is provided for 13 commodities and is available only at the level of incoming and outgoing flows per province, but not at the level of origin-destination pairs (i.e., commodity specific flow data by O-D pair is not known). This implies that any modal split analysis and the application of modal split models can be done at an aggregate freight volume level only, disregarding behavioral differences between commodity groups (e.g., the fact that some commodity groups are more time- or cost-sensitive than others, etc.) and instead applying average sensitivity factors across all commodities. Because of the quick-scan character of the present analysis (compared with detailed feasibility studies), this was considered sufficient.

Design of the Logit Model Using VITRANSS and Other Data

Principles of a Logit Model

The proposed modal split model is a multinomial logit model, specified as follows.

The probability of a shipper choosing a given mode m among all available modes can be expressed as

$$P_m(m = r \mid r = 1 \ldots M) = \frac{e^{U_m}}{\sum_{r=1}^{r=m} e^{U_r}} \qquad (1)$$

where
P_m: probability of choosing mode m from all possible modes $r = 1, \ldots, M$
U_m: the "utility" attached to a given mode-specific route m
m: index operator representing a shipper's available modal options

The probability function P_m in equation (1) applies to all cargo flows transported between a given origin o [$o = 1, \ldots, O$] and a given destination d [$d = 1, \ldots, D$] (where o and d may refer, for example, to a pair of Vietnamese provinces). For simplicity, index differentiators for provinces o and d in equation (1) have been omitted.

The Utility Function

The value that shippers and receivers in a given origin-destination freight itinerary combination attach to transport mode m is represented by a "utility function."[1] Utility can be expressed, as will be done here, as a linear combination of mode-specific characteristics believed to determine shippers' choice among available modes, as follows:

$$U_m = \alpha_{0m} D_m + \alpha_{1m} C_m + \alpha_{2m} T_m + \alpha_{3m} F_m + \alpha_{4m} R_m \qquad (2)$$

where

C_m: Shipping costs for mode m, inclusive of freight rate, handling charges, land transport costs, and other ancillary costs
T_m: Transit time for mode m
F_m: Frequency of service for mode m
R_m: Reliability of service for mode m (defined as the standard deviation of transit time)
D_m: Binary variable that can only take the value of 0 or 1, used to capture all other mode-specific characteristics other than transit time, service frequency, and service reliability[2]

In equation (2), $[\alpha_{0m}, \alpha_{1m}, \alpha_{2m}, \alpha_{3m}, \alpha_{4m}]$ is a vector of unknown population coefficients in the utility function whose value can be estimated. The vector of explanatory variables $[D_m, C_m, T_m, F_m,$ and $R_m]$, which describes the operating attractiveness of mode m, is referred to as the vector of modal attributes.[3]

Relative Position among Modes

The utility position of a transport mode relative to a competing one can be assessed on the basis of the ratio of the likelihood of the mode of interest being chosen over another mode. For example, one can consider the ratio of the probability that a shipper located in region d, and wishing to source freight from region o, chooses mode $k = m$ against the probability that she chooses a competing mode $k = n$, where m and k may refer to, for example, IWT and road transport. Substituting m and n in equation (1), dividing the resulting equations, and using simple algebra it is possible to arrive at the desired likelihood ratio:

$$P_m/P_n = e^{U_m}/e^{U_n} = e^{U_m - U_n}. \qquad (3)$$

Equation (3) establishes that the ratio of modal choice probabilities between modes m and n is a function of the differences between each mode's vector of attributes. Assuming a shipper attaches the same utility level to modes m and n (a result that could be obtained if, for example, they both shared the same attributes), the probability for the shipper to choose m or n to complete a given freight itinerary would be exactly the same. Or, put differently, the difference between the utility functions U_m and U_n would be zero, leading to a value of the odds ratio P_m/P_n of exactly 1, implying an equal modal share between these (equally desirable) modes.

If, on the other hand, measurements indicated that modes m and n possessed unique attribute vectors, one would expect the modal shares for these modes to be different. If, for example, a shipper attached a higher utility to mode m than to mode n in such a way that the difference between the utility functions U_m and U_n equaled, for example, 0.5 (as opposed to zero in the previous example), the right-hand side of equation (3) would yield $e^{0.5} = 1.65$, implying that the market share of mode m would be $1.65 / (1.65 + 1) = 62\%$, instead of 50% (and assuming only m and n were the transport modes available to the shipper).

As noted earlier, while available modes for Vietnam-based freight shippers include over-the-road trucking, rail, waterway barge, coastal shipping, and air freight, the domestic freight system is largely dominated by two modes: over-the-road trucking and waterway barge transport.

Taking the natural logarithm of both sides of equation (3), the modal choice relationship between modes m and n becomes a linear function of the difference in modal attributes (cost, time, reliability, service frequency, and value-added services), as shown in equation (4):

$$\ln(P_m/P_n) = U_m - U_n = \alpha_{0m}(D_m - D_n) + \alpha_{1m}(C_m - C_n) \\ + \alpha_{2m}(T_m - T_n) + \alpha_{3m}(F_m - F_n) \quad (4)$$

where the values of $[\alpha_{0m}, \alpha_{1m}, \alpha_{2m}, \alpha_{3m}]$ can be estimated by linear regression. Equation (4) is referred to in the literature as a logit model.

Estimation of Regression Coefficients

The coefficients in equation (4) are best estimated on the basis of actual choices made by shippers in interprovincial and interregional freight itineraries in Vietnam. Statistical data on such "revealed" choices are known as revealed preference (RP) data. Alternatively, logit model coefficients can be based on "stated preference" (SP), defined as the set of choices decision makers claim they would make when asked about hypothetical choice situations (e.g., through a survey tool). While RP data have the key advantage of representing true choices, they are often not regularly collected, particularly in developing country settings, because of the cost and complexity of measurement. SP data, on the other hand, are relatively easy to collect and may be the only viable source of information when RP data are not available.

In a typical SP interview, decision makers are faced with various hypothetical situations and asked which situation they consider to be most desirable. Decision makers may be given several choices and then asked to rank each in order of increasing preference ("ranking of preferences"). They also may describe to what extent they find option A better than option B according to a scale varying from 0 to 1 ("scaling of preferences").

Figure D.1 Options to Estimate the Parameters of a Logit Model

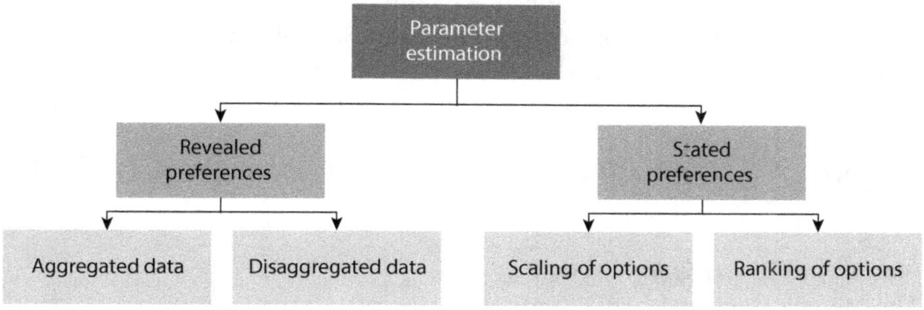

```
                      Parameter
                      estimation
                  /              \
            Revealed           Stated
          preferences       preferences
           /      \           /        \
   Aggregated  Disaggregated  Scaling of  Ranking of
      data        data         options     options
```

Source: Ecorys.

Aggregate and Disaggregate Data

When working with RP data, a distinction is made between aggregate and disaggregate data. Data based on information from individual decision makers, such as firms, are known as disaggregate data. Data based on aggregates of individuals, such as averages of regions or zones, are referred to as aggregate data. Both these data types can inform the regression analysis to determine the relation between modal market shares and the average value of the explanatory variables in the logit equation.

The use of aggregate data implies that information is inevitably lost through aggregation and averaging of the explanatory variables. The advantage, however, is that when the estimated logit parameters are used for prediction purposes at some meaningful aggregation level, no further aggregation of the results is necessary. With disaggregate data, on the other hand, the coefficient values may be more accurate at the microlevel, but some accuracy may be lost when the values are used for prediction purposes, as they have to be aggregated and averaged.

Figure D.1 summarizes the above-discussed options to estimate logit model parameters.

The Modal Split Model as Developed in This Report

A modal split logit model has been developed to analyze modal shift impacts of public sector infrastructure and policy interventions in the Red River Delta, the Mekong River Delta, and the North-South trade linking these two regions. Based on aggregate data at the province-to-province level, the model quantifies shifts between modes as a result of changes in the determining factors that drive modal choice.

The modal shift impacts that are assessed with the help of the modal split model specifically concern shifts between IWT and road transport and, solely in the case of the North-South axis, between road and containerized coastal shipping. The basic equation of the modal split model represents the relation between the ratio of cargo flows by IWT (F_{iwt}) and road (F_{road}) and the differences in transport costs (C), transit times (T), and quality-of-service aspects (Q) between these modes. The functional form of the model expresses the natural logarithm of the ratio of flows by mode (on the left-hand side) as a linear function of the corresponding differences of modal split determining factors (on the right-hand side):

$$\text{Ln}(F_{iwt}/F_{road}) = a_0 + a_1(C_{iwt} - C_{road}) + a_2(T_{iwt} - T_{road}) + a_3(Q_{iwt} - Q_{road}). \quad (5)$$

Modal Split Determining Factors

The literature on modal split applications for freight transportation has consistently found that the main factors that determine modal choice include transport costs (expressed as transport tariffs), transit times, the interarrival time between consecutive sailings in the case of scheduled waterborne transport, schedule reliability, and risk of cargo shrinkage (e.g., damage or pilferage en route). See, for instance, the handbooks by Ortuzar and Willumsen (1990) and Henscher and Button (2000). In Vietnam, regulated tariffs were abandoned in 1995, and prices have since been determined by market forces. As a result, the operating costs incurred by transport service providers, such as IWT carriers, trucking companies, and containership operators, play a dominant role in determining the tariff shippers ultimately pay. It is these operating costs that are therefore the basis for the estimation of transport costs used in the modal split model discussed below.

Transport costs depend mainly on transport distance, the size of the vehicle/ship, the load factor, fuel consumption (which is determined by the engine power in combination with vehicle/vessel speed), and the cost of loading and unloading. Transit times can be derived in a similar way as transport costs, including a fixed and distance-dependent component. Distance tables for IWT and road transport are shown in tables D.1–D.22.

Inland waterway operating costs of self-propelled barges are modeled as comprising a fixed amount of an estimated $2 per ton for loading and unloading and a variable amount per ton-kilometer (ton-km) of cargo carried, varying from $0.064 for 50-ton barges (Class 5) to $0.016 for 700-ton barges (Class 1) (table D.23). These figures have been calculated using fleet operational data from VITRANSS-2, complemented by in-country interviews with IWT operators. Additional assumptions, also based on interviews with cargo operators, concern load factors and sailing speeds. The average load factor for self-propelled barges is estimated to be 45 percent, implying that vessels typically sail one way empty

Table D.23 Main Performance Indicators of IWT Vessels in Vietnam

Vietnam ship class	5	4	3	2	1
Ship capacity in tons	50	100	300	500	700
Cost per cargo ton-km	0.0640	0.0410	0.0220	0.0180	0.0160
CO_2 per vehicle/km	0.1531	0.1108	0.0662	0.0521	0.0444

Source: Ecorys.
Note: IWT = inland waterway transport.

and one way loaded up to 90 percent. This is considered realistic because volume/weight ratios of IWT-intensive commodities limit the load factor that can be realized. The average sailing speed of all ships is estimated at 9 kilometers/hour (where the design speed of IWT vessels is typically 10 kilometers/hour).

An example of the resulting transport costs per trade is given in table D.24 for the O-D pairs of Corridor 1 in the Red River Delta. The type of ship employed was ship size Class 2, with an average load capacity of 500 tons. A corresponding table of road costs is based on a truck weighing 15 tons and with a 50 percent load factor (as confirmed by in-country stakeholder interview data).

Similarly, transit times can be assessed per O-D pair based on an average sailing speed of 9 kilometers/hour equal for all size classes (see table D.25). For road transport, the average speed of trucks is assumed to be 40 kilometers/hour, as consistently corroborated in interviews with road transport carriers.

Equivalent tables to tables D.24 and D.25 can be obtained for all corridors of interest in both the Red River and Mekong River deltas and, as far as trucking costs are concerned, also for the North-South axis.

Differences in IWT transport costs between the deltas stem from the average size of the vessels deployed: IWT vessels operating in the Mekong Delta tend on average to be smaller than those in the Red River Delta, which is explained by the lower waterway classes found in the South region (including a widespread network of smaller canals), along with the larger involvement of smaller private operators that have launched services with small ships. For this analysis, it was assumed that Class 2 vessels (500 tons) are used for Corridor 1 in the Red River Delta and Class 3 (300 tons) for the corridors in the Mekong River Delta.

Table D.24 Example of Road and IWT Shipping Costs per O-D Pair for Corridor 1

	Hanoi	Vinh Phuc	Bac Ninh	Hai Duong	Haiphong	Quang Ninh	Phu Tho
IWT cost ($/ton)							
Hanoi	n.a.	2.8	4.0	3.9	4.5	5.2	3.3
Vinh Phuc	2.8	n.a.	4.4	4.2	4.9	5.6	2.5
Bac Ninh	4.0	4.4	n.a.	3.2	3.9	4.6	4.9
Hai Duong	3.9	4.2	3.2	n.a.	3.8	4.5	4.7
Haiphong	4.5	4.9	3.9	3.8	n.a.	2.7	5.4
Quang Ninh	5.2	5.6	4.6	4.5	2.7	n.a.	6.1
Phu Tho	3.3	2.5	4.9	4.7	5.4	6.1	n.a.
Road cost ($/ton)							
Hanoi	n.a.	9.0	5.2	11.0	20.3	26.2	12.9
Vinh Phuc	9.0	n.a.	11.3	18.9	28.2	32.2	5.0
Bac Ninh	5.2	11.3	n.a.	12.0	20.6	22.7	15.3
Hai Duong	11.0	18.9	12.0	n.a.	10.3	18.8	22.9
Haiphong	20.3	28.2	20.6	10.3	n.a.	11.0	32.2
Quang Ninh	26.1	32.2	22.7	18.8	11.0	n.a.	36.1
Phu Tho	12.9	5.0	15.3	22.9	32.2	36.2	n.a.

Source: Ecorys.
Note: Rows refer to province of origin and columns refer to province of destination; O-D = origin-destination; IWT = inland waterway transport; n.a. = not applicable.

Table D.25 **Example of Road and IWT Transit Times per O-D Pair for Corridor 1**

	Hanoi	Vinh Phuc	Bac Ninh	Hai Duong	Haiphong	Quang Ninh	Phu Tho
IWT (hours)							
Hanoi	n.a.	28.9	36.3	35.7	39.8	44.2	32.0
Vinh Phuc	28.9	n.a.	38.8	38.1	42.2	46.7	27.1
Bac Ninh	36.3	38.8	n.a.	31.8	35.7	40.3	41.9
Hai Duong	35.7	38.1	31.8	n.a.	35.2	39.7	41.2
Haiphong	39.8	42.2	35.7	35.2	n.a.	28.4	45.3
Quang Ninh	44.2	46.7	40.3	39.7	28.4	n.a.	49.8
Phu Tho	32.0	27.1	41.9	41.2	45.3	49.8	n.a.
Road (hours)							
Hanoi	n.a.	13.1	12.6	13.4	14.6	15.4	13.6
Vinh Phuc	13.1	n.a.	13.4	14.4	15.7	16.3	12.5
Bac Ninh	12.6	13.4	n.a.	13.5	14.7	15.0	14.0
Hai Duong	13.4	14.4	13.5	n.a.	13.3	14.4	15.0
Haiphong	14.6	15.7	14.7	13.3	n.a.	13.4	16.3
Quang Ninh	15.4	16.3	15.0	14.4	13.4	n.a.	16.8
Phu Tho	13.6	12.5	14.0	15.0	16.3	16.8	n.a.

Source: Ecorys.
Note: Rows refer to province of origin and columns refer to province of destination; O-D = origin-destination; IWT = inland waterway transport; n.a. = not applicable.

Interregional differences also apply to trucks deployed, with smaller vehicles used in the Mekong Delta compared with the Red River Delta, on average. Based on testimony from stakeholder interviews, 15-ton trucks for the Red River Delta and 10-ton trucks for the Mekong River Delta are the norm, and this is what has been assumed here. Unlike transport costs, transit times are not affected by differences in truck and barge sizes because the operational speed is the same across vehicle classes.

For the North-South axis, road transport costs reflect a somewhat higher average load factor of 75 percent for 15-ton trucks (carrying one 40-foot or two 20-foot containers), as indicated by carriers and consistent with experience elsewhere in the world, where load factors tend to be better optimized for long-haul shipments in general and for containerized transport in particular. Moreover, transport costs of coastal shipping for containerships ranging in size from 400 to 2,000 20-foot equivalent units (TEUs) have been assessed; these are the sizes typically seen in coastal container trades and correspond with a range of 7,200–36,000 deadweight tons (DWT). At present, container ships deployed in Vietnam carry second-hand tonnage in the range of 600–1,100 TEUs, with an average of about 800 TEUs (figures based on Vinalines vessel movement data). These ships are mainly involved in two-port round trips with Ho Chi Minh (HCMC) and Haiphong as ports of call. Sometimes calls are made at Da Nang on the northbound leg of a round trip. Very occasionally calls are also made at Phy To and Can Tho in the South region and Quang Ninh in the North region, utilizing ships of smaller size classes.

Table D.26 Summary of Shipping Costs and Operational Data of Containerships

Ship size (DWT)	Ship capacity (TEU)	Shipping cost ($/ton)	Transit time (days)	Matching time (days)	Bunker Ton per vehicle mile
7,200	400	29.1	4	4	0.043
10,800	600	27.0	4	4	0.059
14,400	800	25.7	4	4	0.073
18,000	1,000	24.8	4	4	0.087
21,600	1,200	24.1	4	4	0.100
25,200	1,400	23.6	4	4	0.112
28,800	1,600	23.1	4	4	0.124
32,400	1,800	22.7	4	4	0.136
36,000	2,000	22.4	4	4	0.147

Source: Ecorys.
Note: DWT = dead weight tonnage; TEU = 20-foot equivalent unit.

The costs of container transport between the ports of Haiphong in the North region and HCMC in the South region, including the cost of loading and unloading, are given in table D.26 and range from $29.1 per ton for a 400 TEU ship to $22.4 per ton for a 2,000 TEU ship. The ports of call on the round trips all face problems with sailing draft. Hence interventions that intend to increase the accessibility of ports would impact the scale of vessels deployed, resulting in lower transport costs.

Testing a Modal Split Model for the Red River and Mekong River Deltas

The logit model can be tested for the choice between IWT and truck transport for both delta regions. Transport costs of IWT vessels and trucks can be used to explain the modal split according to equation (1). As stated, the cargo flows by mode of transport cannot be split further by commodity type, which makes it impossible to distinguish between high and low value freight or to include commodity-specific explanatory variables. This leads to some degree of averaging that, as explained above, is considered sufficient for the type preliminary assessment conducted by this study.

Quality-of-service aspects with respect to scheduled services may result in Mohring effects, which can be understood as the opposite of congestion costs: Higher transport volumes lead to higher frequency of service, thereby lowering shippers' storage costs. The higher the transport volumes, the higher the frequency of service and the greater the Mohring effects. The marginal increase in Mohring effects reduces with the increase of frequency and is worked out at high volumes of transport. To reflect this, the logarithm of the total volume has been used. It should be noted that for the (mainly bulk) industrial cargo carried by IWT, the impact of Mohring effects may be limited, while for coastal shipping services, which comprise liner shipping services with high service frequency (of about 12 weekly services), the Mohring effect has already been captured in the current service level, and additional frequency growth will not add any significant value. To reflect this, an index equal to the logarithm of the total cargo volume has been applied.

Three models were tested: (1) transport costs only, (2) transport costs and Mohring effects, and (3) transport costs, transit times, and Mohring effects. Based on R^2 and t values, the results of these tests were disappointing. In all three cases, the cost variable had the right negative sign, but the value of the coefficient did not differ significantly from zero. The time variable was statistically significant but had the wrong sign, and the Mohring variable in both cases had the wrong (negative) sign. Such results are attributed to the limited level of data granularity as available for the sectors under analysis. Accordingly, a different approach was considered to derive logit model coefficients applicable to the Vietnam case.

The Coefficients Applied

Literature on modal split for IWT is scarce, including as it relates to modal split coefficients. In the practice of transport planning in the Netherlands, price demand elasticities have been applied to assess the impact of a price increase of a mode of transport on demand for this mode (see Van den Bossche et al. 2005). The elasticities of demand are obtained at an aggregate level and based on a review of past studies, which are not based on modal split models of IWT. Lobe (2002) studied modal splits on some freight corridors in Western Europe (some of them including IWT) with SP-based analysis, but without an assessment of statistical fit.

Nevertheless, the results of two in-depth studies on the modal split of land transport versus maritime transport have been published recently. The first, by Brooks et al. (2011), considers the competition between rail and coastal shipping transportation in Australia. The choice determining factors for that study included freight rates, transit times, and schedule reliability. The resulting coefficient for the freight rate, after correcting for the exchange rate and tons per container, was −0.3 for rates expressed in dollars per ton. Similarly, Feo Valero et al. (2010) give results for the modal split of road compared with rail transportation for the inland leg of maritime transport itineraries. They used transport cost, transport time, reliability of service, and frequency of service as explanatory variables. After correcting for exchange rates and tons per container, a coefficient value of transport costs of −0.22, where transport costs are expressed in dollars per ton, was obtained.

For the analysis of the impact of price changes on the modal split, this report relies on the outcome of the above described studies. Specifically, a value of −0.26, which lies between the −0.3 and −0.22 coefficients found in the literature, is used. It can be argued that, given that Vietnam is a lower-middle-income country rather than an industrialized nation, different coefficient values should apply. For example, one could argue that a relative scarcity of capital and less availability and production of consumer goods would lead to higher demand elasticities, and therefore to a higher absolute value of the split coefficient. Conversely, however, it could also be argued that a lower sophistication of logistic services would lead to a slower modal shift response to cost changes, implying a lower split coefficient in absolute value. Both arguments are speculative. It was therefore decided that the choice of the above coefficient (−0.26) was appropriate. The policy and infrastructure provision interventions that the modal split model assesses all lead (or are designed to lead) to cost reductions. Therefore, other (non-cost-related) coefficients were deemed unnecessary for this analytical application. The use of a single coefficient has the added advantage of lending simplicity to the model, while it is observed that, as confirmed in the literature, the marginal benefit of including additional coefficients in the modal split equation other than transport costs is limited.

The Impact of Lower Transport Costs on Modal Split

Modal Competition in the Red River and Mekong River Deltas

For each of the delta areas an assessment was made of the impact of interventions that reduce IWT and coastal shipping transport costs on the modal split of the interventions' freight catchment areas (e.g., specific sets of O-D pairs). For illustration purposes, an example is given below of changes in the modal split of a single O-D pair along Corridor 1 of the Red River Delta as a result of a hypothetical package of measures leading to a one-class increase in the average size of vessels deployed on the corridor, from 500 tons (Class 2) to 700 tons (Class 1).

The cargo flows by IWT and road transport of Table 2.4 reflect the situation where competition takes place between IWT ships of (on average) a Class 2 of 500 tons and trucks of 15 tons, both with an operational performance as described in the text. Assuming that a set of measures is introduced resulting in the average vessel size increasing from Class 2 to Class 1, the baseline IWT transport costs (upper panel of table D.24) would be reduced to the levels given in table D.27.

Comparing tables D.24 and D.27 reveals that the implementation of such an intervention would lead to a reduction in barge transport costs, for instance, for cargo carried from Hanoi to Haiphong, from $4.5 to $4.2 per ton, a reduction of $0.3 per ton. The existing ratio of transported volumes by IWT to volumes by road on this particular O-D pair (see table 2.8) is 5,640/2,200 = 2.564, or in logarithm form 0.942. The reduction in costs of IWT leads to a change in the

Table D.27 IWT Shipping Costs per O-D Pair at Corridor 1 for Class 1 Vessels
U.S. dollars per ton transported

	Hanoi	Vinh Phuc	Bac Ninh	Hai Duong	Haiphong	Quang Ninh	Phu Tho
Hanoi	n.a.	2.7	3.7	3.6	4.2	4.8	3.1
Vinh Phuc	2.7	n.a.	4.1	4.0	4.6	5.2	2.4
Bac Ninh	3.7	4.1	n.a.	3.1	3.6	4.3	4.5
Hai Duong	3.6	4.0	3.1	n.a.	3.6	4.2	4.4
Haiphong	4.2	4.6	3.6	3.6	n.a.	2.6	5.0
Quang Ninh	4.8	5.2	4.3	4.2	2.6	n.a.	5.6
Phu Tho	3.1	2.4	4.5	4.4	5.0	5.6	n.a.

Source: Ecorys.
Note: Rows refer to origins, and columns refer to destinations; IWT = inland waterway transport; O-D = origin-destination; n.a. = not applicable.

ratio of flows as expressed in equation (5). The right-hand side of equation (5) increases by $a_1 \times -0.3 = -0.26 \times -0.3 = 0.078$. The ratio on the left-hand side is thus increases to $(0.942 + 0.078) = 1.02$. Since the latter is expressed in logarithm form, to get to the desired ratio one must calculate $\exp(1.02) = 2.772$, which is the new ratio of IWT flows relative to road flows. Given a total volume sum (IWT and road traffic) of $5,640 + 2,200 = 7,840$, and assuming total volumes transported do not change because of the corridor improvement, the new ratio leads to a demand flow by IWT of 5,761 tons per day, compared to 2,079 tons per day by road, and to an increase in the share of IWT relative to road transport on the same O-D pair.

When the above exercise is applied to all O-D pairs in the various corridors of both delta regions, and for the target years 2020 and 2030, an estimate is obtained of the impact of a one-class increase in average ship sizes on total IWT freight volumes. The results, for illustrative purposes only, are shown in tables D.28 and D.29.

The modest estimated gains in IWT volumes can be explained by the fact that on most O-D pairs the volume captured by one mode is often significantly higher or lower than that of the other mode. In other words, on any given O-D pair, either road transport or IWT tends to be dominant. The impact of cost changes then takes place either at the high or low area of the logit curve and not in the middle, where the curve is steep. This implies that, in the case of high

Table D.28 IWT Volumes for the Red River Delta with and without a One-Class Increase in Ship Size
Tons per day

	Corridor 1			Corridor 2			Corridor 3		
	Without	With	% Δ	Without	With	% Δ	Without	With	% Δ
2008	225,671	226,819	0.5%	19,890	20,000	0.6%	62,176	62,922	1.2%
2020	304,726	307,306	0.9	37,858	38,224	1.0	81,096	82,261	1.4
2030	370,606	374,229	1.0	52,832	53,375	1.0	96,862	98,359	1.5

Source: Ecorys.
Note: IWT = inland waterway transport.

Table D.29 IWT Volumes Mekong River Delta with and without a One-Class Increase in Ship Size
Tons per day

	Corridor 1			Corridor 2		
	Without	With	% Δ	Without	With	% Δ
2008	115,810	117,074	1.1%	23,452	23,617	0.7%
2020	231,839	236,375	2.0	45,961	47,711	3.8
2030	328,529	335,696	2.2	64,719	67,705	4.6

Source: Ecorys.
Note: IWT = inland waterway transport.

volumes of IWT relative to the roads, there is little potential for further share gains, while in the case of low volumes of IWT relative to roads, the base of the increase is small.

Impact of Increase in Port Improvements for the North-South Axis

On the North-South axis, the report assesses the competition between containerizable cargo carried by road between the provinces in the Red River Delta and the provinces in the Mekong River Delta. On this corridor, cargo can be carried by road from origin to destination in 15-ton trucks, or transported by short sea vessel between the seaports of Haiphong and HCMC combined with a truck drayage haul at each end of the coastal shipping itinerary.

The costs of container shipping between the North and South regions, given for a range of vessel sizes in table D.26, can be reduced by deploying larger ships. At present, the size of ships is on average about 800 TEUs, so that an increase in ship size from 800 to 1,000 TEUs would lead to a reduction in transport costs from $25.7 to $24.8 per ton, which is a reduction of $0.91 per ton. However, nearly half of these costs are terminal handling charges. The total cost per TEU, from quay to quay, for an 800-TEU ship is $371, including $182 of terminal handling charges for loading and unloading of containers. As such, measures to reduce terminal handling charges can be particularly effective at improving the overall cost attractiveness of coastal shipping relative to over-the-road transport. For example, an increase in cargo-handling efficiency that led to a reduction of terminal handling charges of 10 percent, or $18.2 per TEU, would result in a reduction in overall transport costs on the coastal route of $1.82 per ton.

To illustrate the impact of container-handling cost reductions on this corridor, one may start by assessing the traffic of a single O-D pair; for example, that between the provinces of Hanoi in the North region and Binh Duong in the South region. The volume shipped by road on this O-D pair, in both directions, was 214 tons per day in 2008, whereas 384 tons per day were transported by coastal shipping. This gives a coastal-road ratio of 1.794. A reduction in transport costs for coastal shipping of $1.82 per ton would lead to a change in the ratio of flows as expressed in equation (5). Specifically, the right-hand side of equation (5) changes by $a_1 \times -1.82 = -0.26 \times -1.82 = 0.473$. Recalling that the ratio of interest on the left-hand side of equation (5) is expressed in logarithm form, the new ratio is obtained by multiplying the old ratio [1.794] by $\exp(0.473) = 2.88$. Given total daily tonnage of 214 + 384 = 598 on this O-D pair, the new ratio leads to a flow by coastal shipping of 444 and by road of 154. Application of this formula to all O-D pairs in the corridor leads to an increase in coastal shipping volumes, under this hypothetical intervention, of 6.8 percent and a decrease in road volumes by 13.7 percent. The resulting volume changes are given in table D.30.

The remainder of this section presents detailed input tables used for the modal split model. They include detailed assumptions on operational costs for IWT, road transport, and coastal shipping.

Table D.30 Estimated Impact of a Hypothetical 10 Percent Decrease in Terminal Handling Charges on the Modal Split of the North-South Trade

Mode	Without cost change	With cost change	%Δ
Road	10,965	9,459	−13.7%
Coastal	22,208	23,714	6.8%
Total	33,173	33,173	0.0%

Source: Ecorys.

Maritime Transport Costs and Time

The container ships deployed between Northern and Southern Vietnam range in size from about 600–1,200 TEUs. Many of these ships carry second-hand tonnage. The cost calculations presented here are derived from Veldman (2011), with data on container shipping in Vietnam based on discussions with Vinalines officials. The data are for conditions in 2008.

Data on costs and operational performance of container services are expressed as a function of the particulars of the ships and their operational environment. The ship particulars include the following:

- Ship size in deadweight and TEU capacity
- Design and operational vessel speed in knots and
- Main engine capacity and fuel consumption

The information is modeled in such a way that by changing ship size and speed the corresponding costs and operational data are adapted simultaneously by using broad statistical relationships estimated with 2008 data from Lloyd's/Fairplay.

The price of a container ship can be expressed as a function of vessel size (S), as given by its TEU carrying capacity, and its design sailing speed (V), in knots, according to equation (6).

For β_1 a value of 0.677 was estimated based on Lloyd's data for fully cellular containerships up to Panamax (see Veldman 2011), indicating that the ship's price increases less than in proportion to its size, and for β_2 a value of 0.249 was obtained. For a container ship of 1,000 TEUs and a design vessel speed of 14.4 knots, the price in 2008 is approximately €25 million. For the calculations, a ship size range of 400–2,000 TEUs was analyzed, at a constant ratio of 18 DWT per TEU. The results of the regression analyses are based on this range of ships.

$$P = \beta_0 \, S^{\beta_1} V^{\beta_2}. \tag{6}$$

The resulting new price of the ships is given in column 3 of table D.31.

The relation between vessel speed and size is given in equation (7). For γ_1 a value of 0.174 was estimated, meaning that larger ships have on average

Table D.31 Main Cost Components

Size (TEUs)	Speed (Knots)	New price ($ million)	Capital-related costs ($ million)	Crew cost ($ million)	Total cost including overhead ($ per day)	Engine power (kW)	Fuel consumption (tons per day)	Bunker costs including auxiliaries ($ per day)
400	15.4	13.1	2.6	0.2	12,058	5,190	16	9,207
600	16.5	17.2	3.4	0.2	15,546	7,584	23	13,454
800	17.3	20.8	4.1	0.2	18,662	9,925	30	17,608
1,000	18.0	24.2	4.8	0.2	21,529	12,229	38	21,695
1,200	18.6	27.4	5.4	0.2	24,212	14,503	45	25,729
1,400	19.1	30.3	6.0	0.2	26,750	16,752	51	29,720
1,600	19.6	33.2	6.5	0.2	29,171	18,981	58	33,674
1,800	20.0	35.9	7.1	0.2	31,493	21,192	65	37,596
2,000	20.3	38.5	7.6	0.2	33,732	23,387	72	41,490

Source: Ecorys.

a slightly higher design service speed. For the range of ship sizes under consideration the design service speed ranges from 15.4 to 20.3 knots. See column 2 in table D.31.

$$V = \gamma_0 S^{\gamma 1}. \quad (7)$$

Equation (8) expresses the engine power in kilowatts as a function of size and speed. The estimated value of δ_1 was 0.586 and of δ_2 was 2,008, which correspond fairly well with results of other research. For the 1,000 TEU ship the engine power is 12,229 kilowatts, and for the other size classes engine power figures are listed in column 7 of table D.31.

$$kW = \beta_0 S^{\delta 1} V^{\delta 2}. \quad (8)$$

Fuel consumption is 160 grams per kilowatt per hour at an engine use of 80 percent with the design service speed. This is 37.6 tons per day for the 1,000-TEUs ship (see column 8 in table D.31). In 2008 the price of heavy fuel oil (HFO) was $550 per ton.

The main design parameters of a service are the size and the speed of the ships deployed. The relevant cost and operational parameters can be derived by using the above-described statistical relationships.

The time spent in port depends on the cargo-handling speed, which depends on factors such as crane productivity, the number of cranes working the ship simultaneously, and the distribution of containers over the length of the vessel. The cargo-handling speed can be expressed as:

$$H = \varepsilon_0 S^{\varepsilon 1} \quad (4)$$

where the handling speed H concerns the number of containers loaded and unloaded per day. The value of ε_1 is 0.33, based on the assumption that the number of cranes working is proportional to the length of a ship.

Capital related costs are assessed on the basis of the following assumptions:

- Capital costs: 15-year economic lifetime and 12 percent interest results in an annuity of 14.7 percent
- Insurance costs: 2 percent of new price
- Maintenance, repairs, and supplies: 3 percent of new price
  - All capital-related charges come at 19.7 percent and are given in column 4 of table D.31
- Annual crew cost: $200,000 independent of ship size
- Management fee: 35 percent of annual fixed costs
  - The sum of the total fixed costs per day is given in column 6 of table D.31
- HFO price: $550 per ton
- Fuel cost auxiliaries: 5 percent of total fuel bill
  - Total daily fuel costs for the time spent at sea are given in the last column of table D.31.

The operational performance is for a round trip between Haiphong and HCMC:

- Number of terminals per round trip between both ports: four
- Round-trip distance: 1,700 nautical miles (time spent at sea is given in column 2 of table D.32)
- Fixed time spent at port: three hours per call, resulting in a fixed amount of time per round trip of half a day
- Variable time spent at port: based on a cargo-handling rate of 15 containers per hour, which corresponds to 20 TEUs per crane per hour; the number of cranes operational ranges from two for a 400 TEU ship to 3.4 for a 2,000 TEU ship. The resulting variable time spent at port is given in column 4 in table D.32.

Table D.32 Round-Trip Time Components and Related Costs

Size (TEUs)	Time at sea (Days)	Time in port (Fixed days)	Time in port (Variable days)	Slack time (Days)	Total time (Days)	Daily costs ($)		Round-trip costs ($)	
						In port	At sea	In port	At sea
400	4.6	0.5	0.9	1.0	7.0	12,518	21,265	29,942	97,992
600	4.3	0.5	1.2	1.0	7.0	16,218	28,999	43,884	124,529
800	4.1	0.5	1.4	1.0	7.0	19,543	36,270	56,977	148,148
1.000	3.9	0.5	1.7	0.9	7.0	22,614	43,224	69,449	169,828
1.200	3.8	0.5	1.9	0.8	7.0	25,498	49,941	81,434	190,090
1.400	3.7	0.5	2.1	0.7	7.0	28,236	56,470	93,022	209,252
1.600	3.6	0.5	2.3	0.6	7.0	30,854	62,845	104,274	227,526
1.800	3.5	0.5	2.5	0.5	7.0	33,373	69,089	115,238	245,060
2.000	3.5	0.5	2.6	0.4	7.0	35,807	75,222	125,948	261,967

Source: Ecorys.
Note: TEU = 20-foot equivalent unit.

- Off-hire days per year: 15.
- Tons per TEU: 12 for empty containers, 15 for laden containers.
- Load degree of ship: 90 percent each way.
  - Of which percentage of laden containers: 70 percent (i.e., paying containers)
- Maximum round-trip duration: seven days. To maintain a weekly schedule some slack time is the result. See column 6 in table D.32.
- Stevedoring costs: $109 per move, which is 90 percent of the Western European rates. This corresponds with $102.5 per laden TEU.
- Port charges concern a mooring charge of $220 per round trip, while berthing fees vary from $75 for a 400 TEU ship to $376 for a 2,000 TEU ship. See column 3 in table D.33.

The resulting shipping costs per TEU are given in column 7 (and per ton in column 8) of table D.33 and are used for the modal split calculations. The fuel consumption per vehicle mile, in tons, is given in column 9 of table D.33 and the related bunkers in kilograms per ship-km are listed in column 10. The latter are used for the assessment of changes in emission volumes.

1. Size (TEU): size of the ship in terms of the number of containers it can carry
2. Cost per round trip ($): total costs including both costs at the port and costs at sea
3. Port charges ($): includes berthing fee + mooring charges
4. Total cost sea leg ($): cost per round trip (2) + port charges (3)
5. Cost per loaded TEU ($): total cost (4) divided by the size of the ship (1) and the assumed load factor (90 percent)
6. Handling charges ($): per TEU, based on 90 percent load factor and 0.75 boxes/TEU ratio

Table D.33 Cost Components of Coastal Transport (HCMC to/from Haiphong)

Size (TEUs)	Cost per round trip ($)	Port charges ($)	Total cost sea leg ($)	Cost per loaded TEU ($)	Handling charges ($)	Sea freight $ TEU	Sea freight $ tons	Bunkers (tons per vehicle mile)	Bunkers (kg per ship-km)
400	127,934	295	128,229	254	182	436	29.1	0.0432	23.3
600	168,413	333	168,746	223	182	405	27.0	0.0588	31.8
800	205,124	370	205,495	204	182	386	25.7	0.0733	39.6
1,000	239,276	408	239,684	190	182	372	24.8	0.0868	46.9
1,200	271,524	446	271,970	180	182	362	24.1	0.0998	53.9
1,400	302,274	483	302,757	172	182	354	23.6	0.1122	60.6
1,600	331,800	521	332,321	165	182	347	23.1	0.1242	67.1
1,800	360,298	558	360,856	159	182	341	22.7	0.1358	73.3
2,000	387,914	596	388,510	154	182	336	22.4	0.1472	79.5

Source: Ecorys.
Note: HCMC = Ho Chi Minh City; TEU = 20-foot equivalent unit.

7. Sea freight:
   - $/TEU: costs per loaded TEU (5) + handling charges (6)
   - $/ton: $ per TEU/tons per loaded TEU
8. Bunkers in tons per vehicle-mile: fuel consumption in tons per day × round trip in days at sea/round trip in distance (nautical miles)
9. Bunkers in kilograms per ship-km: bunkers in tons per vehicle-mile (8) × 1000/kilometers per nautical mile (1.852)

Impact of Port Improvement Projects

The figures in table D.33 show that an important share of total shipping costs per ton is captured by terminal handling charges. For ships of 800 TEUs, the sea freight comes at $386 per TEU and at $25.7 per ton. The terminal handling charge is $182 per TEU for loading and unloading, which is about half the total sea freight charge. This corresponds with a charge of $12.1 per ton.

Projects can target the reduction of coastal shipping costs by achieving economies of ship size. An increase in ship size by employing 1,000 TEU vessels instead of 800 TEU vessels leads to a reduction in cost of $0.9 per ton (costs per TEU shipped by an 800 TEU ship are $204, lowering to $190 for a 1,000 TEU ship; see column 5 of table D.33; if a weight of 10 tons per TEU is assumed, this equals savings of $0.9 per ton). Otherwise, projects can aim to reduce container handling costs through improvements in port efficiency. For example, an increase in cargo-handling efficiency of 10 percent would lead to a reduction in terminal handling charges of $1.82 per ton.

Cargo-handling efficiency in ports can also be achieved through the provision of dedicated multimodal facilities, such as an extended gateway concept (see appendix E). Such interventions emphasize not only physical infrastructure, but also the improved interaction between maritime transport, international shipping, cargo transfers at port, and inland waterway transport. Obtaining a precise quantification of the cost-reduction impact of these aspects is difficult, but could quite well be on the order of 5 percent of terminal handling charges, which comes at $0.61 per ton.

Road Transport Costs

Road transport costs are based on interviews with road haulage companies, users of trucking services, Royal Haskoning *et al.* (2008), and, to a lesser extent, Louis Berger Group and Royal Haskoning (2006) and JICA (2009).

A truck operator offering services on the North-South axis, a round-trip distance of 4,000 kilometers, deployed 15-ton second-hand trucks with a price of Vietnamese dong (VND) 1.6 billion. With an interest rate of 12 percent and a remaining economic lifetime of 10 years, the annual capital costs are VND 283 million. Insurance costs, maintenance and repair costs, manning costs, and food costs are given in table D.34. Expressed in 2012 prices, the total annual fixed costs for truck operations were estimated at VND 893 million.

Fuel consumption is 32.5 liters per 100 kilometers with a price of $0.5 per liter in 2008. Monthly, these operators make on average three trips. The costs per trip in 2012 dollars are $2,500 for a trip on the North-South axis. Given an average load factor of 75 percent in both directions, the cost per ton of cargo is $110.5.

On short-distance trips in the Red River Delta the operators make three round trips per week with a load factor of 50 percent in both directions. The costs per ton of cargo add up to $27.5 per ton (assuming the use of 15-ton trucks). The average speed is 50 kilometers per hour.

The road infrastructure in the Mekong Delta is less developed than in the Red River Delta, such that smaller trucks of 10 tons are reportedly employed. Based on data presented in the Red River Delta study, the costs of table D.35 are adapted to other truck sizes (see table D.36).

For the modal split analysis between road and IWT in the delta regions, the resulting costs in dollars per ton-km are used as an input to calculate the costs per ton per O-D pair.

Inland Waterway Transport Costs

IWT costs are based on information from Louis Berger Group and Royal Haskoning (2006) and Royal Haskoning *et al.* (2008), coupled with interviews with Vietnam-based inland waterway operators and users of inland

Table D.34 Trucking Costs for 15-Ton Trucks on North-South Axis
Vietnamese dong, 2012 prices

Category of costs	Cost
Second-hand price	1,600,000,000
Annual capital charges	283,174,663
Insurance truck	6,000,000
Insurance goods	400,000,000
Maintenance and repairs	140,000,000
Manning costs	25,600,000
Meals	38,400,000
Total annual cost	893,174,663

Source: Ecorys.

Table D.35 Trucking Costs per Ton on the North-South Axis and within the Red River Delta
U.S. dollars

Category of costs	North-South axis	Red River Delta
Fixed cost per trip	1,630	348
Fuel cost	837	63
Lubrication oils	19	1
Total cost per trip	2,487	412
Total cost per ton	110.5	27.5

Source: Ecorys.

Table D.36 Trucking Cost as a Function of Truck Size for Transport in River Deltas

	Truck size (tons)				
	3	5	10	15	20
Engine power (horsepower)	37	44	55	74	92
Cost ($) per ton-km of cargo	0.45716	0.32950	0.20594	0.18315	0.17175
Fuel consumption (liters ton-km of cargo)	0.05417	0.03865	0.02416	0.02167	0.02020
Emissions (kg/ton-km of cargo)	0.15158	0.10815	0.06760	0.06063	0.05654
Fuel consumption (liters/vehicle-km)	0.163	0.193	0.242	0.325	0.404

Source: Ecorys.

Table D.37 Ship Particulars and Capital Related Costs of Self-Propelled Barges

		Maximum channel class				
		5	4	3	2	1
Ship size	tons	50	100	300	503	703
Design speed	km/hr	10	10	10	10	10
Ship dimensions						
Length	m	19	27	37.5	47.0	52.0
Width	m	4	4.8	7.2	8.5	8.5
Max draft	m	1.2	1.35	1.9	2.1	2.7
Free board	m	0.5	0.5	0.5	0.5	0.5
Engine power	HP	76	110	197	260	310
New value	$1,000	23	36	76	107	134
Lifetime	Years	15	15	15	15	15
Interest rate, %		12.0	12.0	12.0	12.0	12.0
Annuity, %		14.7	14.7	14.7	14.7	14.7
Maintenance and repairs, %	new	3.0	3.0	3.0	3.0	3.0
Insurance, %	new	1.5	1.5	1.5	1.5	1.5
Capital related charges	$1,000/year	4.4	7.0	14.5	20.5	25.6
Fixed daily capital costs	$/day	14.7	23.3	48.4	68.3	85.4

Source: Ecorys.

waterway services. Shipping costs are assessed for self-propelled barges for the five ship size classes, which vary in size from 50 to 703 tons. The design service speed is 10 kilometers per hour, and the related engine power varies from 76 to 310 horsepower. The new value of these ships in prices of 2008 varies from $23,000 to $134,000. With an interest rate of 12 percent and an economic lifetime of 15 years, the annuity value is 14.7 percent. The annual costs for insurance are 1.5 percent of the new price, and the costs of maintenance and repairs 1.5 percent. All annual capital-related costs range from $4,400 to $25,600. The fixed daily costs are based on 300 days. See table D.37.

Fuel-related costs at the ship design service speed of 10 kilometers per hour are based on 0.2 liters per horsepower per hour and range from 15 to 62 liters per hour. Daily manning costs are $74 for a crew of five.

Cargo Data and Modal Split Model

The operational time per day is 24 hours, implying that night navigation is assumed to be possible. The cargo volume per trip when carrying cargo is 90 percent of the vessel's capacity. The time spent in port for loading and unloading is based on a fixed amount of time of four hours in both ports together and a cargo-handling rate of 40 tons per hour. The operational speed is 9 kilometers per hour, allowing for hindrances in the fairway's profile and curves. The fuel consumption is adapted accordingly by applying the third power rule. The fuel consumption in kilograms is assessed by applying a specific weight of 0.88 kilograms per liter, and the subsequent CO_2 emissions are based on 3.18 kilograms per liter of diesel. The fuel costs are $0.2 per liter, adding 5 percent for the costs of lubrication oils.

The operational costs assumed for five ship size classes (from 50 to 700 tons) are given in table D.38. These data are used as input for the calculation of changes in transport costs across vessel sizes (as shown in table D.39). Such changes in transport costs are then used in the modal split model to assess the impacts of waterway corridor scale increase. For example, the deployment of larger vessels may decrease costs per ton transported, resulting in a shift between road and IWT of a magnitude estimated by the logit function presented above.

Data on fuel consumption as a function of ship size and route length are given in table D.39. These data are used in the modal split model to calculate fuel costs by ship size, and hence costs per ton transported. This information

Table D.38 Non-Capital-Related Costs and Operational Data

		Ship size (tons)				
		50	100	300	500	700
Fuel-related costs						
Engine power	HP	76	110	197	260	310
Fuel consumption, design speed	liter/hr	15	22	39	52	62
Design speed	km/hr	10	10	10	10	10
Crew costs						
Crew size	Persons	5	5	5	5	5
Crew cost/year	$1,000	26	26	26	26	26
Crew costs per day ($)	$/day	87	87	87	87	87
Operational data						
Operational time per day	hours	24	24	24	24	24
Cargo per round trip	tons	45.0	90.0	270.0	452.7	632.7
Time in port	hours	6.3	8.5	17.5	26.6	35.6
Design speed	km/hr	10	10	10	10	10
Operational speed	km/hr	9	9	9	9	9
Fuel consumption	liters/hour	11.1	16.0	28.7	37.9	45.2
Fuel consumption	kg/hr	9.8	14.1	25.3	33.4	39.8
CO_2 emissions	kg/hr	31.0	44.9	80.4	106.1	126.5
Fuel costs	$/hr	1.2	1.7	3.0	4.0	4.7

Source: Ecorys.
Note: HP = horsepower.

Table D.39 Operational Data, Costs, and Emissions by Ship Size and Trip Length

	Trip length (km)	Ship size (tons)				
		50	100	300	500	700
Sailing time for round trip (hours, assuming 24 hours navigation)						
	100	22.2	22.2	22.2	22.2	22.2
	150	33.3	33.3	33.3	33.3	33.3
	200	44.4	44.4	44.4	44.4	44.4
	250	55.6	55.6	55.6	55.6	55.6
Fuel consumption per round trip (liters)						
	100	246	356	638	842	1,004
	150	369	535	957	1,264	1,507
	200	492	713	1,277	1,685	2,009
	250	616	891	1,596	2,106	2,511
Fuel costs ($) per round trip						
	100	123	178	319	421	502
	150	185	267	479	632	753
	200	246	356	638	842	1,004
	250	308	446	798	1,053	1,256
Round-trip time (days) (assuming waiting for cargo effects)						
	100	1.8	1.9	2.5	3.1	3.6
	150	2.5	2.6	3.2	3.7	4.3
	200	3.2	3.3	3.9	4.4	5.0
	250	3.9	4.0	4.6	5.1	5.7
Round-trip costs ($)						
	100	303	389	654	894	1,124
	150	435	555	908	1,213	1,495
	200	567	720	1,161	1,531	1,866
	250	699	886	1,415	1,849	2,236
Cost per ton ($)						
	100	6.7	4.3	2.4	2.0	1.8
	150	9.7	6.2	3.4	2.7	2.4
	200	12.6	8.0	4.3	3.4	2.9
	250	15.5	9.8	5.2	4.1	3.5
Cost per ton-km ($)						
	100	0.067	0.043	0.024	0.020	0.018
	150	0.064	0.041	0.022	0.018	0.016
	200	0.063	0.040	0.022	0.017	0.015
	250	0.062	0.039	0.021	0.016	0.014
Fuel consumption (kg per ton-km)		0.0482	0.0348	0.0208	0.0164	0.0140
CO_2 emission (kg per ton-km)		0.1531	0.1108	0.0662	0.0521	0.0444

Source: Ecorys.

is used to assess the impacts of interventions resulting in scale increase or shift between road transport and IWT, causing overall transport costs to change. It is noted that the cost figures in the table reflect only operational costs and do not cover external costs related to emissions, safety, or any other external impacts.

Table D.40 General Data

Exchange rate 2012	21,000 VND/$
Exchange rate 2008	16,300 VND/$
Fuel price 2012	1,800 per liter
Dollar inflation	1,050 (2012–08)
Fuel price 2012	1.038095 $/liter
Fuel price 2008	0.5 $/liter
Interest rate	14%

Source: Ecorys/World Bank analysis, Ministry of Finance of Vietnam, and www.xe.net.

In the same way as it was done for the road transport cost data presented in table D.36, the transport costs in dollars per ton-km for IWT shown in table D.39 have been used to calculate the cost per ton carried for any given O-D pair. Other general data utilized for cost calculations are given in table D.40.

Notes

1. Sometimes referred to as "generalized costs." It should be noted that nonlinear functional forms may be used to represent utility levels, such as multiplicative specifications.
2. These can include value added services such as track and trace capabilities, Electronic Data Interchange connectivity, specialized handling, time-definite delivery guarantees, and the like.
3. All attributes are inclusive of pre- and on-carriage transportation (which by definition is assumed to take place over the road).

References

Brooks, M. R., S. M. Pucket, D. A. Hensher, and A. Sammons. 2011. "Understanding Mode Choice Decisions: A Study of Australian Freight Shippers." Paper presented at IAME Congress, Santiago de Chile, October 25–28.

Feo Valero, M., L. García Menéndez, L. Sáez Carramolino, and S. Furio Prunonosa. 2010. "A Stated Preference Analysis of Spanish Freight Forwarders' Modal Choice Determinants on the Inland Leg of Maritime Shipments." Paper presented at International Association of Maritime Economists Conference, Lisbon, July 7–9.

Henscher, D. A., and K. J. Button. 2000. *Handbook of Transport Modeling.* Oxford, U.K.: Pergamon.

JICA (Japan International Cooperation Agency). 2009. *The Comprehensive Study on the Sustainable Development of Transport System in Vietnam (VITRANSS-2).* Hanoi: JICA.

Lobe, P. 2002. "Stated Preference Analysis on Mode Choice for European Freight Corridors." UNITE Case Study 7J, Mohring Effects for Freight Transport, Institute of Transport, Leeds, U.K.

Louis Berger Group and Royal Haskoning. 2006. *Mekong Delta Transport Infrastructure Development Project (MTIDP) Feasibility Study.* Washington, DC: World Bank.

Ortuzar, J. D., and L. G. Willumsen. 1990. *Modelling Transport.* London, U.K.: John Wiley & Sons.

Royal Haskoning, SMEC, and Center of VAPO Vietnam. 2008. *Northern Delta Transport Development Project Consultancy Services for Feasibility Study and Preliminary Engineering Design Final Report: Main Report.* Nijmegen: Haskoning Nederland B.V.

Van den Bossche, M., J. Bozuwa, W. Spit, and K. Vervoort. 2005. *Effects of User Charges on Transport of Goods.* Rotterdam: Ecorys.

Veldman, Simme. 2011. "On the Ongoing Increase of Containership Size." In *Advances in Maritime Logistics and Supply Chain Systems.* Ek Peng Chew, Loo Hay Lee, and Loon Ching Tang, Editors. Singapore: World Scientific Publishing Company.

APPENDIX E

Detailed Description of Proposed Interventions

An overview of the interventions proposed by this report is presented in table E.1. For each case, an implementation period has been assumed that either (a) builds on ongoing interventions (i.e., those already under implementation), whereby the implementation period of the new project is assumed to start one year after completion of the precursor project(s), or (b) if there is no direct link to ongoing projects, implementation is assumed to begin from 2014 onward (2013 for inland waterway transport [IWT] infrastructure works).

Detailed Discussions of Each Intervention

The Red River Delta of Northern Vietnam comprises three main corridors in terms of shipping intensity. These are the following:

- Corridor 1:   Quang Ninh–Haiphong–Pha Lai–Hanoi–Viet Tri
- Corridor 2:   Quang Ninh–Haiphong–Ninh Binh
- Corridor 3:   Hanoi–Day/Lach Giang

Red River Delta Corridor 1 Upgrade

The busiest northern corridor, as measured by current volumes and forecasted growth, is Corridor 1 (Viet Tri–Hanoi–Pha Lai–Haiphong–Quang Ninh). The ongoing World Bank–funded Northern Delta Transport Development Project (NDTDP) is expected to upgrade this corridor from Class III to Class II by 2014. (Reflecting current implementation projections, it has been assumed that the NDTDP improvements will reach completion by mid-2015. It is further assumed that by then the entire corridor meets Class II, including adequate bridge clearances and 24-hour navigation. See box E.1. Given the large freight volumes transported on the corridor, further upgrading to Class I could potentially result in even higher socioeconomic and environmental benefits. In interviews conducted for this report, the Vietnam Inland Waterway Administration

Table E.1 Summary Overview of the Proposed Interventions

No.	Intervention name	Intervention summary	Implementation time frame	Estimated costs ($)
1	Upgrade waterway Corridor 1 of the Red River Delta	Raises Corridor 1 (Quang Ninh–Haiphong–Pha Lai–Hanoi–Viet Tri) **from waterway Class II to Class I**	2016–20	150–250 million
2	Upgrade waterway Corridor 2 of the Red River Delta	Raises Corridor 2 (Haiphong–Ninh Binh) **from waterway Class III to Class II**	2014–16	150–300 million
3	Upgrade waterway Corridor 3 of the Red River Delta	Raises Corridor 3 (Hanoi–Day/Lach Giang) **from waterway Class III to Class II**	2013–15	100–200 million
4	Enable extended gateway facility in the Red River Delta to serve the Hanoi market	Development of an inland waterway and cargo-handling facility near Hanoi to serve (mostly import/export) container flows between Haiphong and Hanoi	2014	10 million
5	Upgrade waterway Corridor 1 of the Mekong Delta	Raises Corridor 1 (HCMC–Ben Tre–My Tho–Vinh Long) **from waterway Class III to Class II**	2013–16	150–250 million
6	Upgrade a coastal shipping container terminal in Northern Vietnam	Modernization of a container terminal in Haiphong dedicated to domestic container shipping services	2014–15	40 million
7	Introduce user charges to fund waterway maintenance	Imposition of user charges on IWT vessel operators to cover the existing waterway maintenance financing gap	2014–ongoing	0.0003 (VND 6) per ton-km
8	Promote engine and fleet modernization in IWT	Provision of public subsidies to (with private sector matching) for engine improvement	2014[a]	20 million
9	Showcase IWT as an enabler of efficient logistics	Promotion campaign on the use of inland water transport and demonstration projects to illustrate its attractiveness	2014–23[a]	30 million

Note: HCMC = Ho Chi Minh City; IWT = Inland waterway transport.
a. Or when the funds are being used fully.

(VIWA) confirmed that the government's funding availability for infrastructure development in the waterway sector is limited and that the majority of funding for capital investment comes from the World Bank and other sources of Official Development Assistance (ODA). It is therefore assumed that only ODA-funded projects are being undertaken in the sector and that NDTDP is the only ongoing program in the Northern region. Hence, the intervention proposed for this corridor entails upgrading the waterway from Class II (realized after completion of the NDTDP) to Class I.

Using the modal split model presented in appendix D, it was assumed that raising the waterway class will result in the use of larger vessels on the corridor. The greater accessibility created by this intervention will likely induce IWT carriers and private fleets to scale up, as evidenced by the upgrades already undertaken in Vietnam in the past, as well as those in other countries. The use of larger ships contributes to lowering the transport cost per ton of cargo carried through economies of scale. This will also lead to the attraction of additional cargo from the roads sector as the competitive position of IWT relative to road transport is improved.

Box E.1 Estimating Investment Costs

The investment costs of the proposed interventions in the Red River Delta have been estimated for this analysis based on the following assumptions:

- Based on known implementation costs from a sample of actual river upgrading projects in Northern Vietnam, a unit cost in the range of $0.6–1.1 million per kilometer, in 2012 prices, was assumed. Past cost data reflect total implementation costs, including the cost of detailed engineering design, physical construction, land acquisition and resettlement compensation, and contingencies. Specific activities conducted under these projects included dredging, widening, bank protection, bend correction, bridge clearance extensions, river training, and installation of navigational aids. While particular engineering solutions at target corridors will vary by section, these are standard capacity expansion interventions in IWT. As such, the above cost range is considered reasonably representative of the "average" waterway upgrading project.
- The investment costs associated with the upgrading of a particular corridor were calculated by multiplying the estimated unit cost per kilometer by the length of the target corridor. In the case of Corridor 1, given a length of approximately 250 kilometers, total investment costs were estimated at approximately $150–250 million.

For the economic assessment, the median value of the above range was used for base case calculations, while the upper and lower ends of the interval were used for sensitivity analysis.

Source: Ecorys/World Bank analysis.

Red River Delta Corridor 2 Upgrade

The second most important corridor in Northern Vietnam is Corridor 2, running parallel to the coastline from Quang Ninh to Ninh Binh, via Haiphong. On this corridor an upgrade from Class III to Class II was assessed. Costs have been measured using the same unit values as for Corridor 1. With a length of 280 kilometers, the estimated investment costs are $150–300 million.

Red River Delta Corridor 3 Upgrade

Corridor 3 (Hanoi–Day/Lach Giang) is the third most important waterway corridor of the Northern Delta region in terms of volume potential. Under the World Bank–financed NDTDP only selected parts of this corridor are being upgraded, notably the access to Ninh Binh port for seagoing vessels via the Ninh Co estuary. Upgrading the remainder of this corridor from Class III to Class II should also be considered and is therefore included as a proposed intervention under this study. Applying estimated unit costs to the total length of approximately 180 kilometers, the investment costs would amount to $100–200 million.

Red River Delta Extended Gateway

This intervention entails the development of an extended multimodal gateway for Haiphong port at or within the vicinity of Hanoi, on the Red River.

Box E.2 Extended Gateway Concept

An extended gateway is a multimodal terminal that acts as an extension of a seaport terminal, with the goal of increasing logistics efficiency by taking over certain activities normally conducted at the (likely heavily congested) sea port, such as security scans, customs procedures, technical cargo clearance, and other administrative procedures. An extended gateway connects a sea port terminal to a river port facility located in its hinterland, particularly for the handling of container freight flows. This solution may contribute to (a) alleviating congestion at the sea port terminal by shifting handling activities to a hinterland location and (b) alleviating congestion and reducing emissions on the road transport corridor linking the sea port with its hinterland. A key strategic requirement behind the extended gateway concept is that the hinterland river port and the sea port operate as one facility for the user. To the extent that critical government services, such as customs and security clearances, are provided at the extended gateway, public and public-private investment in such facilities may be attractive if economically justified.

In the particular case of Corridor 1 of the Red River Delta, the corridor's concentration of containerized volumes allows inland shipping services to become feasible more readily than when developed independently by individual ship operators. For example, an independent IWT operator may not be able to capture enough volume of cargo to justify weekly sailings of 32 20-foot equivalent unit (TEU) barges (the size that could typically be accommodated on the current fairway). However, if cargo owners or their intermediaries bundle their cargo flows for the region on this route, higher frequencies can be offered, and one or more IWT operators can be attracted to provide shuttle-type services. For container services in particular, high sailing frequencies are usually required to serve just-in-time manufacturing supply chains. Investments in an extended gateway connected to the sea port terminal can be used to attract freight from multiple cargo owners, resulting in volumes that are consistent with more frequent sailings. Furthermore, the inland gateway can act as a centralized storage point near large industry or population centers. Finally, because of the cargo volumes that are attracted, other services on or near the site become feasible, such as container repair, consolidation-deconsolidation, and storage activities.

Source: Ecorys/World Bank analysis.

Investments would include quay wall improvements and container-handling equipment at the inland port where the extended gateway is to be located. Additionally, necessary IT systems—hardware and software—would be introduced at both ends of the route (the inland port and the main port) to provide reliable tracking and tracing, customs clearance automation, and the transfer of data between the main terminal and the extended gateway (see box E.2).

Container-handling facilities at the port of Phudong, near Hanoi, are already under development, and components of an extended gateway concept, such as customs facilities, are being deployed. Investment costs for a full-fledged inland gateway servicing Haiphong are taken to be roughly $10 million, based on the assumption that portions of the infrastructure required are already being developed at Phudong river port, and that addition funding is needed primarily to acquire container-handling equipment, service facilities, and IT systems.

Based on interviews with stakeholders concerning their expectations regarding an extended gateway, and based on general trade statistics, an estimate has been made (subject to sensitivity analysis) on the handling cost savings that can be realized through the introduction of an extended gateway. The expectation is that the extended gateway services will contribute to a reduction in overall terminal handling costs at both the main port of Haiphong and at the inland port itself, resulting in an overall lower cost for shipping containers between the two facilities. Savings of $0.61 per ton have been assumed, as explained in appendix D. The modal split model was then used to assess the share of container flows between Haiphong and Hanoi expected to switch from road to IWT and the associated cost savings and emissions reduction that would result from both the diverted traffic away from the roads and the already-captured IWT traffic (see the results in appendix F).

Although JICA (2009) data do not indicate the share of containerized cargo for specific O-D pairs, reasonable assumptions were made based on the current and projected share of manufactured products in the corridor's freight mix (the portion most likely to be containerized). It was assumed that, at present, approximately 10 percent of the freight flows between Hanoi and Haiphong are containerized, and that 4 percent of containerized freight on the corridor is transported on the waterways. These shares are projected to change to 14 and 19 percent, respectively, by 2020, and to 18 and 32 percent by 2030. According to the modal split model, the extended gateway advantage would contribute to taking some 6,000 20-foot equivalent units (TEUs) off the roads and into the waterways by 2020 (assuming a cargo weight of 12 tons per container; see appendix F), and 17,000 TEUs by 2030, relative to the do-nothing baseline. It is assumed that all the freight thus shifted will be serviced by the new gateway. Furthermore, based on the reasonable assumption that portions of the IWT freight that would have moved via this mode with or without the intervention are designated to use the extended gateway as well, a capacity of 50,000 TEUs is suggested for the gateway, so as to allow for further growth.

Mekong Delta Corridor 1 Upgrade

Corridor 1 (HCMC–Ben Tre–My Tho–Vinh Long) is the busiest corridor in the Mekong Delta region. A Class III waterway at present, Corridor 1 is heavily congested on some sections (notably the Cho Gao Canal). As this is the most direct route between Ho Chi Minh City (HCMC) and the Mekong Delta, raising the navigability conditions of this corridor could potentially generate large economic and environmental benefits. The proposed intervention would upgrade the corridor's waterway class from Class III to Class II. Improvements are assumed to start in 2013 and be completed by 2016.

Cost assumptions were initially developed for this intervention using costs known from past inland waterway corridor upgrading projects in the Mekong

Delta region. From these, an average unit cost of $0.23 million per kilometer was obtained. However, this unit cost reflected a sample of projects that comprised much lower class upgrades (e.g., from IV to III). To reflect the higher costs associated with a Class III to II upgrade, the same cost range as that of the North region (see box E.1) was applied to the South region. Given that Corridor 1 is approximately 200 kilometers in length, estimated investment costs are in the range of $150–250 million.

Expected impacts from this project include vessel scale increases and modal shift from road to IWT, both of which would reduce overall transport costs and emission levels. The model assessment will be similar to those for Projects 1, 2, and 3 as described above.

Haiphong Coastal Shipping Container Terminal

This intervention comprises the upgrading of one of the existing container terminals at the port of Haiphong to cater primarily to cargo flows in the domestic coastal corridor (see box E.3). This may include, inter alia, investments in handling equipment, terminal area redesign, and improvements to the terminal access channel (e.g., to increase water depth). The project may also include investments in mooring facilities for inland waterway vessels at the sea port near the container terminals.

The investment costs of upgrading existing facilities at Haiphong to enable a more effective domestic container port are estimated to be in the order of $40 million for a first phase, which would enable a handling capacity of up to 400,000 TEUs annually. This estimate is based on the assumption that four container gantry cranes servicing two berths will be required, with a unit cost of approximately $5 million, along with terminal yard improvements and selected upgrades in connectivity at the port's immediate hinterland (for both road and IWT).

Expected impacts of this project include a rise in container throughput brought about by improvements in handling efficiency: faster turnaround times of sea-going vessels, reduced container dwell times at the terminal, and/or faster loading/unloading of inland waterway vessels. Such efficiencies, which would ultimately manifest themselves in the form of lower terminal handling charges, would result in lower overall container transport costs for shippers in the North-South trade. The size of the potential savings in terminal handling charges as a result of this intervention is conservatively estimated to be in the range of 5 percent off current handling costs.

The modal split model was used to estimate the container volumes that can be diverted from road to coastal shipping as a result of lower overall shipping costs, and the associated transport cost savings and emission reductions this would bring about. Given that no data are available on coastal shipping container volume projections for Vietnam, modal split calculations were undertaken for the base year of 2008 (latest year for which data are available). The resulting road-coastal modal share was then assumed to stay constant for the remainder of the project's life.

Box E.3 Coastal Container Shipping in Vietnam

Southern Vietnam handles a substantial amount of international maritime container volumes and has attracted mainline container shipping services connecting the region with the world's main East-West trades. Container volumes in Northern Vietnam, on the other hand, remain modest. Yet there are frequent services for the coastal domestic shipping of containers between the North and South regions, with a directional imbalance of larger volumes going northward than southward. Ships of about 600 TEUs in capacity are used for this trade, and shipping rates range from $500 to $700 per 40-foot container, according to interviews with coastal container shipping operators. Even though one could consider the 1,700 kilometer distance a disadvantage for more expensive trucking services, road transport is an important competitor to North-South coastal shipping, as confirmed by logistics service providers interviewed for this report. One of the key barriers to more intense use of the coastal option includes the relatively slow loading and unloading operations at Haiphong port.

Source: Ecorys/World Bank analysis.

Charging Regime for Waterway Infrastructure Maintenance

While the previous interventions almost invariably include the provision of new physical infrastructure, this intervention focuses on strengthening the sustainability of existing assets through better and more predictable maintenance of Vietnam's inland waterway network. The project entails two components:

1. Ensuring That Assigned Waterway Class Levels Are Met Everywhere by Conducting Timely and Sufficient Maintenance Works. The first component will increase the reliability of network navigability. At present, uncertainty over water depth levels on critical points of the network forces vessel operators to keep a loading margin to account for unexpected shallow sections along their routes. This increases transport costs and reduces the environmental efficiency of IWT. With more stable, predictable fairway conditions, vessel operators will be able to optimally load their ships, possibly use larger ships, and raise the number of navigable days. This contributes to increased transport efficiency, lowering costs per ton-kilometer (ton-km), and attracting cargo from the roads.

Assessing the economic impact of improved maintenance is difficult, since it requires an understanding of how "inefficient" the use and maintenance of waterways currently is. Using the modal split model as a tool to estimate the impact of better maintenance across the network, the following assumptions were made:

- The JICA (2009) "do nothing" scenario is based on assuming insufficient maintenance funding, as it is the case today (see chapter 4). This means that the underlying forecasts take account of waterway classes not fully maintained in future periods, resulting in lower IWT volumes for 2020 and

2030 than would be the case if maintenance were optimally implemented. Whether implicitly or explicitly, ship operators take account of this suboptimal outcome in their cost models, and prices per ton-km are higher than they would be if waterways were fully and regularly maintained. This inefficiency is removed by the proposed intervention, thus reducing transportation costs.

- The magnitude of the reduction in transport costs, however, is difficult to determine a priori because maintenance insufficiencies vary by river section and possibly also over time. For the purposes of this report, it was assumed that adequate maintenance provision results in benefits similar to those associated with raising the effective waterway class. Specifically, it was assumed that fully funded maintenance would generate benefits on the order of a 10 percent waterway class upgrade for all major corridors. In other words, if a waterway upgrade from Class III to Class II would result in transport cost savings of, say, $1 per ton-km, it was assumed that adequate maintenance provision at a Class III waterway would deliver cost savings of $0.1 per ton-km. While it is true that the returns to better waterway maintenance are hardly expected to be uniform across the network, the rationale for the 10 percent estimate, aside from its simplicity, is that higher returns in some sections will be offset by lower returns in other sections. Thus the proposed estimate can be understood as the expected weighted average cost reduction impact network-wide.

2. Ensuring Sufficient Funding for These Works through Contributions from Waterway Users. The second component entails charging a levy on vessel owners. As described in chapter 5, an annual sum of approximately $7.5 million ($75 million for the period 2010–20) would be required to more adequately maintain the core network, based on information obtained from VIWA that maintenance levels are only 50–60 percent of what is required (a shortfall of roughly $150 million over 10 years across the entire network, based on projections from the Inland Waterway Sector Master Plan). Chapter 5 proposed several mechanisms for exacting maintenance fees on waterway users, including annual vessel registration fees, channel usage charges, fuel levies, and frontage fees. While these options differ with regard to implementation complexity and the distribution of levy payment burden, assessing the impact of a levy on integrated transport costs is largely independent of the type of levy charged. For example, the logit model defines generalized cost functions per O-D pair irrespective of where these costs originate. In principle, and assuming a competitive IWT market, any cost incurred will eventually be transferred to the end user—in this case the shipper—in the form of higher transport costs per ton-km. Given current and projected IWT ton-km volumes, raising $7.5 million annually over the next 10 years requires an average charge rate of approximately $0.0003 per ton-km, equivalent to VND 6 per ton-km (both figures in prices of 2010).

Engine and Fleet Renewal

Unlike the previous interventions, which focus on network improvements, this intervention aims to promote fleet modernization to raise the energy efficiency of the operational fleet. This would be promoted by addressing the following:

- *Economies of scale*, by stimulating the deployment of larger ships (i.e., ability to carry larger freight volumes), resulting in lower emissions per ton-km transported
- *Energy efficiency measures*, by improving engine performance. This can result in more efficient combustion processes, increasing the power output per unit of fuel burnt, thereby reducing the required amount of fuel and hence also the associated emissions.

This intervention proposes the introduction of an incentives program for engine efficiency, with an indicative budget of $20 million. Such investment scale is considered large enough for proof-of-concept, but small enough to assess further budget increases based on initial impacts realized. It is assumed that this level of funding applies only to the inland fleet.[1]

The Vietnamese inland waterway fleet contains a large number of very small vessels (below 50 deadweight tons [DWT]). Although larger vessels only account for 10 percent of the fleet by vessel count, they provide 60 percent of total carrying capacity. Given that the costs of engine efficiency improvements rise much less than linear relative to ship size (e.g., the additional power needed for propulsion decreases since vessel weight and friction rise less than linearly with engine power), it is recommended to focus the project on larger ships.[2] This would indirectly also contribute to the aim of further supporting a scale increase.

Benefits include lower emissions and reduced operating costs because of the fuel savings realized. This can be an attractive commercial benefit for operators who may likely be willing to co-invest. Hence, it is assumed that 50 percent of the costs are covered by ship operators, so as to ensure private sector commitment and avoid piggy-backing behavior (similar programs have been successfully tested and implemented in Europe), with the balance funded by public funds.

We also assumed the following:

- Improvements on average result in 10 percent fuel savings and 80 percent fewer emissions of sulfur oxides (SO_x) and nitrogen oxides (NO_x). Such savings levels are consistent with modernization programs in Europe and match, for instance, regulatory targets set by the Central Commission for Navigation on the Rhine. They are similar to target levels for maritime shipping as set by the International Maritime Organization (IMO).
- Only the larger ship types (starting with vessels of 500 tons and above) are part of the support program.

- Overall, 5 percent of the fleet carrying capacity will be improved by the project. This percentage is based on assumptions with regard to the average costs per ship and available budget. Since ships above 500 tons account for 50 percent of fleet carrying capacity and there are approximately 5,000 such ships in Vietnam, a targeted 5 percent capacity coverage would require the participation of up to 500 vessels in this modernization program.

The impacts of this intervention have been assessed in the modal split model by inserting fuel consumption improvements in the transport cost function for the share of transport performed by larger vessels. The modal split model was then used to assess the impacts on the scale increase induced by this and the subsequent savings in fuel consumption by both the energy efficiency and the scale increase effect. Other benefits, including modal shift, followed from this.

Promotion and Demonstration Program

The final intervention proposed entails a promotion and demonstration program. As such an intervention has no precedent in Vietnam, quantitatively assessing its economic impact through a modal split model exercise, which requires historical data, is not feasible. Hence, assumptions were made as to the effectiveness of the project to inform the modal split model.

A stakeholder outreach campaign is proposed that consists of the establishment of a dedicated IWT promotion body, whose primary role would be communicating and liaising with cargo owners to showcase the benefits of the use of IWT. This may include marketing campaigns (which have proven to be effective in the Netherlands), as well as direct consulting services offered to cargo owners, to assess their particular benefits of shifting to IWT, required investments, and earn-back period (and/or other key modal choice indicators for private enterprises).

A modest budget of $10 million can be proposed for this initiative. This is considered sufficiently large to obtain tangible results but still manageable enough to be used for a trial period of about two or three years, after which the Government of Vietnam (GoV) can decide if and how to extend it, depending on the results obtained.

In conjunction with the promotion effort, specific demonstration projects can be funded using the concept of Marco Polo (see box E.4), where cargo owners receive start-up co-financing to shift certain flows from road to IWT, depending on the amount of cargo transferred. The aim is that within a period of two or three years the shift becomes financially attractive and is maintained on that basis thereafter. Specific payment structures could be designed to monitor this (e.g., part of the budget is to be paid only if it is maintained for a period of three or five years). Through a break-even analysis, modeling was made of the share of road transport that should shift to IWT to make the promotion package cost-effective.

Box E.4 The Marco Polo Program

The Marco Polo Program of the European Commission aims to ease road congestion and its attendant pollution by promoting a switch to greener transport modes for European freight traffic. Railways, sea-routes, and inland waterways have spare capacity. Companies with viable projects to shift freight from roads to greener modes can turn to Marco Polo for financial support. More than 500 companies have already done so successfully since the program was launched in 2003. Every year, a new batch of projects qualifies for funding.

Marco Polo co-funds direct modal-shift or traffic avoidance projects and projects providing supporting services that enable freight to switch from road to other modes efficiently and profitably. Funding is in the form of an outright grant. It is not a loan to be repaid later. Applicants must meet a series of conditions to obtain a grant. Grants cover a share of costs associated with the launch and operation of a new modal-shift project but must be supported by results.

A grant gives financial support in the crucial start-up phase of a project before it pays its way to viability. Grants last from two to five years. Projects should be commercially viable by the time the funding stops. Successful participation in a Marco Polo project may further serve as a platform for companies' corporate social responsibility campaigns.

Source: European Commission, http://ec.europa.eu/transport/marcopolo/about/index_en.htm.

Notes

1. Since the market of building and purchasing sea-going vessels is international in scope, modernization through fleet renewal takes place much more readily when linked to international ship improvements compared with the inland vessel market. This has been the experience of countries with large IWT sectors.
2. This also relates to age of the vessel and engine. Although it is presumed that larger vessels are relatively younger than smaller vessels, no detailed breakdown for the Vietnamese fleet could be obtained.

Reference

JICA (Japan International Cooperation Agency). 2009. *The Comprehensive Study on the Sustainable Development of Transport System in Vietnam (VITRANSS-2)*. Hanoi: JICA.

APPENDIX F

Detailed Impacts of Proposed Interventions

Project Impacts in 2020 and 2030 Resulting from the Modal Split Model

Impacts Assessed

The nine interventions proposed by the report have been economically assessed using the modal split model described in appendix D and a standard cost-benefit analysis (CBA) methodology.

The following impacts have been taken into account to economically evaluate each intervention:

- The *economic investment costs* of the proposed interventions and their *implementation timeframes*, as outlined in appendix E. The maintenance program is assumed to continue permanently. The pilot programs for inland waterway transport (IWT) promotion and engine modernization are assumed to be phased out once their available budgets are fully disbursed.
- The annual *maintenance costs* for interventions involving the construction of infrastructure are assumed to be 0.5 percent of investment costs. This is in line with maintenance costs of waterway networks in other countries and typical public spending levels for this purpose. This applies to interventions 1 through 6.
- Improvements in waterways or ports can result in either lower transport times (e.g., if port handling becomes more efficient) or lower transport costs (e.g., if larger ships can be used, resulting in lower costs per ton of cargo carried). Such improvements result in generalized transport cost savings. Time improvements will result in lower round-trip times, leading to lower operating costs (e.g., depreciation costs and crew costs) and increases in effective IWT capacity. There are two types of transport cost savings resulting from the implementation of the proposed projects:

Transport cost savings due to increase of scale within the shipping mode concerned (mainly relevant for IWT-related projects addressing waterway class). Cost savings in terms of transport time savings within shipping are not expected from the projects because these result neither in shorter IWT distances nor in higher sailing speeds. Instead, transport cost savings are expected to be realized through vessel scale increases. While travel time changes are relevant to modal shift decisions, the majority of impacts are related to scale increase within IWT itself because Vietnam's modal shift potential is limited.

Transport cost savings due to modal shift from road to IWT or coastal shipping. This is relevant for packages including infrastructure upgrading, but also for the packages otherwise lowering waterborne transport costs (e.g., extended gateway, coastal shipping container-handling, maintenance funding, and engine modernization).

- Since the projects do not affect logistics processes beyond this, no further *storage savings* are expected.
- *Emission reductions*, realized through scale increase, engine improvement, and traffic diversion from roads to waterways. This includes the reduction of carbon dioxide (CO_2) emissions as well as local air pollutants (nitrogen oxide [NO_x] and sulfur oxide [SO_x]). The economic value of CO_2 is a global figure since CO_2 is a global pollutant. For 2010, a price level of approximately $35 per ton was used, rising to about $55 per ton in 2020 and beyond.[1] The value of local air pollutants like SO_x and NO_x, on the other hand, needs to be corrected for local price levels. This was done using purchasing power parity (PPP) ratios (economic values were multiplied by the PPP ratio of Vietnam versus the Netherlands).[2] Economic costs of SO_x emissions thus amount to about $1,800 per ton, while the value of NO_x emissions was estimated at about $900 per ton in 2012 (the Dutch emission values—respectively $22,300 and $11,500—were corrected for the Vietnamese case by multiplying these by the PPP ratio for Vietnam and the Netherlands, which is 0.08). Although this is much higher than the CO_2 value, local pollutant emission volumes are only a fraction (0.1–2.0 percent) of CO_2 emission volumes. Emission levels of these gases relate to the fuel type used, combustion process, and use (or lack thereof) of exhaust gas processing.
- *Traffic safety improvements* result from shifts from road to IWT, since waterborne traffic is generally safer than road traffic (fewer accidents and fatalities per ton-kilometer [ton-km]). Further, an increase of scale within shipping contributes to safety improvements because of the resulting reduction in shipping traffic (as fewer ships are required to move the same volume of cargo). The difference between the modes is assumed to be limited, however. Safety valuations for both modes are in the range of $0.005 or half a cent per vehicle kilometer (based on the value of safety estimated in the Netherlands[3]—$0.06 per vehicle kilometer for road transport and $0.07 per vehicle kilometer for IWT—and multiplied by the PPP ratio of 0.08 to correct for the Vietnamese context). It is noted that these figures are based on typical accident rates for the Netherlands because no accident ratios could be obtained for Vietnam.

Impacts by Intervention in 2020 and 2030

This section presents modal split model estimation results for each of the interventions assessed. Specifically, an overview table is given per intervention (see tables F.1 through F.8) highlighting the following main impacts:

- Change in IWT volume: tons per day shifted from road to IWT as a result of the project (relative to the business-as-usual baseline) and the percentage increase that the shift represents
- Modal share of IWT in the "do nothing" scenario and modal share of IWT in the with-project scenario
- Change in vehicle kilometers for road and IWT: this reflects the impact of modal shift as well as scale increase on vehicle kilometers per day
- Transport cost savings: this indicates the yearly transport savings for (a) the existing IWT traffic (freight transport already using IWT in the without-project scenario that has become more efficient because of the project) and (b) traffic that diverts from road to IWT as a result of the project and
- Change in CO_2 emissions: change in CO_2 emissions resulting from modal shift and scale increase effects, as well as the relative change in total emissions

Modal split estimations are based on the behavior of the "rational shipper." As such, modal shift, transport demand, and emission-level projections ignore real-world rigidities such as information asymmetries, existing shipper-carrier contractual relationships, existing long-term supply chain arrangements, and any other forms of market structure rigidities or instances of market failure that may prevent shippers, carriers, and other stakeholders from immediately adjusting decision making to changes in market conditions (such as those assumed to be brought about by the proposed interventions). However, the CBA, which attempts to estimate the economic returns to investing in the proposed interventions, controls for market rigidities by making assumptions regarding how quickly the benefit streams (e.g., transport cost savings and emission reductions) are likely to be realized over time. A detailed explanation of the CBA approach and results obtained is presented below in this appendix.

Red River Delta Corridor 1 Upgrade

Corridor 1 is the most important corridor of the Red River Delta. Large volumes are shipped along this corridor, resulting in relatively high transport savings (compared to Corridors 2 and 3 of the North region) after the proposed upgrade. Still, IWT volumes in the with-project scenario are 0.85 percent higher in 2020 and 0.98 percent higher in 2030 than in the scenario without the project (see table F.1). This also results in a rise of the modal share of IWT in the with-project situation of six-tenths of a percentage point.

The vehicle kilometers for both road and IWT go down as a result of modal shift and scale increase. The upgrade allows larger vessels to enter the corridor,

Table F.1 Estimated Impact of Project 1 by 2020 and 2030: Red River Delta Corridor 1

Intervention 1: Quang Ninh–Haiphong–Pha Lai–Hanoi–Viet Tri	2020	2030
Change in IWT volume (tons per day diverted from road)	2,580	3,623
Relative change of IWT volume compared to "do nothing" scenario, %	+0.85	+0.98
Modal share IWT Corridor 1, % ("do nothing" scenario)	64.6	61.7
Modal share IWT Corridor 1, % (with project)	65.2	62.3
Change in vehicle kilometers per day (road)	−43,756	−61,450
Change in vehicle kilometers per day (IWT)	−50,391	−61,079
Transport cost savings (million $ per year, price level 2012)		
Existing IWT traffic	$28.5	$34.4
Traffic diverted from road	$0.1	$0.2
CO_2 emissions change (tons per day)	−344	−414
Road	−20	−28
IWT	−324	−386
(Relative change CO_2 emissions on the corridor, %)	−11	−11

Source: Ecorys/World Bank analysis.
Note: IWT= inland waterway transport.

which results in fewer vehicle kilometers than the situation without an upgrade (the "do nothing" scenario).

Benefits from traffic diversion from road to IWT remain relatively small on both corridors, suggesting that the cost sensitivity of road traffic is relatively low compared to its time sensitivity (as diversion would imply lower costs but higher transport times).

Still, a substantial reduction of CO_2 emissions is realized, which is not primarily caused by road transport volume reductions, but rather by an increase in vessel scale that reduces the number of vessel kilometers.

Red River Delta Corridor 2 Upgrade

The impacts of upgrading Corridor 2, from Haiphong to Ninh Binh, resulting from an upgrade from Class III to Class II, are presented in table F.2.

The volume impact of upgrading Corridor 2 is smaller than that of upgrading Corridor 1, owing to the lower volumes overall that are moved via Corridor 2. The modal share gain for IWT in the with-project scenario, of at least one full percentage point, is more significant than that obtained for Corridor 1, likely because of the lower waterway class of Corridor 2 and therefore the bigger marginal reduction in unit transport costs associated with fairway improvements. Still, the majority of the impact relates to the increase of scale within IWT, with only a small contribution resulting from modal shift from road to IWT.

Red River Delta Corridor 3 Upgrade

The impacts of upgrading Corridor 3 from Hanoi to Day/Lach Giang, resulting from an upgrade from Class III to Class II, are presented in table F.3.

Detailed Impacts of Proposed Interventions

Table F.2 Estimated Impact of Project 2 by 2020 and 2030: Red River Delta Corridor 2

Intervention 2: Haiphong–Ninh Binh	2020	2030
Change in IWT volume (tons per day diverted from road)	1,166	1,497
Relative change of IWT volume compared to "do nothing" scenario, %	+2.0	+2.2
Modal share IWT Corridor 2, % ("do nothing" scenario)	76	74
Modal share IWT Corridor 2, % (with project)	77	76
Change in vehicle kilometers per day (road)	−19,772	−25,397
Change in vehicle kilometers per day (IWT)	−31,898	−38,037
Transport cost savings (million $ per year, price level 2012)		
Existing IWT traffic	$17.8	$20.1
Traffic diverted from road	$0.1	$0.1
CO_2 emissions change (tons per day)	−179	−202
Road	−6	−8
IWT	−173	−194
(Relative change CO_2 emissions on the corridor, %)	−18	−18

Source: Ecorys/World Bank analysis.
Note: IWT = inland waterway transport.

Table F.3 Estimated Impact of Project 3 by 2020 and 2030: Red River Delta Corridor 3

Intervention 3: Hanoi–Day/Lach Giang	2020	2030
Change in IWT volume (tons per day diverted from road)	366	543
Relative change of IWT volume compared to "do nothing" scenario, %	+0.97	+1.03
Modal share IWT Corridor 3, % ("do nothing" scenario)	42.6	44.5
Modal share IWT Corridor 3, % (with project)	43.0	45.0
Change in vehicle kilometers per day (road)	−6,203	−9,209
Change in vehicle kilometers per day (IWT)	−14,997	−20,909
Transport cost savings (million $ per year, price level 2012)		
Existing IWT traffic	$3.9	$5.3
Traffic diverted from road	$0.01	$0.01
CO_2 emissions change (tons per day)	−39	−55
Road	−1	−3
IWT	−38	−52
(Relative change CO_2 emissions on the corridor, %)	−11	−11

Source: Ecorys/World Bank analysis.
Note: CO_2 = carbon dioxide; IWT = inland waterway transport.

As noted in chapter 2, Corridor 3 carries only about 5 percent of total IWT volumes in the Red River Delta. Upgrading this corridor hence provides advantages of scale for only a modest amount of freight. The resulting transport cost savings and reduction in emissions remain relatively low in absolute terms.

Red River Delta Extended Gateway

The extended gateway project considers the impact of an inland waterway port near Hanoi operationally connected to the sea port terminals of Haiphong on the flow of containerized cargo on this corridor.

Table F.4 Estimated Impact of Project 4 by 2020 and 2030: Red River Delta Extended Gateway

Intervention 4: Red River Delta extended gateway	2020	2030
Change in IWT volume (tons per day diverted from road)	254	681
Relative change of IWT volume compared to "do nothing" scenario, %	+11.5	+9.3
Modal share IWT, % ("do nothing" scenario)	19	32
Modal share IWT, % (with project)	22	35
Change in vehicle kilometers per day (road)	−7,131	−19,108
Change in vehicle kilometers per day (IWT)	319	854
Transport cost savings (million $ per year, price level 2012)		
Existing IWT traffic	$0.4	$1.3
Traffic diverted from road	$0.02	$0.1
CO_2 emissions change (tons per day)[a]	0.3	0.7
(Relative change CO_2 emissions on the corridor, %)[a]	0.3	0.5

Source: Ecorys/World Bank analysis.
Note: IWT = inland waterway transport.
a. Impacts too small to distinguish between modal shift and scale increase.

As shown in table F.4, the Hanoi gateway is expected to lead to an increase in the modal share of IWT on the Hanoi-Haiphong corridor of approximately 3 percentage points. As the intervention does not result in increases in average vessel sizes, only the road vehicle kilometers decrease (as a result of road to waterway modal shift). The IWT vehicle kilometers increase slightly because the distance by IWT between Haiphong and Hanoi is greater than by road, and because of the impact of volume diverted from road to IWT.

The impact on transport cost savings and CO_2 emissions is relatively small, and CO_2 emissions rise rather than reduce because the relative emission advantage of IWT vessels is smaller than the negative impact of a longer length of haul.

Mekong Delta Corridor 1

This intervention assesses the impact of improving the waterway class of Corridor 1 of the Mekong Delta (HCMC–Ben Tre–My Tho–Vinh Long) from Class III to Class II.

This corridor carries the largest share of IWT volumes shipped in the Mekong Delta. Transport savings hence are projected to be substantial. As in the Red River Delta, the expected traffic diversion from trucks to IWT on this corridor is modest. Nonetheless, the project results in an increase in the modal share of IWT (see table F.5). The reduction in CO_2 emissions, of almost 20 percent, is substantial.

As also noticed for the Red River Delta corridors, vehicle kilometers for both road and IWT decline as a result of vessel scale increases. Corridor class upgrades enable the navigation of larger vessels, resulting in fewer vehicle kilometers than in the no-upgrade scenario.

Detailed Impacts of Proposed Interventions

Table F.5 Estimated Impact of Project 5 by 2020 and 2030: Mekong Delta Corridor 1

Intervention 5: HCMC–Ben Tre–My Tho–Vinh Long	2020	2030
Change in IWT volume (tons per day diverted from road)	4,537	7,167
Relative change of IWT volume compared to "do nothing" scenario, %	+2.0%	+2.2%
Modal share IWT Corridor 1, % ("do nothing" scenario)	81.2	80.4
Modal share IWT Corridor 1, % (with project)	82.8	82.2
Change in vehicle kilometers per day (road)	−174,975	−276,436
Change in vehicle kilometers per day (IWT)	−77,674	−109,692
Transport cost savings (million $ per year, price level 2012)		
Existing IWT traffic	$50.8	$75.1
Traffic diverted from road	$0.5	$0.9
CO_2 emissions change (tons per day)	−531	−785
Road	−48	−77
IWT	−483	−708
(Relative change CO_2 emissions on the corridor, %)	−19	−18

Source: Ecorys/World Bank analysis.
Note: IWT = inland waterway transport.

Coastal Shipping Container Terminal Development

This intervention concerns the upgrading of an existing container terminal at the port of Haiphong. Through improvements in handling efficiency, cost savings can be obtained for coastal shipping relative to road transport, which can increase coastal shipping volumes and terminal container throughput. Estimated impacts are shown in table F.6.

The upgrading of a coastal shipping container terminal, under the assumptions laid out, would result in a modal share gain for IWT of nearly 3 percentage points over the long run. It will also generate positive savings in transport costs, mostly from existing waterborne traffic. The induced modal shift will lead to a reduction of CO_2 emissions by roughly 4 percent relative to business-as-usual.

Charging for Waterway Maintenance

As explained in appendix D, the analysis of this intervention entails two elements: (a) introducing a charge to be paid by IWT carriers and (b) delivering maintenance improvements.

In calculating the impact of introducing a maintenance charge, it was assumed that the levy manifests itself through a rise in the cost per ton-km transported. Based on projected volumes through 2020, a levy of about $0.0003 (VND 6) per ton-km would be sufficient to cover expected shortfalls in the maintenance of Vietnam's core waterway network over the next 10 years. After 2020, revenues will continue to increase with rising volumes, and it was assumed that the rate of revenue increases will continue to be sufficient to cover shortfalls in maintenance funding through 2030.

Second, to assess the impacts of improved maintenance it was assumed that this results in an average improvement of the actual fairway class, which in

Table F.6 Estimated Impact of Project 6 by 2020 and 2030: Coastal Shipping Container Terminal Development

Intervention 6: Coastal shipping container terminal development	2020	2030
Change in coastal shipping volume (tons per day diverted from road)	830	2,153
Relative change of coastal volume compared to "do nothing" scenario, %	+5.7	+5.7
Modal share coastal shipping, % ("do nothing" scenario)	51.3	51.3
Modal share coastal shipping, % (with project)	54.2	54.2
Change in vehicle kilometers per day (road)	−59,735	−155,005
Change in vehicle kilometers per day (coastal shipping)	5,275	13,688
Transport cost savings (million $ per year, price level 2012)		
Existing coastal shipping traffic	$4.0	$10.3
Traffic diverted from road	$0.1	$0.3
CO_2 emissions change (tons per day)[a]	−49	−128
(Relative change CO_2 emissions on the corridor, %)	−4.1	−4.1

Source: Ecorys/World Bank analysis.
Note: IWT = inland waterway transport.
a. Emission reductions relate to modal shift only as no increase of scale within coastal shipping is assumed.

practice implies that the network would be available for more days per year, with better loading ratios, and/or for larger ships. The modeling assumption made is that maintenance will in effect raise the waterway class by 10 percent across the core IWT network. Estimated impacts are shown in table F.7.

Results show that maintenance charges of the level proposed would be expected to generate modest but still positive transport cost savings while keeping modal share unchanged. In other words, the negative impact of higher IWT cost per ton-km (due to the levy) on IWT modal share is expected to be offset by the positive impact on modal share of better maintained waterways. Transport emissions are also expected to reduce overall as a result of this measure.

Engine and Fleet Modernization

This engine renewal project aims to reduce emissions of IWT ships by deploying more energy-efficient equipment. The use of such measures has no precedent in Vietnam. As a result, assumptions were made based on the experience of fleet renewal programs in Europe and the United States. Specifically, it was assumed that 5 percent of the fleet carrying capacity will receive support for upgrading their engines[4] and that performance will be improved by 10 percent with regard to CO_2 emissions and 80 percent for SO_x and NO_x. Such gains will require exhaust gas treatment, which is common in maritime shipping in Emission Control Areas in the United States and Europe and has been noted by the European Commission PLATINA project and by Ecorys (2010). The technology is therefore proven. Its application on IWT ships is also tested, although not yet in the Vietnamese context specifically. Whether or not this technology can be introduced in the currently operational inland vessels of Vietnam is not known. Similar investigations in Bangladesh, the Netherlands, and Romania have found that this primarily depends on the size of vessel engine rooms. It is expected that the likelihood of compatibility with the technology is largest for larger ships.

Table F.8 shows estimated impacts of the proposed modernization program. It finds that shifts between road and IWT are small, mainly because of the limited nature of the program, accounting for 5 percent of the national installed capacity. Transport savings within IWT are also small, as the project only indirectly contributes to an increase of scale and its main benefits originate from lower fuel costs. The program's main economic impact is borne through reductions in daily

Table F.7 Estimated Impact of Project 7 by 2020 and 2030: Charging for Waterway Maintenance

Intervention 7: Charging for maintenance	2020	2030
Change in IWT volume (tons per day diverted from road)	133	225
Relative change of IWT volume compared to "do nothing" scenario	+0.02%	+0.02%
Modal share IWT all corridors, % ("do nothing" scenario)	69	67
Modal share IWT all corridors, % (with project)	69	67
Change in vehicle kilometers per day (road)	−6,445	−10,610
Change in vehicle kilometers per day (IWT)	−19,686	−26,096
Transport cost savings (million $ per year, price level 2012)		
Existing IWT traffic	$1.5	$2.4
Traffic diverted from road	$0.1	$0.2
CO_2 emissions change (tons per day)[a]	−95	−159

Source: Ecorys/World Bank analysis.
Note: IWT = inland waterway transport.
a. Total for IWT scale increase and road diversion. Figures cannot be disaggregated.

Table F.8 Estimated Impact of Project 8 by 2020 and 2030: Engine Modernization Program

Intervention 8: Engine modernization	2020	2030
Change in IWT volume (tons per day diverted from road)	71	106
Relative change of IWT volume compared to "do nothing" scenario	+0.01%	+0.01%
Modal share IWT all corridors, % ("do nothing" scenario)	69	67
Modal share IWT all corridors, % (with project)	69	67
Change in vehicle kilometers per day (road)	−1,943	−2,992
Change in vehicle kilometers per day (IWT)	54	82
Transport cost savings (million $ per year, price level 2012)		
Existing IWT traffic	$0.7	$1.0
Traffic diverted from road	$0.0	$0.0
CO_2 emissions change (tons per day)[a]	−51	−71
SO_2 emissions change (tons per day)[a]	−1.0	−1.4
NO_x emissions change (tons per day)[a]	−0.4	−0.6

Source: Ecorys/World Bank analysis.
Note: IWT = inland waterway transport.
a. Emissions refer to IWT only; road diversion is negligible.

emissions, as more modern engines would reduce greenhouse gases (GHG) and pollutant emissions by a much larger rate than it would reduce transport costs.

Promotion and Demonstration

Quantifying the impact of an IWT promotion and demonstration project through the modal split and CBA methodology, which require historical data inputs, is difficult because no such programs have been conducted in Vietnam in the past. Instead, a break-even analysis has been developed, as follows:

- The project consists of a budget of $10 million for promotion (to be spent over a period of roughly 10 years) and $20 million for a demonstration/pilot project. The latter may take two to three years to develop, after which the project would be expected to continue on purely commercial terms (i.e., without further subsidy).
- For the break-even analysis, it was assumed that the total budget is spent in 10 years, averaging $3 million per year.
- The cost advantage of IWT over road transport is approximately $0.17 per ton-km. This means that if [3 million/0.17 =] 18 million ton-km are shifted from roads to IWT, the promotion investment would be recovered through transport cost savings for the Vietnamese economy.
- Total road transport on the five core national road-IWT freight corridors (three in the North region, two in the South region) amounts to approximately 3.3 billion ton-km (according to VITRANSS-2 data).
- Hence, a shift of at least [18 million/3.3 billion =] 0.55 percent freight share from roads to IWT would be required for this project to break even.

CBA Methodology and Results

Intervention-specific volume and emission impacts for 2020 and 2030, as presented above, have been used as inputs to the CBA. But before the proposed interventions are analyzed on CBA grounds in this appendix, a discussion of the CBA methodology is in order. After a general methodological description, the discussion then focuses on the CBA assumptions that were needed to conduct the analysis for the nine proposed interventions. The results of the CBA are then presented, followed by the results of the conducted sensitivity tests.

CBA Methodology

In a CBA environment, the relevant impacts of a given intervention are compared with a reference scenario where a counterfactual or no-intervention case is assumed. This allows benefits and costs to be netted out of what is expected under the "do nothing" alternative, thereby isolating the impact of the intervention assessed.

Net economic costs and benefits of a measure over a certain period are expressed in monetary values and discounted to today's values. To do this, a discount rate is applied reflecting the economic opportunity cost of capital appropriate for the context in which the measure takes place. The present value of net economic costs is compared with the present value of net economic benefits to arrive at an intervention's net present value (NPV). A positive NPV denotes an intervention that generates net economic benefits to the economy—and therefore one whose implementation is desirable. Another, equivalent, way of assessing the economic viability of an intervention is to compare the applied discount rate to the measure's economic internal rate of return (eIRR): to the extent that the eIRR is above the discount rate, the intervention is deemed economically viable. The higher the eIRR, the stronger the economic case in favor of a given intervention.

In this context, the CBA is used to prioritize the proposed measures (i.e., policy and/or infrastructure interventions) with respect to their effectiveness and economic value added.

Identifying Impacts

The proposed measures can have several impacts (costs and benefits), which may apply to different stakeholders. Economic costs usually concern the capital and maintenance costs of investment packages. Economic benefits of IWT-related projects are concerned with (a) savings in generalized transport costs related to modal shift and scale increase, (b) the economic value of reductions in GHG and local pollutant emissions, and (c) safety benefits of avoided accidents.

Investment and Maintenance Costs

The costs of a particular intervention are mainly capital investment and maintenance costs. The investment costs have been assigned to the actual year of investment. The maintenance costs were determined for the particular interventions as well as for the reference scenario (since maintenance costs still have to be made under the "do nothing" baseline). A standard 0.5 percent of investment costs (yearly) was applied.

Transport Costs Savings

The proposed interventions are expected to result in transport cost savings. These savings are borne by (a) shippers who decide to shift from (higher-cost) trucks to (lower-cost) barges and (b) "captive" waterway shippers who benefit from the use of large, more operationally efficient vessels. The combined cost savings are referred to as generalized transport cost savings. Their magnitude is estimated through the modal split model (see the discussion above).

Emission Reductions

One of the underlying aims of the study is to propose interventions that can lead to reduced transport sector emissions. All proposed interventions intend to contribute to this aim. For example, modal shift from trucks to IWT will have an impact on total emissions because the emissions per ton-km of barge transport are lower than those of truck transport. Scale increase and/or interventions that reduce congestion will also affect emission volumes because the required propulsion power increases less than proportionally with the carrying capacity of a ship. In this respect, changes in fuel consumption are used to calculate reductions in emissions. This is an output of the modal split model.

Safety Improvements

Safety outcomes of Vietnamese roads are suboptimal, resulting in personal and material damages with costly social and economic consequences. Through modal shift from roads to IWT, safety on the roads is expected to increase, which can be valued via the economic benefits of fewer accidents. Standard estimates have been used for the valuation of transportation safety available for the Netherlands, subsequently corrected using appropriate PPP ratios for Vietnam to arrive at a domestically applicable value of $0.005 per vehicle-kilometer. The valuation of safety on a ton-km basis, however, is much lower for IWT than for trucks because vessels can load more tons per vehicle than trucks can. This implies that modal shift from roads to IWT contributes to increased traffic safety.

The CBA Sheet and Output Indicators

After identifying all relevant impacts and transforming them into monetary values, a CBA sheet was developed. The CBA sheet summarizes the different impacts and segregates costs and benefits. Impacts are then discounted over the project period at the assumed economic cost of capital of 10 percent to arrive at a value for an intervention's NPV.

CBA Assumptions

The modal split model used to assess intervention impacts provides modal share estimates for the year 2008 (in essence, assuming that measures were to be realized at that point in time) and projections for 2020 and 2030. For all other years, impacts were estimated through interpolation and extrapolation for the period 2012–50, although the exact investment period varies by intervention (see chapter 7). Expenditures are taken to be spread out linearly over the corresponding investment years.

When a corridor is upgraded in class, it is assumed that in the long run all vessels operating on the corridor will converge to a higher average capacity than in the without-project situation. However, such scale increase will not be realized at once. In other words, if a corridor upgrade is completed in, for example, 2015, it does not mean that from 2016 onward all long-term scale increase benefits will materialize. Replacing existing ships with larger ones takes time, and the pace of replacement is further determined by their age, replacement costs, and earn-back periods.

As such, project specific assumptions were developed on the gradual realization of economic benefits up to the level suggested by the modal split model. It was assumed that for interventions 1 through 6 it will take 15 years to attain the maximum level of benefits, since these projects involve the operation of larger and/or additional vessels on which carriers will need to make substantial investments (e.g., in new purchases). Such investments can only play out over time. For interventions 7, 8, and 9, a shorter, 10-year benefit realization horizon was assumed, since these projects entail measures for which impacts can be obtained more readily with the existing fleet. For all interventions, the growth in the benefit realization rate was assumed to be linear, starting at 10 percent of the maximum impact in the first year after implementation.

Additional aspects of relevance for the CBA calculations are as follows:

- The period 2012–50 was used as the time horizon.
- The applied economic cost of capital, or discount rate, is 10 percent.
- Where investment costs were estimated as a range, the middle value of the range has been applied in the CBA calculations.
- Because no freight flow forecast data are available beyond 2030, in extrapolating benefits over the out-years through 2050, the same yearly growth rate was used as during the period 2020–30. For the CBA output, this has little impact because the discount rate of 10 percent causes impacts beyond 2030 to be of negligible influence on the CBA result.

CBA Results

Modal split model projections for eight interventions were calculated and subsequently applied to a standard CBA framework. Table F.9 presents the most relevant CBA results [net present value (NPV), economic internal rate of return (eIRR), and benefit/cost (B/C) ratio] for each intervention. Vietnam's economic cost of capital is assumed to be within the 10–12 percent interval. As such, eIRR levels at or above 10 percent denote economically efficient, and therefore desirable, interventions. Table F.10 provides the breakdown of economic benefits associated with each intervention by source: transport cost savings, emission reductions, and safety improvements.

Table F.9 CBA Results for the Proposed Interventions

No.	Intervention name	Implementation time frame	Financial cost ($ million)	Net present value at 10% ($ million)	eIRR, %	B/C ratio
1	**Red River Delta Corridor 1 upgrade**	**2016–20**	**$200**	**$0.6**	**10**	**1.0**
2	Red River Delta Corridor 2 upgrade	2014–16	$225	–$83	6	0.5
3	Red River Delta Corridor 3 upgrade	2013–15	$150	–$102	2	0.2
4	Red River Delta extended gateway	2014	$10	–$2.3	8	0.7
5	**Mekong Delta Corridor 1 upgrade**	**2013–16**	**$200**	**$209**	**16**	**2.3**
6	**Coastal shipping container terminal**	**2014**	**$40**	**$22.7**	**13**	**1.7**
7	**Charging for maintenance**	**From 2014**	**n.a.**	**$32**	**n.a.**	**n.a.**
8	**Engine and fleet modernization**	**From 2014**	**$20**	**$0.6**	**10**	**1.0**

Source: Ecorys/World Bank analysis.
Note: B/C = benefit/cost; CBA = cost benefit analysis; eIRR = economic internal rate of return. Economically viable interventions shown in boldface; n.a. = not applicable.

Sensitivity Tests

For each intervention, numerous assumptions were required to assess their feasibility. Hence, sensitivity tests were conducted for each to assess to what extent the above results are robust to changes in underlying assumptions. The results are shown in table F.11.

Table F.10 Sources of Economic Benefits by Intervention

| No. | Intervention name | Benefit source (%) | | | IWT modal share gain by 2020 (percentage points) |
		Transport costs savings	Emission reductions	Safety improvements	
1	**Red River Delta Corridor 1 upgrade**	75.5	27.1	0.4	0.6
2	Red River Delta Corridor 2 upgrade	76.1	23.5	0.4	1.1
3	Red River Delta Corridor 3 upgrade	75.5	23.8	0.7	0.5
4	Red River Delta extended gateway	99.6	−1.5	1.9	3.0
5	**Mekong Delta Corridor 1 upgrade**	75.3	24.1	0.6	1.8
6	**Coastal shipping container terminal**	71.7	26.8	1.4	2.9
7	**Charging for maintenance**	33.9	65.4	0.8	0.0
8	**Engine and fleet modernization**	31.8	68.1	0.1	0.0

Source: Ecorys/World Bank analysis.
Note: IWT = inland waterway transport. Economically viable interventions shown in boldface.

Table F.11 Sensitivity Analysis

No.	Intervention name	Net present value at 10% (million $)	eIRR, %	B/C ratio
1	Red River Delta Corridor 1 upgrade	$0.6	10.0	1.0
	Investment costs increase by 25% (high-cost case)	−$30.1	8.5	0.8
	Investment costs decrease by 25% (low-cost case)	$31.3	12.2	1.4
	Maximum obtainable level of benefits set at 80%	−$21.2	8.7	0.8
2	Red River Delta Corridor 2 upgrade	−$83.4	5.8	0.5
	Investment costs increase by 33% (high-cost case)	−$141.6	4.2	0.4
	Investment costs decrease by 33% (low-cost case)	−$25.3	8.3	0.8
	Maximum obtainable level of benefits set at 120%	−$66.2	6.9	0.6
3	Red River Delta Corridor 3 upgrade	−$101.9	1.6	0.2
	Investment costs increase by 33% (high-cost case)	−$145.2	0.3	0.2
	Investment costs decrease by 33% (low-cost case)	−$58.7	3.6	0.3
	Maximum obtainable level of benefits set at 120%	−$96.7	2.5	0.3
4	Red River Delta extended gateway	−$2.3	8.4	0.7
	Investment costs doubled	−$11.0	5.2	0.4
	Maximum obtainable level of benefits set at 120%	−$1.1	9.3	0.9
5	Mekong Delta Corridor 1 upgrade	$208.6	15.7	2.3
	Investment costs increase by 25% (high-cost case)	$165.7	13.9	1.8
	Investment costs decrease by 25% (low-cost case)	$251.5	18.1	3.1
	Maximum obtainable level of benefits set at 80%	$138.5	14.1	1.8

table continues next page

Table F.11 Sensitivity Analysis *(continued)*

No.	Intervention name	Net present value at 10% (million $)	eIRR, %	B/C ratio
6	Coastal shipping container terminal development	$22.7	13.2	1.7
	Investment costs increase by 25%	$14.0	11.7	1.3
	Only 2.5% realized savings in handling charges (rather than the 5% originally assumed)	−$6.3	8.8	0.8
7	Charging for maintenance	$31.6	—	—
	Increase charge from VND 6 to VND 10 per ton-km	−$2.6	—	—
	5% (instead of 10%) benefits of a class upgrade	−$9.9	—	—
8	Engine and fleet modernization	$0.6	10.4	1.0
	Investment costs increase by 25%	−$3.6	7.8	0.8
	50% higher volume capture	$9.1	16.2	1.6

Source: Ecorys/World Bank analysis.
Note: — = not applicable.

Notes

1. Van Essen et al. (2008). Values were converted by authors to U.S. dollars of 2012.
2. IMF (2012), calculated as $3,359 [PPP Vietnam, 2011]/$42,183 [PPP the Netherlands, 2011] = 0.08.
3. Ecorys (2009), see annex "Kengetallen." Data corrected for Vietnamese PPP.
4. Total fleet of Vietnam in 2010 equals 7.8 million DWT, of which 50 percent concerns vessels of 500 tons and above. Assuming an average size of 800 tons, this implies that roughly 5,000 ships would qualify. To cover 5 percent of the carrying capacity of the Vietnamese fleet, 10 percent of the carrying capacity of vessels above 500 tons, or 500 large ships, would need to be upgraded. A public budget of $20,000 per vessel would be made available for this. By requesting an equal contribution from ship owners, the total available budget would be $40,000, which compares well, for example, with the installation of a dual fuel set (see Ecorys [2010]).

References

Ecorys. 2009. *Werkwijzer OEI bij MIRT-verkenningen* (in Dutch). Rotterdam, the Netherlands: Ecorys.

———. 2010. *Energy Efficient Inland Waterway Transport in Bangladesh*. Washington, DC: World Bank.

IMF (International Monetary Fund). 2012. *World Economic Outlook*. Washington, DC: International Monetary Fund.

JICA (Japan International Cooperation Agency). 2009. *The Comprehensive Study on the Sustainable Development of Transport System in Vietnam (VITRANSS-2)*. Hanoi: JICA.

Van Essen, H.P., B.H. Boon, R. Smokers, A. Schroten, M. Maibach, C. Schreyer, D. Sutter, C. Doll, B. Pawlowska, and M. Bak. 2008. *Handbook on Estimation of External Costs in the Transport Sector*. Delft, the Netherlands: CE Delft.

Environmental Benefits Statement

The World Bank Group is committed to reducing its environmental footprint. In support of this commitment, the Publishing and Knowledge Division leverages electronic publishing options and print-on-demand technology, which is located in regional hubs worldwide. Together, these initiatives enable print runs to be lowered and shipping distances decreased, resulting in reduced paper consumption, chemical use, greenhouse gas emissions, and waste.

The Publishing and Knowledge Division follows the recommended standards for paper use set by the Green Press Initiative. Whenever possible, books are printed on 50 percent to 100 percent postconsumer recycled paper, and at least 50 percent of the fiber in our book paper is either unbleached or bleached using Totally Chlorine Free (TCF), Processed Chlorine Free (PCF), or Enhanced Elemental Chlorine Free (EECF) processes.

More information about the Bank's environmental philosophy can be found at http://crinfo.worldbank.org/wbcrinfo/node/4.

www.ingramcontent.com/pod-product-compliance
Lightning Source LLC
Chambersburg PA
CBHW082119230426
43671CB00015B/2742